The Principles
of Basic Institutions
of the System of Government
in Poland

The Principles
of Basic Institutions
of the System of Government
in Poland

Translated by ALBERT POL

Sejm Publishing Office
Warsaw 1999

POLISH ASSOCIATION OF CONSTITUTIONAL LAW

Edited by Professors
Paweł Sarnecki
Andrzej Szmyt
Zbigniew Witkowski

Graphic design by
Krzysztof Siwiec

ISBN 83-7059-452-2

A NEW CONSTITUTION FOR THE REPUBLIC OF POLAND.
A LEGISLATIVE HISTORY

For a long time, Poland — the first post-socialist country to enter the path of democratic reform, was unable to adopt a modern and fully democratic constitution. The work on the constitution has lasted beyond measure, i.e. over 8 years. We should, therefore, be grateful for the fact that, after three years of work in the Constitutional Committee of the National Assembly, a new constitution for the Republic of Poland was passed on 2nd April 1997 and then confirmed by the Nation in a referendum on 25th May the same year.

After the beginning of the intensified process of democratic transformation which followed the conclusions of the "round-table" discussions in April 1989, Poland made three attempts to draw up and adopt a constitution which would create an adequate foundation for reforms of the entire political and economic system.

The first attempt to adopt a Constitution was made by the Sejm and the Senate in the years 1989–91. At that time, constitutional committees were appointed in both houses of Parliament. Each house prepared its own draft constitution. Political parties and individuals, in particular experts in constitutionalism, also prepared their own drafts. There were some 10 draft constitutions in public circulation.

Today, from the perspective of hindsight, it is rightly held that the turn of the 1980s and was the most convenient moment for adoption of a new constitution. It is argued that, at that time, there existed conditions for obtaining the necessary consensus for constitutional solutions fulfilling the requirements of a democratic state ruled by law and the needs of a period of transformation in the system of government. The chance to adopt a constitution, no matter durable or not, disappeared in a short time, since a viewpoint prevailed that a Parliament chosen through a not fully democratic election (the so-call contractual Sejm) should not be the one to adopt a new constitution.

The second attempt to adopt a constitution was made by the Parliament chosen in free elections in October 1991. A constitution had to be passed in accordance with the procedures specified in the Constitutional Act adopted by that Parliament on 23rd April 1992. The Act envisaged a democratic, but very complex procedure for preparing and adoption of a constitution. The Constitutional Committee appointed by both houses of Parliament on the basis of that Act began its work in January 1992. Within the required period of 6 months following the establishment of the Committee, 7 drafts were submitted to the National Assembly. Their authors included political parties and the President of the Republic. Unfortunately, shortly after the beginning of work on the constitution, President Lech Wałęsa dissolved Parliament in May 1993 when the Sejm adopted a motion of no confidence in the government of Ms. Hanna Suchocka.

After parliamentary elections held on 19th September 1993, won by left-centrist parties, work on the constitution was resumed and continued until 2nd April 1997. The work of the Constitutional Committee of the National Assembly — and that of the National Assembly itself — was concentrated on 6 drafts (from among 7) offered to the Assembly of the previous term. The above mentioned Act governing the procedure for work on a constitution, with some amendments, abolished the principle of discontinuance of work on a constitution and thereby made it possible to consider drafts proposed in the Parliament of the previous term. Moreover, one (the seventh) draft was submitted to the National Assembly by "Solidarity" Trade Union — supported by almost one million citizens. This was possible owing to the amended Act governing the procedure for work on a constitution and after the concept of citizens' legislative initiative was introduced therein.

At this place, it is difficult to discuss details of all these drafts. Drafts submitted by the Democratic Left Alliance — SLD and Polish Peasant Party — PSL (in cooperation with the Union of Labour — UP) were based on the concept of a democratic state ruled by law with essential elements of a social state (concerning, in particular, individual rights) and on parliamentary government. The draft proposed by the Union for Freedom — UW, the third political party in Parliament, was liberally oriented as regards its economic and social aspects. The draft presented by Lech

Wałęsa, which afterwards lost his support in the course of work in the Constitutional Committee, and the draft prepared in 1991 by the Constitutional Committee of the Senate of its first term, were distinguished by a concept of government based on the dominant power of the President. The citizens' draft proposed by "Solidarity", inconsistent in its concept, contained substantial elements of a social and corporate character, and those related to the "settlement" of matters occurring in the period of the People's Republic of Poland.

All the drafts were presented by their sponsors in the Constitutional Committee of the National Assembly. Then, in September 1994, they were discussed (in the course of the first reading) in the National Assembly and, afterwards, referred to the Constitutional Committee for preparing a single, uniform draft constitution. A month later, a debate was held in the Sejm on the subject of fundamental questions of the system of government indicated by the Constitutional Committee.

In the course of two debates, and during the work in the Constitutional Committee, there appeared all the controversies typical of the constitutional discussion held after 1989, as well as all differences between particular draft constitutions. Despite this and various breakdowns of work on a uniform draft constitution in the Constitutional Committee, it was successfully concluded within a period of three years. The Committee also managed to adopt a draft of a preamble to the constitution, what was initially considered impossible, as the text proposed by Tadeusz Mazowiecki was considered acceptable (with small modifications) by all participants in the debate. The draft constitution was ready, in principle, in December.

The crisis which had arisen after the completion of substantial work on the draft was overcome before a final vote in the Committee. This was possible owing to the willingness of the participants to compromise and to make mutual concessions. This resulted from really unexpected initiative of two parties, PSL and UP which proposed to repeat the voting on some provisions of the draft, concerning in particular social rights (the right to education and health protection), territorial division of the country and the structure of local government, as well as the right of the Sejm to override the President's veto against statutes adopted by Parliament. The purpose of this initiative was to change previously agreed provisions in the above mentioned matters.

7

As a consequence of the talks started at the beginning of January 1997 with participation of SLD, UW and UP, and following the appeal to the Constitutional Committee addressed by the President of the Republic who was concerned about the crisis in the work of the Committee, the wording of amendments was determined as a result of mutual concessions. The amendments took into account the proposals for wider scope of free of charge principle in education in public schools and basic health care (as proposed by UP), for leaving unsettled the question of territorial division and three-level structure of local government in the Constitution. The concept of the family farm as a basis for the structure of agriculture was also introduced (in accordance with the proposal of PSL), as well as the principle of overriding the President's veto by a three-fifths majority of votes in the Sejm (instead of a two-thirds majority originally drafted). Following the suggestion of PSL, a party opposing the establishment of districts [powiats], the proposal made by UW was accepted, according to which only a general formula of basing territorial structure on the principle of decentralisation of public power, recognition of the commune as the basic unit of division and local government with the possibility to establish — by means of ordinary statute — other units of regional and local government. SLD, coming to a compromise in this respect, submitted its proposal of some transitional provisions to be included in chapter XIII of the Constitution ("Final and transitional provisions"). The purpose of these provisions was to maintain continuity of operation of organs elected (or appointed) on the basis of the existing constitutional provision up to the expiry of their statutory term of office.

A different position was taken by the opposition in the Constitutional Committee. The representative of the draft constitution prepared by "Solidarity" Trade Union (called a "citizens' draft" which was treated as opposite to that proposed by the Constitutional Committee, even if in fact the latter was taken into account to the same extent as other drafts) proposed that all provisions of the draft constitution of the Committee be repeatedly voted and replaced by relevant provisions of the draft submitted by "Solidarity". When this motion was voted down, it offered 19 amendments to particular provisions of the Constitutional Committee's draft. They related to political parties (the prohibition against totalitarian parties), relations between the State and the Church, freedom of con-

science and religion, the right to life (from conception to natural death), obligations of the State to the family, and the structure of State organs. The proposed amendments provided for the inclusion in the text of the Constitution of the above-mentioned "temporary provisions" of the "Solidarity" draft and envisaged the shortening of the term of office of the then — existing authorities of the Republic, the replacement of the composition of the Constitutional Tribunal and verification of judges of other courts. The representative of the draft of the Senate of its first term submitted amendments limited to replacing the entire chapters of the Constitutional Committee's draft with relevant chapters of the Senate's draft.

As a result of the debate held in the Constitutional Committee on 14–16 January 1997, and votes on the above proposals, the position taken by Senator Alicja Grześkowiak representing the draft of the Senate of the 1st term was rejected by a large majority of votes. From among the amendments proposed by the representative of "Solidarity's" draft, a proposal (partly modified) to prohibit the existence of political parties and associations of a totalitarian character (the present Article 13) was passed. However, the prohibition against such parties and associations resulted implicitly and entirely from the provisions of the Constitutional Committee's draft. They also accepted the proposal to supplement the list of the duties of citizens with the duty to show concern for the common good as well as the proposal to reformulate the wording of a provision about the social and economic policy of the State in relation to the family. All the negotiated proposals for amendments, as mentioned above, offered by PSL, UP, UW and SLD, were adopted.

During the final voting on an ultimate version of the uniform draft constitution, 45 members of the Constitutional Committee (out of 48 members present at the sitting) supported the draft, 2 were against and 1 abstained.

II. On 24–28 February 1997, the National Assembly held its sitting devoted to the consideration of the report of the Constitutional Committee on the draft constitution (its second reading). In the course of the discussion, with 230 members of the National Assembly participating, 400 amendments were offered to the draft constitution. They related to matters which had been the most controversial during the work of the Constitutional Committee, including the preamble, freedom of religion and relations the State — Churches, the right to education and other social rights, State finances and relations between international and Community law on the one hand and domestic law on the other.

After the conclusion of the sitting of the National Assembly on 28ᵗʰ February, talks were continued between parliamentary clubs (caucuses) and talks with representatives of extra-parliamentary Opposition, aimed at reaching further constitutional compromise. Dialogue with the Opposition, represented by the Solidarity Electoral Action (AWS), only produced partially positive results. The Opposition's stiffening of its position portended its future criticism in respect of the constitution.

The amendments to the constitution offered during the second reading of the draft were referred in accordance with the existing procedure to the Constitutional Committee. During its sittings on the 7ᵗʰ, and from 10ᵗʰ to 14ᵗʰ March, the Committee considered all the proposed amendments and approved 118 amendments. The results of the work of the Committee were presented on 21ˢᵗ and 22ⁿᵈ March 1997 in an additional report of the National Assembly to be voted on together with the previous minority motions of the Committee. After adoption of the amendments by the required two-thirds majority of votes, on 22ⁿᵈ March, the National Assembly adopted the whole draft constitution by a considerable majority of the votes. 497 members of the National Assembly took part in the vote. The required majority of votes was 332. 497 members voted for the adoption of the draft constitution, 31 members voted against and 5 abstained. The result of voting aroused great enthusiasm among the members of the National Assembly, who spontaneously sang the national anthem.

According to the provisions of the existing constitutional act on the procedure for the adoption of the constitution), the President of the Republic proposed (at its second reading) 41 amendments to the draft constitution adopted by the National Assembly. Many of them were of an editorial nature, however, but some also had a substantial meaning. The purpose of the latter was to specify and extend presidential competencies to appoint particular State organs (commanders of the armed forces, presidents of the supreme judicial organs), to limit the scope of Deputy's immunity to matters connected with the exercise of the mandate, the concept of incompatibility, the establishment of the final character of judgments of the Constitutional Tribunal regarding the statutes enacted before the coming into force of the constitution with a lack of a two-year transitional period (as specified in the Constitution), as well as shortening of vacatio legis from 6 to 3 months.

The Constitutional Committee considered the President's proposals and approved some of them, but others (including those concerning limitations on parliamentary immunity and recognition of final character of the above mentioned judgments of the Constitutional Tribunal) received a negative opinion.

On 2ⁿᵈ April 1997 the third reading of the constitution was held in the National Assembly. It was devoted to consideration of the report of the Constitutional Committee on the proposals of amendments to the Constitution offered by the President of the Republic. The National Assembly voted to approve most of those amendments which received support from the Constitutional Committee. In final voting, 451 members of the National Assembly (out of 497 of members present) voted for the Constitution, 40 were against and 6 abstained.

In their speeches given after the final vote in the National Assembly, the President of the Republic, the President of the Assembly and presidents of the major parliamentary clubs (caucuses) recognized the Constitution as a reasonable compromise and a modern basic law which takes into account universal trends of contemporary constitutional theory and the values shared by the Polish Nation. The President of the Republic declared a nationwide referendum to be held on 25 May 1997, and soon confirmed this by issuing an appropriate order. This day was also the first day of a political campaign concerning the referendum, a campaign which ended on the day preceding the day of the referendum. The campaign was characterized by explicit polarization of forces between political parties represented in Parliament and extra-parliamentary Opposition (mostly AWS "Solidarity" and The Movement for the Reconstruction of Poland (ROP) of the former Prime Minister, Jan Olszewski, and also by the harsh tone of remarks made by adversaries of the Constitution, accompanied in part by the Roman Catholic Church. The harshness of their position was not always supported by substantial arguments. The objections most often raised to the Constitution by its opponents concern the disposal of sovereign rights of the Nation (in connection with Article 90), rejection of the concept of natural law as a basis of legal order in the State, limitation of the rights of parents to rear their children in accordance of their [i.e. parents'] convictions.

The results of the constitutional referendum held on 25th May 1997 on the basis of the Act of 29th June 1995 on Referendum, published in the proclamation by the National Electoral Commission, show that 42.68 percent of those having the right to vote (28,324,965) participated in voting and that 12,139,790 valid votes were cast (with 1068 invalid votes). The attendance was lower than expected. 6,398,316 votes (or 52.71 percent) were cast for the Constitution and 5,571,439 votes against (45.89 percent of valid votes).

The validity of the constitutional referendum, pursuant to the Act of 29th June 1995 on Referendum, was approved by the Supreme Court by its decision of 15 July 1997 after consideration of all protests lodged against the referendum. In the conclusion of its decision, the Court held that all the protests, including the fact that more than 50 percent of those eligible had refrained from voting, were groundless or had no impact on the results of the referendum.

The Constitution of the Republic of Poland came into effect (pursuant to the provisions of Article 243, on the expiry of the 3-month period following the day of its promulgation, i.e. on 17th October 1997. There are, however, exceptions specified in Article 236(2) and 237(1), according to which certain provisions of the Constitution will come into force on a later date. After the said day, the legislators have undertaken considerable efforts in order to implement the provisions of the Constitution to the extent to which its application is determined by the adoption of ordinary statutes. The Council of Ministers is obliged to present to the Sejm — within a period of 2 years from the day on which the Constitution comes into force — such bills as are necessary for the implementation of the Constitution (Article 236(1)). Such specific obligation does not exclude introduction of bills by other institutions and MPs. The Legislative Council, an advisory and opinion-making organ of the Council of Ministers, has formulated the scope and directions of necessary change in the existing legislation. After parliamentary election in September 1997, won by the then — Opposition (i.e. by former opponents of the Constitution), these changes have been gradually effected.

Kazimierz Działocha

Paweł Sarnecki

Professor, Jagiellonian University, Cracow

THE ORIGIN AND SCOPE
OF THE POLISH CONSTITUTION

Poland's need to adopt a new Constitution in the Nineteen-Nineties was obvious to everyone. The political experiences of the country in 1989 were an obvious rejection of the previously-existing structure of government. Initially, without even formal changes to the existing constitutional norms, many of the most important of them ceased to operate when the Nation recovered its sovereign position in the State — manifested most directly in the results of the election of 4th June 1989. Certain constitutional phrases, dealing with the "the Socialist state" (as it was understood in those times), the leading role of the communist party, the leading role of the working class and the worker-peasant alliance as a "base of power" declared to be the sovereignty "of the working people of towns and country", implementation and development of "socialist democracy", phrases which treated binding legal regulations completely instrumentally as "an articulation of interests and will of the working people" as well as other similar constitutional contents — were suspended in mid-air. The same might be said about those constitutional phrases that gave primacy to state property as a fundamental factor of the economic system, or full subordination of economic life to economic planning — at a time when economic collapse was evident to everyone. This was also true in relation to constitutional provisions concerning civil rights whose ornamental character was finally uncovered with the introduction of the state of siege in Poland against its mutinous society rather than against a threat from a foreign enemy. The Polish people have demonstrated explicitly their desire to live in a system of pluralistic democracy, a system where the rule of law expresses objective values, freedom of the individual is respected and the economy is rational. In our efforts in this respect we have not darkly felt our way. In Poland, the tradition of a functioning democratic state was one of the oldest in Europe. It covers not only the period of the so-called "gentry's democracy" and the period of operation of the first modern constitution in Europe, i.e. the Constitution of 3rd May 1791, but also the experiences of the various, relatively liberal, systems of government existing in the 19th century (the so-called "Duchy of Warsaw", "Kingdom of Poland" after the Congress of Vienna, the Free City of Kraków, Kingdom of Galicia and Lodomeria, Grand Duchy of Posen etc.) and within the Polish Republic of 1918–1939. Several constitutional acts which existed particularly in the later period, and above all the two complete constitutions of 1921 and 1935, provided wide experience of the functioning of quite disparate forms of government, characterised by an attenuated form of democracy but never rejecting it completely. So, when the tragic reality of the 1945–1989 governmental system had been rejected, the work to create a modern state was not only a manifestation of a determination to join other democratic states of the modern world, but also evidence of a return to the democratic traditions of our own history which had not been expunged from the social consciousness. Therefore, the authors of new constitutions could benefit — and have benefited — from model solutions adopted in modern states as well as previous Polish constitutional structures.

The Constitutional vacuum, which appeared in the summer of 1989, as a result of an effective — even if only *via facti* — negation of the operation of the fundamental principles of the old Constitution (formally — the Act of 22nd July 1952, though much amended), was filled with the formulation of new provisions. This happened by way of a comprehensive amendment adopted by Parliament at the end of December of that year. By deletion, in full, of the introduction and chapters on the principles of the political system and the socio-economic system, the Act formally approved the rejection of the premises of the then-existing system of government. They were replaced by the following principles, declared to have binding force:

(1) a democratic state ruled by law and implementing the principles of social justice;

(2) sovereignty of the Nation;

(3) legality of the functioning of State organs;

(4) political pluralism and freedom to create political parties;

(5) decentralisation of State functions through local government;

(6) freedom of economic activity;

(7) full protection of property rights and equal status of all forms of ownership.

From that point on, these seven principles, along with the provisions concerning the role of the Armed Forces, have constituted the first chapter of the Constitution, titled "The foundations of the political and economic system" in its new shape.

The so-called December Amendment confined its creative scope to constitutional principles. Moreover, several positive consequences undoubtedly arose from its numerous decisions quashing existing restraints, particularly in the field of civil rights. But, in principle, it did not interfere with concrete constitutional provisions concerning the organizational structure of the state and with the system of civil rights.

(However, it is worth mentioning here the abolition of both the parliament's and government's right to adopt economic plans). However, there is no doubt that the new constitutional assumptions contained in this new chapter, due to their nature (i.e. providing a necessary basis for interpretation of the constitution) have sometimes led to changes in the understanding of other, formally unchanged constitutional provisions and to unveil new contents. This, naturally, had to have far reaching consequences for the method of interpreting other legislation. The utmost significance has been acquired by the principle of a democratic state ruled by law and implementing the principles of social justice. In fact, owing to the enactment of the December Amendment, we have received a new constitution and the Poles acquired a different shape for their system of government. This transition was accentuated by the change effected by the same Amendment to the official name of the state (and, therefore, the name of the Constitution) and the symbolic change of its coat-of-arms. The passing of the December (1989) Amendment allows us to recognize Poland as the first ex-socialist country to adopt — in fact — a new democratic constitution.

From that moment, the work on shaping a constitution, successfully concluded on 2nd April 1997, was done on two levels. The first of them included further amendments of the existing Constitution, which did not interfere with the contents of chapter I — on "the foundation of the system", but rather dealt with transformation of the structure and competencies of individual organs or the scope of particular civil rights. Here, should be particularly mentioned the introduction of self-administration at the level of the basic territorial division of the state (8th March 1990) and direct election of a President of the Republic by the Nation and not by parliament (27th September 1990), or depriving the judiciary of its character of a political power (19th April 1991). Of special significance is the Constitutional Act of 17th October 1992 on the mutual relations between the legislative and executive institutions of the Republic of Poland and on local government. Pursuant to its title, it established the status of parliament, the President and government, including local councils, at the same time repealing relevant parts of the old Constitution. Only the fundamental principles of government, introduced by the December Amendment, along with the provisions concerning the judiciary and those concerning civil rights were continued in force. However, the idea of a special constitutional act of the parliament to adopt a separate "Charter of Civil Rights", declared at that time by the President of the Republic, did not find parliamentary approval. The Constitutional Act of 17th October 1992 which, due to the scope of its provisions, received the semi-official name of the "Little Constitution" — even by its title alone and also by its specific provisions — introduced to the existing system of constitutional law a particularly important principle of separation of powers, and also such measures as appointment of a Cabinet by the President of the Republic, and not by the first chamber of parliament (the Sejm), judicial control of the validity of general elections, introduction of requirement for countersignature of several acts of the President, making the Prime Minister an organ co-ordinating the activities of ministers, etc. During the five years of its existence, the Constitutional Act has also undergone substantial changes, of which the most important was that of 21st June 1996, establishing a completely new structure for the Council of Ministers — i.e. distinguishing among "ministers directing a ministry" and "ministers performing tasks assigned by the Prime Minister". This means a further considerable strengthening of the position of the chief of government.

Another level of constitutional work were the debates of special constitutional committees of parliament, appointed in order to prepare a comprehensive draft of a new constitution. Initially, such work was performed by two separate committees in each chamber of parliament, set up on 7th December 1989. They prepared two separate draft constitutions. However, as a consequence of parliament's self-dissolution in October 1991, they could not be integrated and adopted as one constitutional act. Subsequently elected new houses of parliament started formulating the procedure for adopting a constitution, to which they wanted to attach the utmost importance. As a result of such work, a special constitutional act was adopted on 23 April 1992, which envisaged a constitution to be adopted by both houses of parliament jointly convened as the National Assembly, and the appointment of a special Constitutional Committee, preliminary debates on the draft constitutions in the houses of parliament as well as holding a nation-wide referendum for final confirmation of the constitution. On the basis of this Act, the Constitutional Committee functioned during the terms of 1991–1993 and 1993–1997. In the latter term, the Committee achieved success in its work, preparing a complete draft. The Committee made use of drafts previously adopted by the houses of parliament, as well as other draft constitutions proposed by various political forces (political parties, trade unions or individuals). During the 4 years of its functioning, the Committee held 101 sessions, while its 6 subcommittees — working on different parts of the Constitution — held dozens of sittings. The results of its work were twice approved by the National Assembly: in the second reading and, finally, after consideration of amendments offered by the President of the Republic — in a third reading — on 2nd April 1997. After the affirmative result of the constitutional referendum of 25th May, the new Constitution finally came into force on 17th October 1997.

The long duration of the work on the constitution should be attributed not only to the over-elaborate procedure of its preparation. The main factor responsible for prolongation of the work was the attempt by many participating political forces to reach a wide constitutional compromise. Their efforts were successful and the compromise is most evident in the sphere of constitutional axiology, i.e. in the reference of several constitutional provisions to different ideological trends existing in Polish society. In the wording of the Constitution, one can easily identify the influence of Christian social thought, solidarism and Catholic personalism, the influence of liberal conceptions and radically democratic options and, to a relatively large extent, socialist thought or the ideas of agrarianism.

The Constitution explicitly rejects only the principles applied by Nazism, fascism and communism. The compromise was also facilitated by a universal tendency to refer to Polish traditions in systems of government. As a result of a gradual approximation of attitudes, the four biggest parliamentary groups, including two members of the then-ruling coalition and two from the outside, actually established a wide "constitutional bloc" enabling the support of a considerable majority in parliament for the draft elaborated in the Constitutional Committee. However, significant political forces — represented in parliament and, even those lacking such representation — have remained outside the "bloc", a fact reflected in the results of the constitutional referendum. Nevertheless, with the final coming into force of the Constitution on 2 April 1997, many reservations about its contents have evidently lost their intensity and presently no serious attempts to change any of its major provisions can be observed.

The most radical changes effected by the new Constitution, compared to its predecessor, concern — in my view — four groups of issues. The first of them is the introduction of several new constitutional principles imposing a slightly different character on the system constructed by that Act — even in comparison with the system existing just before its adoption. From a clearly formal point of view, this was demonstrated in the substantial extension of the first chapter, as compared with the first chapter of that Constitution, introduced by the December (1989) Amendment. Both chapters deal with the basic foundations of the system of government. At this point, one should chiefly note a newly introduced principle declaring the state to be the common good of all its citizens, as specified in Article 1. Other new features characterising Polish statehood include the principle of uniformity of the state — however, with the decentralisation of public power, a "social market economy" as a characteristic feature of the state economic system, provision of special protection for the family farm in agriculture, the requirement for co-operation between the state and churches for the good of society with a simultaneously declared impartiality of the state in matters of personal conviction, etc. The principle of a democratic state ruled by law originated in December 1989 and was developed by the declaration of the requirement to respect international law and that the Constitution be applied directly by all state authorities, irrespective of the fact whether laws operate, or not, in this field of activities. A very distinctive feature of the new chapter I is the inclusion within its scope of many so-called "programmatic norms" proclaiming a series of state actions designed for the benefit of its citizens and dealing with particularly important aspects of social life. They are specifically linked to the proclamation of the state as the "common good of the citizens". These norms have thereby become not only a basis for the construction of the public rights of an individual, but also elements characterising the system of state government. It is worth noting that the norms of this constitutional chapter are protected — in a special way — against any change, since in the procedure for amending the constitution there exists an additional possibility of holding a confirmative referendum. Hence, they are more "entrenched" than other provisions.

The second, and principal, complex of transformations generated by the Constitution, are the provisions concerning freedoms and rights of citizens. Chapter II of the Constitution is designed to deal with this issue and, like Chapter I, is secured by a more difficult procedure for modification and constitutes an extended "Charter of Civil Rights", with its own, formalised internal regularity. In the construction of individual subjects in this Chapter, one can easily see a tendency to ensure a maximum conformity of its provisions with provisions of international conventions concerning the status of the individual. Such an open attitude to so-called international humanitarian law is another important feature of the new Constitution, clearly distinguishing it from the evident mistrust manifested in this respect by its predecessor — Poland's "socialist" constitution. More evident are differences as to the concept of civil rights. The provisions of the "socialist" constitution emanated from a concept that regarded these rights as a result of the class struggle between the proletariat and capital, and the stage of this struggle was to determine the scope of civil rights in general and the extent of possible exercise and protection of particular rights. Obviously, after 1989, they were applied in the practice of public authorities with a modified interpretation, but only if possible, to the extent enabled by the formal sense of the provision. The new "Charter of Civil Rights" derives them from the inherent and inalienable dignity of persons, and the role of public authority is not primarily to specify the scope of the rights granted, but rather to "respect and protect" such dignity. The Constitution must contain at least all these rights which indispensably emanate from such dignity and the authors of the Constitution do not have a discretion available to their predecessors. Due to this fact, a series of new rights of citizens, previously unknown (rights of ethnic minorities, the right to have one's privacy protected, the right of parents to rear their children in accordance with their own convictions, the right to obtain information on the activities of public authorities, and so on) have been included in chapter II. Certain civil rights have undergone a substantial reformulation (e.g. freedom of conscience and religion, freedom of association, freedom of speech) whilst others, previously contained in the Constitution, have been repealed. At this point, one should particularly note the right to work, as well as e.g. "the right to rest and leisure".

Another category of issues, considerably extending the previous constitutional area of interest, deals with transformations relating to "the third power", i.e. the judiciary. They are closely linked to the concept of civil rights, as the new Constitution attaches a great importance to the question of guaranteeing such rights, and among these guarantees, the independent administration of justice constitutes the prime guarantee. The new Constitution integrates the provisions concerning "the third power" in a framework of one chapter, in which administrative and constitutional courts are combined with common courts. It introduces a universal right to have one's case heard by a court as a civil right, the principle of at least two-instance operation of courts, a citizen's right to lodge a constitutional complaint, final character of adjudication of the Constitutional Tribunal, the right of all courts to involve this Tribunal — by means of so-called "questions of law" — to deal with the constitutionality of statutes, applied by them in individual cases. Moreover, there has been a considerable strengthening of guarantees for independence of judges and, in this context, also an extension of the provisions concerning the National Council of the Judiciary as an institutional guarantee for the observance of such independence.

And the last question worth noting at this point, and a new one in the Polish tradition of government, is the financial structure of the state, including organization of its banking sector. A special constitutional chapter contains fundamental provisions concerning the content of budgets, the procedure for contracting of loans and granting financial guarantees by the State, their permissible levels and methods of covering a budget deficit. Moreover a new body, unfamiliar to our constitutional tradition, was appointed to be responsible for formulating the aims of monetary policy, excluding this sphere of activity from the government's cognisance.

Other trains of ideas in the Constitution, in particular the provisions concerning the character and competencies of central State organs, are rather a continuation of previous solutions. This is not only a simple statement of a fact that previously existing constitutional acts also contained provisions concerning electoral law, principles of representation, organization of the legislative and executive branches of government and their mutual relations etc. — but also an indication that such continuity consists, above all, in the similarity between the contents of old and new solutions. It can be easily noted that the authors of the Constitution of 1997 did not aim to show originality everywhere this might be possible, but rather repeated a fairly large number of existing solutions which were gradually introduced in 1989–1996 and met with public acceptance. A classic example is probably the election of the President of the Republic in universal election, which does not seem to correspond in full with the set of concrete competencies of the head of state. The new constitutional provisions and those continued in force will undergo a detailed analysis in further parts of this book.

New segments of the text of the Constitution, together with fragments that have incorporated matter contained in existing legislation, form a very wide scope of regulation. The Constitution of 2nd April 1997 plainly differs in this respect from all preceding Polish constitutional acts; it is more extensive and contains several issues that have not been dealt with by any of them. This concerns, e.g., an explicit declaration on the unitary system of the state, ties between the Polish state and Poles who have left the country, relations between domestic and international law, numerous civil rights of the so-called "third generation", provisions on the procedure for holding a referendum and citizen's legislative initiative and so on. Therefore, the Constitution is undoubtedly a comprehensive, rather than an incomplete, legislative act. Within its framework there are also such solutions which constitute a "canon" or "standard" of modern constitutionalism. Hence, it is a modern constitution — not only in view of its solutions, but also as regards its scope of regulation. One can only wonder whether it is not too extensive, as it includes a large preamble and 243 articles, some of them very detailed. This should be, however, perceived as a response to the period (lasting until 1989) of disrespect not only for constitutional norms, but also for law in general. Hence, there has been an inclination to protect even very detailed solutions with legal provisions of the highest rank. This, of course, may pose a threat, particularly when we bear in mind the difficult procedure for amending this Constitution and the functioning of the Constitutional Tribunal which guarantees the observance of all constitutional provisions, not only the most important of them. However, in order to ensure a certain growth in the level of legal culture of the public, it may be worthwhile to live under the rule of a detailed constitution so that one might experience what this means in practice.

In concluding this essay, I must address the issue of the "origins" of the Constitution, which naturally does not conform to its history. Obviously, there is no possibility here to describe the roots of all the current constitutional solutions or to indicate trends in Polish or European constitutional thought from which they emanate, what are their predecessors in previous acts or their derivation by rejection of other solutions. Deliberations about its origins must be necessarily focused on the most generalized problems. In an earlier study, I reduced all principles and norms contained in the Constitution of 2nd April 1997 to three basic "ideas" (as I defined them) diffused throughout its provisions. In my view, these include the idea of subjection of the state to the needs of its citizens, the idea of a state ruled by law and idea of a democratic state. The origins of all of them can be found primarily in our own tradition of government.

The first idea means a precedence of citizens over the state ("the state is for its citizens, and citizens are not for the state") and manifests itself both in respect for and guarantee of civil freedoms and rights as well as perceiving the state as an important good for these citizens. The first Polish Constitution of 1791 was a constitution of a country whose population was composed of the estates and which had not guaranteed personal liberties and equality before the law to all of its citizens. However, it declared that the largest part of the population, i.e. the peasantry, had to be under protection of law and state authority by way, inter alia, of a declaration safeguarding mutual agreements on the rights and obligations of peasants and landowners. As regards townspeople, they were granted personal freedoms previously reserved for the gentry. The proportion of the latter estate was, in Poland, considerably higher than in other European countries (at around 10 percent of the population). For a long time, it enjoyed many fundamental civil freedoms, such as exemption from the jurisdiction of the Crown's courts. Any limitation of the liberty of its members required a sentence passed by their own court. The gentry were freed from military service outside the national territory, enjoyed full discretion to make decisions concerning their property, etc. Guarantees of the latter right were particularly accentuated in the above-mentioned Constitution.

A more comprehensive catalogue of civil rights was contained in the Constitution of 1921. Obviously, it was not a constitution of a state with an estate system, since the division into estates had been progressively abolished by several 19th century constitutional acts passed at different times in the various parts of Polish lands. Civil rights in the Constitution of 1921 included, above all, such classical freedoms as: equality before the law, personal freedom, freedom of speech and prohibition of censorship, freedom of conscience and religion, freedom of association, etc. However, certain social rights (inter alia, the right of citizens to have their work protected by the state, right to social insurance, right to education without payment and to scholarship assistance) were also contained (to a limited extent) in that Constitution. Most of these rights were continued in the Constitution of 1935. Therefore, one can claim that the present, very broad catalogue of constitutional rights emanates also from provisions contained in previous Polish constitutions. However, in all these constitutions the role of the state in serving its citizens was also linked to a call to support that state. This is based on the rightful belief that only a competent state, capable of operating effectively, could provide protection and create conditions for the development of its citizens. Nevertheless, such a link is above all a result of concrete historical circumstances in which these constitutions were adopted. In Poland, and not so many other countries, adopting a constitution has always been connected with the question of national independence and sovereignty. Hence, constitutions could not limit their provisions only to a category of state obligations to citizens, but they also had to underline the significance of the state for the life of the nation and to impose certain burdens on citizens. The founders of the first Polish Constitution made a fundamental effort to avoid the loss of Poland's independence at the end of the 18th century. The second Constitution was a basic measure used to organize Poland's independence, regained after over a hundred years of captivity. The authors of the third constitution designed it as an instrument for the considerable strengthening of the state in the face of being surrounded (from the east and west) by totalitarian neighbours. In this constitution we can notice a substantial weakening of the aforementioned idea of service to the nation, but not its complete rejection. The fourth, and current, constitution is also a basic act consolidating, to a large degree, the state sovereignty regained in 1989. Despite this, however, and due mostly to the changed international situation of Poland, the idea of subordination of the state to its citizens is clearly demonstrated in its text, while citizens' duties to the state and the entire society were formulated in the most moderate way.

Similarly, looking through all the Polish constitution, we can identify the existence of the idea of a law-obedient state. As early as in the Constitution of 1791, this idea was expressed by stressing the specific role of the law ("The happiness of the nation depends on just laws"), in a declaration of the highest legal force of the constitutional act ("And this present Constitution shall be the standard of all laws and statutes for the future Diets"), in the adoption of the principle of division of powers into three branches with separate functions — the legislative, the executive and the judiciary, in the adoption of the principle which binds administration with statutes ("[administration] shall operate where the laws allow"), in confirmation of independence of judges ("every citizen should know where to seek justice"), in declaration of a will to enact civil and penal law codes. The nature of the then-existing Polish society (i.e. composed of estates) resulted in separate systems of courts for the gentry, townspeople and peasants.

The Constitution of 1921 was based on the concept of a "state ruled by law" in its classic form. In this respect, it extended the solutions adopted in 1791 to include: uniformity of legal procedure for all citizens, administrative jurisdiction having the form of specific administrative courts, guarantee of the independence of judges, a special tribunal to consider disputes as to jurisdiction. These measures were repeated in the Constitution of 1935. The concept of establishing a constitutional tribunal was not alien to inter-war Polish constitutional thought. From that perspective, the new Constitution, preserving a declaration of 1989 to maintain the principle of a state ruled by law proposes new institutions of a state ruled by law — or substantially transforms many of those previously existing. It also attempts to arrange the system of sources of law. It introduces the principle of direct operation of international agreements in domestic relations. By reference to the Constitutional Tribunal, established as early as 1982, it declares the final character of its judgments and extends its scope of activity. Referring to the Commissioner for Citizens Rights, the Constitution is concerned about guaranteeing him/her a completely independent position. Referring to administrative jurisdiction, it clearly establishes a two-instance arrangement. It brings the jurisdiction of misdemeanour boards under the control of common courts of law and declares their abolition by 2001. It also introduces a system of constitutional complaint by the citizens to the Constitutional Tribunal — a new, and most important, instrument for the protection of their constitutional freedoms and rights in the event of their violation.

The third major constitutional concept, namely the idea of democracy, permeates the new Constitution, and emanates from the development of Polish constitutionalism. It should be stressed that this idea is even more deeply rooted in Poland where, from the beginning of the 16th century, there existed a so-called "gentry's democracy", which manifested itself, above all, in the functioning of a parliament whose share in enactment of law and, particularly imposition of taxes, should not be neglected, and which concluded international agreements and exercised control over the executive power. The Polish king, like his English counterpart, constituted a part of such parliament. From the end of the 16th century, the "gentry's democracy" also manifested itself in the direct election of a king by all the gentry. In the 17th and, particularly, 18th century, the functioning of that system underwent profound decay. The Constitution of 1791 was aimed at its reconstruction and rationalisation, but did not intend to build a state of "enlightened absolutism". While formulating, *expressis verbis*, the principle of sovereignty of the Nation (Article V), it replaced the election of an individual monarch with the election of a dynasty. The functions performed by parliament were not limited but only fundamentally improved by establishing the principle of taking decisions by a majority vote instead of the requirement of unanimity. These functions were also reconstructed due to the adoption of the aforementioned principle of tripartite division of powers. A parliamentary mechanism of government was applied, after the example of English solutions, which granted to the Parliament a right to demand the dismissal of ministers and such demand was binding on the king. The control powers of Parliament included a right to indict ministers before a special Sejm Court. A requirement for a ministerial countersignature on every royal edict was introduced.

The solutions of a democratic state appeared in the Constitution of 1921 under the influence of the constitution of the 3rd French Republic. It maintained the principle of the sovereignty of the Nation, linking it — unlike the Constitution of 1791 — with a republican form of government. It is based on the principle of representation, tripartite division of powers, parliamentary government, political non-liability of the head of state, political and legal accountability of a government to Parliament. In its specific solutions concerning the system of government, it is a typical example of constitutions of the "post-Versailles period". The Constitution of 1935 departed from that course of development. Without effecting any substantial change in the status of citizens in the state system of freedoms, without elimination of public liberties and political pluralism, it created an authoritarian system of government in place of parliamentary democracy, whilst emphasizing the role of the President of the Republic. However, it did not regard him as any "chief", and his "superiority" over other organs is limited to the function of "harmonising" their activities. From this point of view, the provisions of the present Constitution (1997) can be seen as a synthesis of main keynotes of both pre-war Polish constitutions — parliamentary democracy as their defining feature, although connected with a strong position for the head of state who functions, inter alia, as a "guarantor of the continuity of State authority". The idea of democracy has been extended to include certain procedures of so-called direct democracy (referendum and popular initiative), coupled with a considerable reduction of all forms of extra-parliamentary legislation having the status of statute (which survives only in the form of presidential decrees issued during a period of the state of siege), adoption of the principle of permanency instead of sessional arrangements in the work in Parliament, etc.

While the origins of current constitutional solutions may be derived from the achievements of earlier Polish constitutions, it should be mentioned that these constitutions were, at birth, determined by the principal ideas of both European and American constitutionalism, known to and absorbed by Poland's social elite. However, their adaptation was not mechanical, but by way of discussion, introduction of supplements and modifications. In short, we can say that the fundamental work of Montesquieu was published in Poland 39 years after its first French edition, the basic work of J.J. Rousseau — 16 years later and an adaptation of the treatise of E. Sieyes — one year after the original. All these three events took place before the adoption of the Constitution of 1791, and it scarcely needs adding that the aforesaid elite could have readily known the originals long before the issue of translations, and there is evidence that they really were known. Moreover, works of decisive importance for Polish constitutional law — those of B. Constant appeared in Poland 16 years after the original, the work of J.S. Mill within only 5 years. The Polish translations of such authors as A. Dicey, G. Jellinek and H. Kelsen were published shortly after their originals. Their treatises were widely discussed and commented on. Therefore, the fundamental concepts of the world's constitutionalism should also be placed among the antecedents of the present Polish Constitution, as one can easily detect in its provisions. Whilst getting accustomed to these ideas, Polish constitutional thought continues to develop, supplementing such "imports" with its own considerations. Its own profound influence was particularly evident in the Constitution of 1935.

The present Polish Constitution knowingly adopts certain solutions contained in modern constitutions of other democratic states. Since the course of an authentic development of Polish statehood was broken by violence on the part of foreign states, we have had to resort to such adaptations in the years when continuation of this broken process was possible (1918–1921 and 1989–1997). The authors of Polish constitutions have always been aware of model solutions applied by other, in particular leading, countries, since such information was rendered to them in relevant studies available in the Polish language. Such activities were not limited to translating dissertations and constitutions. There also appeared — in more or less intelligible form — papers by Polish authors disseminating knowledge about systems of government existing in other countries, obviously, to the extent allowed by the censorship exercised by the states occupying Poland. It is worth noting a study by professor of the Warsaw

Main School (the Russian occupant did not permitted the functioning of a university) A. Okolski, titled "Ustrój państw europejskich i Stanów Zjednoczonych", ["Systems of Government in the European States and the USA"] issued in 1887. Recently, counting from the beginning of the 1960s, the number of such studies has considerably increased. The influence of other systems of government should be, therefore, included in the origins of the present Polish Constitution. Its provisions concerning e.g. administrative and constitutional jurisdiction, the so-called constructive vote of no confidence or the Commissioner for Citizens' Rights have an evident counterpart in earlier constitutional solutions applied in other countries. Finally, a strong influence on the contents of the Polish Constitution has been exerted by the standards of international human rights law — now almost universally accepted — a fact easily proved by comparing international conventions in this respect with the constitutional provisions.

To sum up this aspect of deliberations, we can state that there are many constitutive elements to the origins of the discussed Constitution. These are not, however, as can be easily noted, uniform sources. In practice, they can obtain substance in the course of application of the Constitution, when it will be necessary to refer to historic and doctrinal interpretation. Hence, it is only in the future, and after a sufficiently long period of application of that Constitution, that we will be able to assess whether its authors succeeded in combining all these sources in one coherent unit.

Maria Kruk

Professor, Polish Academy of Sciences, Warsaw

THE SYSTEMATIC ORDER OF THE CONSTITUTION OF THE REPUBLIC OF POLAND OF 2ND APRIL 1997

It rarely happens that the systematic order of a constitution, understood as the order and a structure of its provisions i.e., sequence of provisions as well as separation and collection of certain issues in sequential chapters, is the subject matter of independent consideration[1]. As a rule, the regulation of the defined matters has — in every constitutional act — its logical, strictly defined and usually traditional place. So, general principles appear at the beginning of a constitutional text, regulations specifying the structure of central authorities precede those on organs of local administration and provisions on judicial authority do not appear before the provisions concerning legislative and administrative authorities etc. However, exceptionally, this order may vary[2].

Moreover, the phenomenon that generations of constitutions include certain rules regarding this matter, establishing something akin to a standard, has long been well-known. This phenomenon can be easily observed nowadays as the new constitutions place issues regarding freedoms and human rights before those provisions dealing with the organization of the State authority.

Further, it is not important, as regards the order, where a certain provision is placed within the constitution. Neither its status as a constitutional provision nor its legal validity waxes or wanes on this point. And perhaps that is the reason why the systematic order, as a research problem, is rarely considered to be important.

---

[1] Analysis of the meaning and historical evolution of the systematic order of the Constitution has been made by P. Sarnecki: *Systematyka konstytucji [Systematic Order of the Constitution]* (in:) *Charakter i struktura norm konstytucji [Character and Structure of the Constitutional Norms]*, edited by J. Trzciński, Wydawnictwo Sejmowe 1997, p. 20–34.

[2] In the transformation period of the system of government in Poland for example, the adoption of the interim Constitution (of 1992) in the form of the constitutional act, which in part replaced the previous Constitution (of 1952), caused that the systematic order of the constitutional act in force strayed away from the logical and traditional order.

However, the analysis of the systematic order of the constitution allows one, in many cases — and sometimes at first glance — to tell much about the intentions and motivations of the legislator, about the principles to be included in the text, as well as about the axiomatic priorities which constitute the basis of this act. More precise analysis gives more information; it shows the social and legal values and ideas the constitution emphasizes, as well as identifying the principles, practices or ideologies against which the constitution is supposed to be a shield.

All these problems, I argue, are reflected in the systematic order of the Polish Constitution of 1997 and so the issue of order is worth discussing.

1. It should be recalled that the Polish Constitution was adopted only at the end of a ten year period of transformation in the Polish governmental system. This period was ushered in by the event known worldwide as the Round Table Talks i.e., the talks between the opposition and the government, which resulted in working out of a historical agreement between the forces holding power in Poland since the end of World War II, and the democratic opposition, gathered around the "Solidarity" trade union[3].

As regards the constitutional and legal context, this agreement resulted in the amendment, in April 1989, of the Constitution of the People's Republic of Poland of 1952 then in force. This Constitution was later amended many times[4]. As regards political consequences, it produced the parliamentary elections of June 1989 that initiated a new chapter in the postwar history of Poland. An opposition, for the first time since 1952, sat in parliament and for the first time a non-communist prime minister was in charge of the government.

According to many specialists, it was the best time for the adoption of a new constitution since the society was optimistic in mood and the new political forces were consolidated. However, this was not done[5] and when

---

[3] February–March 1989.

[4] See among others in: M. Kruk *Transformacja polskiego porządku konstytucyjnego w latach 1989–1997 [Transformation of the Polish Constitutional Order in 1989–1997]* chapter IV of the collective work: *Zasady podstawowe polskiej konstytucji [Basic Principles of the Polish Constitution]*, edited by W. Sokolewicz, Warszawa 1998.

[5] One of the most officially emphasized and prominent reasons, was the contractual i.e., not entirely democratic character of the Polish Sejm elected in June 1989, according to the agreement concluded during the Round Table talks. According to the agreement 65% of seats were guaranteed to the pro-government coalition and only 35% of them were subject to free

the best opportunity passed, there came a period of economic transformations difficult for the whole society and there was a simultaneous differentiation in the political groupings. This context adversely influenced the pace and dynamism of the constitution-building process. Work on the constitution began to drag out[6]. Many factors impinged on the process: the very variety of the draft constitutions submitted by different political parties or citizens; the interrupted term of office of the parliament in 1993; amendments to the mode of adopting a constitution (1993); and especially the acquisition of power, after early elections (1993), by a coalition defined as post-communist. Once again, the moral i.e., the political right of this parliament to adopt a constitution came under question. It has been said that this situation resulted not only from the fact that the supporters of the old order constituted the majority in the parliament, but also from the fact that around 30% of voters, who voted for representatives of many small right-wing parties that did not obtain mandates, had no representation in parliament. This caused a political split in the Constitutional Committee regarding the issue of the constitution and also had wider repercussions in society. This problem reappeared at the end of the process of adopting the constitution in the form of a stormy anti-constitutional campaign waged before its text had been submitted to a referendum[7].

The constitution was finally adopted on 2nd April 1997 and accepted in a nationwide referendum held on 25th of May 1997[8]. Those eight years of waiting for a new constitution were not lost. At that time, the first attempt took place to prove the effectiveness of the new principles regarding the system of government, introduced step by step, together with the amendments to the constitution, to the legal order of the state. These principles were focused especially, on the basis of the political system, social life and social relations as well as the economy, new concepts of

electoral competence (they were disposed among the Solidarity supporters). See K. Działocha: *Towards a New Constitution of the Republic of Poland,* "Droit Polonais Contemporain — Polish Contemporary Law" (further DPC-PCL) 1995, No. 1–4, p. 5–14.

[6] See M. Kruk: *The Long Haul: Constitution-Building in Poland,* "The European Yearbook of Comparative Government and Public Administration" 1995, Vol. II, p. 465–474.

[7] See S. Gebethner: *The 1997 Referendum on the Constitution in Poland. The Controversies and the Compromise,* DPC-PCL 1997, No. 1–4, p. 135–136.

[8] See R. Chruściak: *The Constitution of the Republic of Poland of 2nd April 1997 — the Course of Parliamentary Work from 1995–1997,* DPC-PCL 1997, No. 1–4, p. 163–176.

functioning of the public authorities (the separation of powers and local government) and the mechanisms for exercising power and, finally, on the organization of the judiciary and general legal certainty[9].

Even taking account of the fact that these principles were not completely ordered in the previous legal system, neither effective nor complete, they yet constituted a trend that should be connected with the transformation period. Many mistakes made at that time, either within the legislative sphere or within the practical interpretation of the constitutional text, might have been eliminated or minimized in the new constitution. So, the new constitution was based not only on theoretical or doctrinal principles of the democratic, constitutional model of the government system but also on the experiences of the Polish political classes. These eight years were of great importance for Poland, since it had lost its sovereignty at the end of 18th century and only re-established it at the end of World War I.

The question remains whether this delay also exerted a negative influence? It seems that it did since it somehow produced an over--extensive constitutional text. The transformation period revealed many spheres of social and political life in which lack of constitutional authority was regarded as serious. Moreover, this lack of authority was not substituted by customs, tradition or doctrine. During those years, the legislators developed many new ideas on the inclusion of new principles and rules, institutions and procedures, in the new constitution. They were to fill the revealed gaps and to find solutions to many highly specific issues. None of the draft constitutions of 1989–1993 were so extensive or detailed as the final, consolidated draft Constitution of the Republic of Poland i.e. the text of the present constitution.

2. Without discussing whether the extensiveness of this text has positive or negative implications, we should present the constitution in statistical context. It includes 243 articles and a preamble. Its contents are divided into 13 chapters, the last of which is devoted to transitional and final provisions. The division into chapters, and occasionally into subchap-

---

[9] See among others: *Mała konstytucja w procesie przemian ustrojowych w Polsce [Small Constitution in the Process of Transformation of the System of Government in Poland]*, edited by M. Kruk, Warszawa 1994, or the texts published in DPC-PCL 1995, No. 1–4; and 1996, No. 1–4.

ters, is the only basic division which systematize the text of the constitution. There is no division into parts, titles etc., as in many other constitutional texts. Its chapter II is the most extensive one and it includes provisions regarding freedoms and rights of a person and a citizen (56 Articles).

All chapters have titles adequate to the matter they regulate. As mentioned before, certain chapters also have separate subchapters with titles. These subchapters allow for better ordering and understanding of the matter regulated.

This does not mean that we can easily follow the text of the constitution without an index. There are issues that are difficult to locate since the provisions regulating them are found in different chapters. For example, the principles of electoral law and other issues connected with elections have been regulated separately in regard to every organ elected and additionally in the chapter concerning citizens' rights. Another example: the exclusive right of the government regarding legislative initiative has not been regulated in the chapter concerning the legislative initiative but in the chapter devoted to public finances, where the regulations regarding the budget procedure are included. There are other examples: regulations having the force of statute, which may be issued by the President under specific conditions i.e., when the one of the emergency measures is introduced, are not to be found in a special chapter including provisions regarding sources of law, especially universally binding law; the issue of the referendum is discussed in several chapters and, besides that, there are a lot of referrals, see amongst others Article 90 etc. This procedure has its justification since it is plainly necessary to be definite and detailed in those parts of the text dealing with states of emergency, everything connected with finances etc. However, this practice consequentially affects the integrity of other parts of the constitution.

3. The sequence of the chapters of the new Polish constitution is as follows: Chapter I: The Republic; Chapter II: The Freedoms, Rights and Obligations of Persons and Citizens (subchapters: General Principles, Personal Freedoms and Rights, Political Freedoms and Rights, Economic, Social and Cultural Freedoms and Rights, Means for the Defense of Freedoms and Rights, Obligations); Chapter III: Sources of Law; Chapter IV: The Sejm and the Senate (subchapters: Elections and the Term of

Office, Deputies and Senators, Organization and Functioning, Referendum); Chapter V: The President of the Republic of Poland; Chapter VI: The Council of Ministers and Government Administration; Chapter VII: Local Self-Government; Chapter VIII: Courts and Tribunals (subchapters: Courts, the Constitutional Tribunal, the Tribunal of State); Chapter IX: Organs of State Control and for Defence of Rights (subchapters: The Supreme Chamber of Control, the Commissioner for Citizens' Rights, the National Council of Radio Broadcasting and Television); Chapter X: Public Finances; Chapter XI: Extraordinary Measures; Chapter XII: Amending the Constitution; Chapter XIII: Final and Transitional Provisions.

We note, at first glance, that this systematic order has features reflecting the intentions of the legislator, for example: the superior position of the freedoms and rights of a person and a citizen; distinction of a chapter defining the sources of law; considering the provisions regarding the parliament as provisions referring to the legislative power and placing them before the provisions regarding the executive power, especially those regarding the president; differentiation of chapters regarding the local government, public finances and emergency states; considering the National Council of Radio Broadcasting and Television as an organ of defence of rights and not an organ of administration etc.

This does not necessarily mean that this systematic order is especially original or greatly different from that of the constitutions of other democratic countries namely, the constitutions of the new generation adopted in the 90s in the post-socialist countries. Assuming that every constitution, on the one hand, exemplifies its specific character within its systematic order and, on the other hand, exhibits a certain universalism, it should be stated that systematic order of the Polish constitution remains within the general scheme. It means that characteristic features of the systematic order of this constitution show both its similarity with modern constitutions of other democratic countries and its original character, emphasizing its particular distinction.

It would be difficult to identify the existence of any particularly traditional features in the systematic order of the successive Polish constitutions. During the years — or taking into account the first Polish constitution — during the centuries, similarities regarding the order of certain constitutional provisions appeared in the constitutions of other countries of that time. The first Polish constitution, and at the same time the first constitution in Europe, the Constitution of 3rd May i.e., the act of government adopted on 3rd May 1791, was divided into eleven chapters--articles, each having a separate title. The first chapter was devoted to religion and the following three defined the social status and the rights of the noble, bourgeois and peasant estates i.e., *sui generis* citizens' rights. The following chapters were devoted to the State authority including, among others, the principle of sovereignty, provisions regarding the prerogatives of the Sejm as the legislative branch, then prerogatives of the king as the executive branch and finally, provisions regarding the judicial branch. The order of the constitution was strict and regulations regarding the Sejm authority hold the supreme place in it, followed by provisions dealing with regency, the education of the king's children, and armed forces.

The Polish constitutions between World War I and II i.e., the Constitutions of March 1921 and April of 1935, were characterized by a significant discrepancy in regard to basic principles concerning the system of government, especially the system and organization of the State authority, which resulted in differences in their systematic order. The Constitution of 1921, modeled on the French Constitution of the Third Republic, adhered to the principle of parliamentary democracy, placing the regulation regarding the legislative power exercised by the parliament in first place and then, according with tradition, placing the provisions regarding executive branch — the executive branch understood as the President of the Republic of Poland and the Council of Ministers — before the judicial branch. Only then, did there appear the provisions regulating the duties and rights of citizens.

These issues appeared to be different in the April Constitution. It regulated the basic principles of the system of government and the status of a citizen in Chapter I, entitled the Republic of Poland. These principles were discussed more extensively in this constitution than in the March Constitution. However, the April Constitution violated, in its first chapter, the traditional order in which the organization of the State authority had been so far regulated (i.e., the provisions regarding the legislative branch have been put in the first place). This constitution discussed, in the first place, the issue of the President of the Republic, which was in conformity with the political concept of this organ assuming — according to the provisions of the constitution — its supreme authority in the state. The provisions treating the Sejm and the Senate were to be found after those dealing with the executive branch, and the provisions regarding administration of justice, not the judicial power, were placed subsequently. The constitution did not include a chapter on citizens' rights.

The Constitution of the People's Republic of Poland of 1952 can be compared with the constitutions of other East European peoples' democracies of that time, since it followed the same universal scheme. The scheme was not particular enough to create a separate type of constitution as regards systematic order. Its characteristic features were: separation of the chapter devoted to the socio-economic system as well as the lack of separation and, at the same time, existence of a separate regulation of the three branches due to rejection of the principle of separation of powers, as well as placing the provisions regarding the position of the parliament before the provisions regarding other holders of power. In this concept of the system of government, the one-chamber parliament was the supreme organ of the State power. The rights and duties of citizens were regulated in other parts of the Constitution of 1952.

The history of Polish constitutionalism also knows transitional periods when interim constitutional acts were in force i.e., the so-called Small Constitutions, which were mainly characterized by their failure to systematically regulate constitutional matters. As a rule, they restricted themselves to a definition of principles regarding the organization and competence of the central State organs and did not specially discuss citizens' rights. They showed a different attitude to previous constitutions and, at the same time, had a different manner and scope of perception of the provisions of the previous constitutions. Apart from the tradition of calling these acts "Small Constitutions", it is difficult to discuss their long-lasting influence on the character of the constitutional traditions in the context of systematic order. The direct predecessor of the Constitution of 1997, i.e., the Constitutional Act of 17th September 1992, had a particularly complicated structure and included various elements of the previous constitution e.g., it had two separate chapters, an old and a new, which both regulated the basic principles of the system of government.

Since it has been assumed that the two first Polish Constitutions of 1791 and of 1921 contributed to the establishment of a modern and democratic Polish tradition, the modern Polish legislator referred to it, in so far as this tradition was significant and continued up to present times.

4. The Polish Constitution of 1997 is opened with a preamble. Its adoption caused so many problems that, at a certain stage of its preparation, it was agreed that there would be no preamble. However, at the end of this preparatory work, when the political consensus sufficient for final adoption of the constitution had almost been reached, the problem of the preamble surfaced again. Certain parliamentary clubs or individual deputies submitted various proposals regarding the final shape of the preamble. Fortunately, one proposal was chosen, that submitted by Tadeusz Mazowiecki — the first Polish non-communist prime minister in 1989, which became the basis for the preparation of the final version accepted by the so-called constitutional bloc i.e., the parliamentary parties supporting the draft of the Constitutional Committee of National Assembly[10].

The main obstacle in the preparation of the final version of the preamble, acceptable to all political options, was the attitude to the religious content that the preamble was to include. The text of the preamble as finally adopted, however much criticized, reflects an almost classic pattern — given variety of solutions dealing with this issue — and is not too lengthy. Nevertheless, it is longer than the majority of preambles in other constitutions, including previous Polish ones, but is not so long as the preamble preceding the Constitution of 1952. The preamble has no articles and is written in solemn and elevated style.

Its contents refers to our historical roots and national experiences, whilst emphasizing at the same time both differences in outlooks on life and the ethical unity of the nation. It characterizes further aims and main principles included in the Constitution, among them those, which are not later repeated *expressis verbis* in the text of the constitution — such as: subsidiarity or cooperation between the public authorities. Many users of the constitution refer to these aims and principles as being in force. As regards the preamble, it is difficult to discern a coherent model in the Polish constitutional tradition since this issue has been differently treated

---

[10] See S. Gebethner, *op. cit.*

in all our constitutions. Two preambles similar in form and style can be found in the first two Polish constitutions. However, the Constitution of 1935 did not include a preamble and the preamble in the 1952 Constitution was preceded by an extensive historical and ideological lecture. It may be interesting to mention here, that among the proposals for the text of the preamble to be included in the new constitution, was one copying the whole preamble from the Constitution of 3rd May.

As occurs in the majority of constitutions, the first chapter of the Constitution of 1997 introduces the basic principles of the political and social system that express the values preferred in a certain state. However, the title of this chapter — the Republic of Poland — as compared to other constitutions — is exceptional. Generally speaking, constitutions define the provisions gathered in this chapter as general or fundamental principles. This practice is not entirely unusual in the Polish tradition since — as mentioned before — the first chapters of the March and April Constitutions had the same titles. This may, to some degree, be considered as strengthening the Polish constitutional tradition. The Constitution of the Republic of Poland of March 1921, the first Polish constitution after regaining sovereignty after 120 years of political non-existence of Poland as a sovereign and democratic state, has been considered in Poland until now, as a model of democratic constitutionalism, as well as a point of reference for estimating later solutions. However, this chapter of the March Constitution included only two articles defining the character of the state i.e., the Republic, as well as the holders of the sovereign power. The first chapter of the Constitution of 1935 contained more information.

This atypical title of the first chapter of the constitution can be also found — although rarely — in constitutions of other countries. The first chapter of the Lithuanian Constitution of 1992 is called the State of Lithuania; the Constitution of Croatia of 1992 names its first chapter, which includes no articles, Sources and Roots and then the fundamental principles are defined in the next chapter. Other constitutions also have their specific character, the first chapter of the French Constitution of the Fifth Republic is devoted to a particular problem i.e., the problem of sovereignty and is titled "On Sovereignty". The first chapters in the constitutions of the federal states discuss the problem of federalism — like the Belgian Constitution of 1994, the Constitution of Bosnia and

Herzegovina of 1995 and others. Sometimes there is no separate chapter regulating fundamental principles as is the case with the constitution of the United States of America. There, where this chapter appears in the classic form, it is devoted to the regulation of selected fundamental principles constituting the basis of the political system of a certain state.

The first chapter of the new Polish constitution includes a very extensive catalogue of principles referring not only to a precisely understood political system but also to the status of an individual as a person and a citizen; self-governing organizations; relations between the state and the church; economic system and even referring to the status of the family and family relations. This scope of regulation highly justifies the title of the chapter I — the Republic of Poland — since it presents a certain catalogue of values on which the relations of the public life of the state are based.

The next characteristic element of the systematic order of the Polish Constitution of 1997 is giving prominence to provisions regarding the rights of a person and a citizen, as well as placing these provisions before those touching on the organization of the State and public authorities. These issues constitute the contents of the chapter II.

Moreover, the distinction has been made there between the freedoms and rights of a person and the citizens' rights. This first category of rights has been consequently and symbolically placed at the beginning of the second chapter. A similar tendency is to be observed in certain, previously adopted constitutions of the West European countries, for example: the Spanish Constitution of 1978, the Greek Constitution of 1986, and others. This tendency became almost universal in Central and Eastern Europe during the transformation period. The above mentioned freedoms and rights constitute the subject of regulation of chapter II in the constitutions of: Bulgaria (1991), Estonia (1992), Romania (1991), Slovakia (1992), Slovenia (1991), Bosnia and Herzegovina (1995), Macedonia (1991), Croatia (1990), the Russian Federation (1993) and others, though there are also exceptions e.g. Latvia and the Czech Republic regulated this issue in separate acts, Hungary formally still does not have a new constitution and thus citizens' rights have the place typical of the systematic order of former socialist constitutions.

In the Polish constitution, as in the new generation of constitutions of other European post-socialist countries, the provisions regarding freedoms and rights of a person and a citizen are placed intentionally at the very beginning of the constitution since this order includes an important axiomatic principle. All previous constitutions of these countries, based to a greater or lesser degree on the Soviet constitution of 1936, placed the provisions regarding the rights and duties of citizens; in the final articles of the constitution. Although a similar tendency prevailed in the West European countries (the regulations regarding citizens' rights were placed in the first Polish democratic constitution adopted in 1921, in chapters connected with the organization of the State authority), in the case of the constitutions of the former socialist countries (including the Polish Constitution of 1952), this tendency symbolically harmonized with either political and legal concept of these rights — subordinating the rights of an individual to the collective — or with actual non-respect, abuse and limitation of such rights.

Emphasis put on the status of an individual within the state i.e., its freedoms, rights and duties, is today aimed at manifesting a different approach to this issue. The new concept assumes that human rights as natural rights and rights of a person and a citizen constitute the basis for the arrangement of political and social relations within a democratic state ruled by law, in which the state and the legal system provide these rights with special guarantees. Placing the regulations regarding this matter in chapter II was a conscious expression of breaking with the past and reference to modern standards of human rights.

The inner structure of this chapter additionally systematizes the matter discussed. Chapter II includes: General Principles, Personal Freedoms and Rights, Political Freedoms and Rights, Economic, Social and Cultural Freedoms and Rights, Means for the Defense of Freedoms and Rights as well as Duties. This structure also reflects the influence and inspiration of the systematic order regarding the freedoms and rights of a person and a citizen recognized in basic instruments of international law.

Another issue typical of the new Polish constitution is the manner in which it discusses the sources of law. The issues regarding this matter have been grouped and regulated, as a whole, in one separate chapter. Moreover, this chapter has been placed in a very important position within the systematic order of the constitution: this chapter appears as the third one.

The complex regulation regarding legal acts as well as the important place of these issues in the constitution are rarely observed in other constitutions. Such treatment is exceptional for the constitutions of the post-socialist countries although chapters specially devoted to the issue of legislation are to be found in the constitutions of Latvia and Estonia.

The reason that the creators of the Polish constitution took such a decision was to emphasize the high importance of the law, especially those legal provisions that are universally binding. It is connected with the aspiration to establish conditions for the functioning of a state ruled by law (in the meaning: Rechtstaat, Etat de droit), as well as guarantees for citizens' freedoms and rights. Keeping distance from the ambiguity regarding these issues in the provisions of the previous constitution, as well as from the non-democratic practices of the law-making process under that constitution also constituted a highly important motive. The 1952 Constitution allowed for the adoption, in an extra-constitutional manner, of normative acts interfering with the sphere of citizens' rights and allowed for the establishment of authorities entitled to issue such acts. In this way, this constitution allowed for the relative autonomy of the administration in the process of creation of legal norms, sometimes not even properly promulgated, but defining the legal status of an individual or the competence of the State apparatus.

The idea of gathering the provisions regarding this issue in one chapter, as well as limiting the prerogatives of the administration and other non-parliamentary organs regarding the law-making process was aimed at preventing a repeat of such situation. There were many objections concerning this concept raised by legislators which, according to some opinions, was not given adequate treatment in the constitution. Certain resolutions in this respect are nowadays criticized. Nevertheless, the concept seemed promising and it expressed the idea of respect for the law that has been finally adopted in the constitution.

Thus, chapter III — entitled "Sources of Law" — introduces, first of all, a clear distinction between provisions on universally binding law and provisions of domestic law that cannot regulate the citizens' rights; especially, they cannot constitute a basis for taking decisions about citizens.

This chapter enumerates normative acts that include universally binding provisions, and by formulating indirectly the principle of the primacy of a statute, precisely defines conditions of issuing regulations laid down for implementation of statutes and the types of these regulations, as well as specifying the authorities able to issue them.

The chapter further defines the relation between this type of legislation and domestic law i.e., the place of the international agreements within the domestic legal order and the mode of their ratification. This is very important against the backdrop of previous constitutional practice of the period of real socialism that expressed an ambiguous relation to international law. Then, recognition of international instruments on human rights was declared but was coupled with an aversion to respect modern standards within the protection of rights and freedoms of a person.

Finally, the openness of the constitution to future integration with the European Union resulted in the inclusion in this chapter of a special mechanism for ratification of Poland's accession to the EU and the principles regarding adaptation of our national law to the European Community law. In this way, this chapter performs the function similar to the function of provisions of Chapter 14 and 15 of the amended French Constitution of the Fifth Republic or chapters of constitutions of other countries like Belgium, Sweden, Estonia, Croatia or Macedonia, specially devoted to the issues of treaties or international relations. Nevertheless, the Polish constitution does not include a chapter separately discussing the subject of international relations or issues regarding the European Union.

5. The systematic order of the constitutional provisions referring to the system of government i.e., organization, structure, competence and mutual relations between the public authorities, is based on the concept of regulation — in successive chapters — of the individual State organs and then the organs of local government. It is typical that these chapters do not include and in their titles do not make use of complex definitions of the legislative, executive and judicial branches in regard to each of the three powers. Our constitution does not include, like the constitutions of Belgium, Greece, Macedonia, Romania, Slovenia, Croatia, Bosnia-Herzegovina, one general chapter (or title) devoted to the structure of the State authorities. The main idea regarding the separation of powers has been defined in one of the provisions of chapter I of the new Polish Constitution, and this chapter discusses also which organs perform appropriate functions in this respect; and the succeeding chapters include only — as previously noted — provisions regarding individual organs (see the titles of chapters, presented above).

The primary place in this complex of issues is held by the Sejm and the Senate i.e., provisions regarding the organization, functions and mode of the functioning of the parliament. Chapter IV is devoted to the above issues and there the work of both parliamentary chambers is defined. The matter defined there is subject to an inner systematic order which is reflected in the subtitles. These are as follows: Elections and the Term of Office, Deputies and Senators, Organization and Functioning, Referendum.

As can be observed, two issues are found there that are not so closely connected with parliamentary structure, organization and procedures, namely, elections (electoral law) to both chambers and the referendum. Reservations regarding the placing of the provisions concerning the electoral law in this chapter have been mentioned earlier: the problem concerns not only their lack connection with parliamentary issues but the distraction of the issue of the electoral law. Moreover, placing the institution of the referendum there seems to be dubious. However, it might be difficult to state that there is nothing that connects it with the parliamentary issues as both chambers are involved in the procedure for announcing a referendum. However, the referendum as an instrument of direct democracy constitutes, together with representative (indirect) democracy, one of the two contradictory forms of exercise of power by the sovereign, that is — the nation (this principle has been discussed in chapter I). The combined regulation of these forms of the exercise of power diminishes their contradictory character by suggesting their non-controversial relations and emphasizes their rather supplementary character.

As regards the executive power, according to the above mentioned concept, the constitution separately regulates the matter of the President (chapter V) and the government i.e., the Council of Ministers together with government administration (chapter VI) however, the government and the President constitute together a dual executive power — as is clearly stated in chapter I of the constitution.

The constitution does not include separate chapters regulating — as does the French Constitution — the mutual relations or connections of another character between these three organs i.e., the parliament, the President and the Council of Ministers or the two branches of government, the legislative and the executive.

The order of this triad: the parliament–the President–the government, and especially the placing of the provisions regarding the parliament before those dealing with the head of state, are not accidental. It reflects the traditional Polish respect for the parliament and parliamentary democracy, as well as a respect typical of traditional parliamentarism or even acceptance of an insignificant preponderance of the parliament — within the system of authoritative organs — as the direct representative of the sovereign. This issue has been discussed earlier and it was probably the reason that there were no proposals to give primacy to the president as was done, for example, in the French Constitution of the Fifth Republic, in the contemporary constitutions of the Russian Federation and several other countries of the region, as well as in the Polish Constitution of 1935.

This does not necessarily mean that the parliament has been awarded the privilege of domination. On the contrary, there have been attempts to limit its precedence over the executive by introducing the principle of balance of powers to the constitution. However, the significant position of the parliament as the representative organ has been preserved.

The Constitution of the Republic of Poland of 1997, like the majority of modern constitutions of Western and Eastern Europe, with the exception of the constitutions of Belgium, Greece or Romania, regulates the issues regarding the self-government and the local administration in a separate chapter; here, it is chapter VII. These issues are discussed after the regulations regarding the government and government administration which signifies the logical continuation of the subject matter of the public uthority and the system of its execution at local level. The connection of these issues with the matter of the executive is clear there, and only then does the Constitution move to discuss the issue of judicial authority.

We must remember that the constitution pays a lot of attention to the issues of self-administration, especially local government, also in chapter I. The demand of establishing a broad system of self-administration constituted one of the main slogans of the Solidarity movement, and it became obvious that the new constitution would regulate this matter in a very comprehensive way.

Judicial power is regulated in chapter VIII entitled Courts and Tribunals. The provisions of the constitution leave no doubt that by this authority they understood either classic holders of this power i.e., common courts and courts of special character like the Chief Administrative Court or the Tribunal of State, as well as the constitutional court — called in Poland — the Constitutional Tribunal.

Joint regulation of all these institutions in one chapter allows for the establishment of a coherent system for the whole judiciary, although there are many obvious differences in the character of certain courts, for example, as between the common and the constitutional judiciary. It should be admitted that the concept of the Polish legislator regarding this issue is original. The constitutional judiciary is usually not identified with the judicial authority and the regulation regarding it is not connected with the common judiciary.

Beside the regulations regarding all types of courts, the issue of the National Council of the Judiciary is discussed in this chapter. This institution, established in 1989 and whose concept appeared during the Round Table talks, was appointed mainly to safeguard the independence of courts.

The following chapter of the Polish constitution is devoted to the organs of the state control and protection of legality. The Supreme Chamber of Control is discussed there, an organ of state control of long and democratic tradition. It was established in Poland under the provisions of the Constitution of 1921 as an organ subordinate to parliament which remained in existence, with short intervals, during the whole postwar period. It also includes organs for the legal protection of a modern generation of rights — the Commissioner of Citizens' Rights (Ombudsman) appointed in 1987, and the National Council of Radio Broadcasting and Television — appointed in the 90s.

The latter organ has a double character: on the one hand, it is an administrative agency independent from the Council of Ministers, since it gives concessions to radio and television broadcasting stations, issues regulations etc., and on the other hand, it safeguards the freedom of speech and the public interest in radio broadcasting and television. The constitution emphasizes the role of the Council and that is why the Council is included in the chapter devoted to the regulations of organs of the law enforcement.

6. The Constitution of the Republic of Poland of 1997, as many other constitutions, separately discusses the problem of public finances. The principles regarding management of the public financial resources by the state are discussed in chapter X, specially devoted to this problem. It discusses, amongst other things, the collection of financial resources and their apportionment (special precautions have been taken in the constitution regarding the method of taking state decisions on the public finances, bearing in mind the experiences of the past, when the state became indebted in uncontrolled ways), as well as the principles for imposition of taxes and the organization of the State Treasury. The next part of this chapter is devoted to principles and procedure for preparation of a draft State Budget and its adoption, as well as the requirements regarding the budget deficit, which results from the idea of economic voluntarism prevalent in the former system. Finally, it deals with protective measures against political blockages in parliament and provisions on the status and competence of the central bank of the State — the National Bank of Poland — together with guarantees regarding its independence from government. The fact that the Act on public finances, adopted unanimously by the parliamentary majority and the opposition, means that a great importance is given to the problems of an adequate administration of the public finances.

7. There are no doubts that the regulation regarding extraordinary measures somehow reflects our history. Experiences from the period of the state of siege imposed in Poland in 1981 due to the domestic situation and in order to achieve certain political aims [11] resulted in especially carefully drafted regulation of this issue, included in chapter XI. First of all, a distinction between the three extraordinary measures has been drawn namely, a state of siege, a state of emergency and a state of natural disaster together with their detailed description. Thereafter, the procedures and competence of organs that may introduce them have been described in detail, and finally — of importance — very definite limits to citizens' rights during any period requiring extraordinary measures have been set down. The principle of parliamentary control over the introduction and period of such measures is one of the characteristic features of this regulation within the new constitution.

---

[11] Constitution of 1952 according to which (and somehow with its abuse) the state of siege was introduced did not anticipated the institution of the emergency state.

8. Finally, typical of all constitutions, the last chapter is devoted to provisions regarding its amendment. Unlike the Constitution of 1952, which was very laconic in this respect and did not create any special difficulties in procedures for amending the basic law, the provisions of the new Polish constitution are more sophisticated and at the same time very rigorous (some argue too rigorous).

Chapter XII, which defines the procedures for amendment of the constitution introduces — in comparison with procedures for the adoption of the statutes — many procedural obstacles to making such amendment of the constitution difficult, for example, by attributing a special status to such proposals. Thus, the provisions of this chapter change the class of holders of the right to initiate the procedure to amend the constitution, introduces long and obligatory intervals in the realization of the subsequent stages of the amendment procedure, require unanimous resolution of both chambers in this respect, as well as the existence of a qualified majority.

Nevertheless, what is most amazing in this procedure — and which in result affects the whole systematic order of the constitution — is the introduction of more strict restrictions if the amendment relates to the provisions of chapters I, II or XII. There, the requirements regarding terms of amendment are even more restricted and, moreover, provides for the possibility of holding a referendum on the issues defined in those chapters. The right to require the holding of a referendum is vested in every holder of the right to initiate the process of amendment of the constitution.

The result of the introduction of the above mentioned constitutional resolutions is, of course, the significant consolidation and strengthening of provisions included in the above mentioned chapters. Their selection does not require even a comment since they constitute the basic principles regarding the state and the law, the freedoms and the obligations of a person and a citizen, as well as the mode of amendment of the constitution.

Chapters I, II and XII select from the text of the constitution, in a very specific way, the additional difficulties in amending provisions included in these chapters. This activity reminds one of the entrenched clauses regarding the defined principles of the system of government that appear in other constitutions. However, in the Polish context, it has a different character. First of all, it does not mean that this matter is invariable. The matter included in these chapters is — from the formal point of view — entirely changeable, although it requires the implementation of specially difficult procedure. This procedure means that such amendment will have to be made considering the broad political consensus (parliamentary one), and in case of holding of a referendum, considering the support of the society. Moreover, this relative invariability (or difficult variability) refers not to the selected principles or only to one principle, but to their entire complex, including all the basic principles of the broadly understood political and social system of the Republic of Poland, all freedoms, rights and obligations of an individual as well as the provisions regarding the mode of amendment of the constitution. These provisions have precedence over the other provisions within the hierarchy of constitutional principles, as well as within the hierarchy of the moral, political and social values represented by them.

The last chapter of the constitution, chapter XIII, is of a somewhat technical character, if we may use such a definition. It is devoted to final and transitional provisions so it does not include new independent principles and, moreover, its provisions will expire after some time. Thus, many constitutions do not include such provisions in their integral text and separate constitutional acts are adopted in such cases. This approach was considered by the Constitutional Committee of National Assembly, however, the final decision taken was different. A view that the exclusion of these provisions from the text of the constitution might result in a lack of respect for them, may have prevailed.

Nevertheless, these provisions do not only have a technical, ordinal significance, especially in a situation where the constitution is a fundamental act supporting and introducing a new political, economic and social system, a new axiological attitude to many problems of fundamental significance for the state and society, as well as many new procedures, legal institutions and guarantees.

This chapter has a fundamental significance from the point of view of the implementation of a constitution. The clause stating that this act comes into force after three months from the date of its promulgation, marked only the beginning of difficult and complicated processes. The spontaneous influence of the constitution on changes to existing legislation are not in conformity with the constitution, since it acts only in very limited spheres. The tasks of changing the presently existing legal order have been imposed on the State authorities and these tasks are defined in the provisions of chapter XIII. These provisions state now that e.g., the government is obliged, in two years after coming into force of this constitution, to submit essential bills regarding the change of the existing legal order. These two years end soon and it is so difficult thereafter to amend the constitution. Chapter XIII became the special shield and guarantee of the real implementation of the constitution.

This comment ends consideration of the systematic order of the new Polish constitution. This systematic order is in conformity with modern trends in democratic constitutionalism and reflects the hierarchy of values and priorities of the Polish legislator.

Leszek Garlicki

Professor, University of Warsaw

THE PRINCIPLES OF THE SYSTEM OF GOVERNMENT
IN THE REPUBLIC OF POLAND

I. INTRODUCTION

The Constitution of 2nd April 1997 is a document abundant in principles and general clauses. It undoubtedly belongs to a group of basic laws whose authors have aimed not only at the creation of a system of organs and institutions, but also at making it subject to a developed network of principles and values of a more general character. Such an approach had many causes.

The first was the manner of preparing the constitution, a product of the considerations of a collective body, i.e. the Constitutional Committee, and a resultant of drafts previously submitted by particular political subjects. This fact inevitably encouraged the participant in the work on the constitution to leave their own "deposits" in the text. Moreover, the considerable influence on the final configuration of the content of the constitution exerted by the experts also encouraged a comprehensive approach to general principles, which is typical of "scholarly" tendency to systematize the elaborated material.

The second cause was connected with the experiences of previous constitutional practice, when defects and gaps in specific provisions of the Constitution of 1952 were remedied by broad reference to the general principles of the system of government. Let us recall that a new content for these principles was formulated by the amendment of 29th December 1989, so they proved useful enough to adjust old constitutional norms to the new reality. A mission devoted to such adjustments was undertaken especially actively by the Constitutional Tribunal. In certain principles (in particular the principle of a democratic state ruled by law) it has adopted contents so wide that they almost replace the written text of the constitution. Such "success" achieved by general principles in 1989–96 resulted in a situation where it would have been very difficult to omit some of them in the course of drafting

51

a new constitution. Since any omission might have suggested a rejection of the previous understanding of those principles, the authors of the constitution — accentuating mostly the continuation of the tradition of the preceding eight years — tried to avoid it.

The third cause is related to disputes about the axiological substance of the constitution. It is well-known that criticism aroused by the constitution actively concentrated on the charge of "axiological neutrality" and, hence, the ignoring of Poland's heritage, values and experiences. Even if such criticism has not led to the creation of the constitution as a document with an excessively "ideological tinge", it did encourage its authors to include in the text a considerable, perhaps excessive, number of declarations and statements of a very general nature.

Thus, in the Constitution of 1997 one may find many principles and general clauses of very different dimensions and significance. They are expressed, above all, in the extensive preamble (which also contains a particular *invocatio Dei*, and which identifies such universal values as truth, justice, good and beauty as emanating, inter alia, from belief in God) and the first chapter — "The Republic" — comprising 29 articles. Among these clauses and principles, there can be distinguished a particular group of those considered the most important, sometimes defined in doctrine as "the principles of principles"[1]. Some of them express the ideas and values typical of a contemporary democratic state, other manifest the specific character of Polish historical tradition and its path to democracy. Altogether, they compose the constitutional identity of the state.

Any attempt to classify or enumerate these principles will have, in the nature of things, an arbitrary character. Hence, at this point we have to confine ourselves to describing several principles[2] which have already developed a most fundamental and established content, that most comprehensively characterize the axiology of the new Constitution and the directions in which its specific provisions should be interpreted.

[1] Cf. M. Kruk: *Konstytucyjne zasady podstawowe — ich znaczenie prawne i katalog* [*Basic Constitutional Principles: Their Legal Significance and Catalogue*], (in:) *Zasady podstawowe polskiej Konstytucji* [*Fundamental Principles of the Polish Constitution*], edited by W. Sokolewicz, Warszawa 1998, p. 13. This notion appeared in a handbook by Z. Jarosz and S. Zawadzki: *Wstęp... [Introduction...].*

[2] Slightly different catalogue was proposed by W. Osiatyński (in:) *A Brief History of the Constitution*, "East European Constitutional Review" 1997, No. 2–3, p. 70 et seq.

II. THE PRINCIPLE OF SOVEREIGNTY OF THE NATION

1. Every modern constitution specifies, in some manner, in whom the sovereign power in the state is vested. The Constitution of 1997 does not depart from typical solutions in this respect. Article 4(1) reads: "Supreme power in the Republic of Poland shall be vested in the Nation". We must stress, however, that such notion should be perceived also in a negative aspect — recognition of the "Nation" as a sovereign means that any particular social group or political party cannot exercise power. In that sense, the present solution (repeating the formula of December 1989) is a departure from the provisions of 1952 which specified the "working people of towns and villages" as the holder of power.

2. Power is exercised by the Nation mostly through the mechanism of elections and representative democracy based on the concept of free mandate (Article 104 of the Constitution). However, Article 4(2) envisages the existence of certain forms of direct democracy.

They particularly take the form of a referendum. Currently, the Constitution provides for the use of a local referendum (Article 170) and three forms of nationwide referenda. Firstly, a referendum may be held "in respect of matters of particular importance to the State" (Article 125(1)); however, the holding of a referendum is at no time an obligation of an absolute nature. The objective of a referendum is to give voice to the Nation in a certain "matter", but a referendum is not a way by which competencies of constitutional organs of the State might be supplanted. In particular, statutes cannot be adopted by a means of a referendum. A decision to hold a referendum (which also specifies the date and the wording of the questions) may be taken by the Sejm, or by the President of the Republic, provided that the consent of the Senate is obtained. Hence, it is impossible to hold a referendum without consent given by at least one house of parliament. The result of a referendum is binding, if more than half of the number of those having the right to vote have participated in it (Article 125(3)). Details in this respect are determined by the Act of 29th June 1995 on Referendum, however it should be adjusted to the provisions of the new constitution.

Secondly, a referendum may be used as an element in the procedure for amending the constitution, but only in a situation where such amendment relates to its most important provisions (contained in chapters 1, 2 and 13) and only where — after the passing of that amendment by parliament — such referendum has been required by the President of the Republic, the Senate or at least one-fifth of the constitutional number of Deputies (Article 235(6)). In such case, the amendment of the constitution is deemed accepted if the majority of those voting express support for it, and the number of persons participating in the referendum does not matter for the validity of its result.

Thirdly, a referendum may be held in order to grant consent for ratification of an international agreement on Poland's accession to an organization to which the competence of organs of State authority in relation to certain matters is delegated (Article 90(1)). It is the Sejm that decides between the use of legislative procedure and the holding of a referendum (Article 90(4)).

The Constitution provides for the procedure of a people's initiative (100 thousand voters may submit a bill to the Sejm — Article 118(2)), but its realization requires the adoption of an appropriate statute.

III. THE PRINCIPLE OF INDEPENDENCE AND SOVEREIGNTY OF THE STATE

1. This principle has not such a universal character as the principle of sovereignty of the Nation or some other principles discussed in further parts of this study. However, due to the Polish historical experiences, it is relatively intensely manifested in the Constitution of 1997. In its preamble we can find phrases relating to our ancestors struggling for independence and recalling the time when the Nation was deprived of the possibility of a sovereign and democratic determination of the fate of the Motherland. Protection of the independence and integrity of the national territory is specified as paramount among the duties of the Republic (Article 5). The role of the Armed Forces (Article 26(1)) and the duty of citizens to defend the Homeland (Article 85(1)) are also defined within the context of these values. And finally, one of the fundamental duties of the President of the Republic is to "safeguard the sovereignty and security of the State as well as the inviolability and integrity of its territory". Nevertheless, strong accentuation of sovereignty and independence is typical of not only the Polish Constitution — similar solutions may be found, for obvious reasons,

in constitutions of both the states which recently regained their independence[3] and even those with a well-established existence.

Independence means the existence of the Republic as a separate state, and this value has been emphasized by recalling the period of Poland's partitions (1795–1918) and the events of the World War II. Independence means Poland's existence within its present borders; thus, the numerous instances of emphasis on the principle of integrity and inviolability of the state territory are not accidental in the text of the Constitution. Sovereignty means the ability of the State to decide independently about all matters related to it, recalling the negative experiences of the years 1944–1989.

2. Poland's sovereignty in the sphere of international relations does not necessary imply a prohibition against its involvement in the processses of European integration and, nowadays, this means Poland's accession to NATO and the European Union. This is manifested in Article 90 (the so-called European clause), whose paragraph 1 allows to "delegate — by virtue of international agreements — to an international organization or international institution the competence of organs of State authority in relation to certain matters". The scope of such delegation must be limited to "certain matters". Hence, Article 90(1) cannot be treated as a basis for complete renunciation by Poland of its state sovereignty, as has been argued by some opponents of the Constitution.

Moreover, there exist complicated procedural requirements for the enactment of such international agreements, designed to ensure the protection of Poland's sovereignty. Firstly, a statute, granting consent for ratification of such international agreement, is passed by a two-thirds majority of the Sejm and the Senate taken in the presence of at least half of the constitutional numbers of their members (Article 90(2)), which is a more stringent requirement than in respect of passing amendments to the Constitution (Article 235(4)). Secondly, the Sejm may decide to replace the method of granting parliamentary consent by holding a nationwide referendum (Article 90(3) and (4)). Thirdly, both a statute granting consent for ratification of an international agreement and such and agreement may be challenged before the Constitutional Tribunal as to its conformity with the Constitution (Article 133(2) and Article 188(1)).

---

[3] Cf. e.g. provisions of the preamble and Article 3 of the Lithuanian Constitution of 1992 or provisions of Articles 1 and 54 of the Estonian Constitution of 1992.

Additional constitutional limitations relate to use of the Polish Armed Forces. The introduction of a state of war is allowed "only in the event of armed aggression against the territory of the Republic of Poland or when an obligation of common defence against aggression arises by virtue of international agreements" (Article 116(2)). The principles for deployment of the Armed Forces abroad and the principles for the presence of foreign troops on the territory of the Republic of Poland must be specified by statutes or ratified agreements (Article 117).

IV. THE PRINCIPLE OF A DEMOCRATIC STATE RULED BY LAW

1. This principle was introduced to Poland's constitution by the December (1989) Amendment, and the present formulation is a verbatim repetition of that provision. Such unity of content is of great importance, since it makes it possible to receive the rich practice of the Constitutional Tribunal and other courts, developed after 1990, as of continuing relevance to the foundations of the current Constitution[4]. Unlike the above-mentioned principles, whose content should have been reconstructed mostly on the basis of doctrinal views, the principle of the law state has already been subject to judicial interpretation which determines — in a binding fashion — some of its consequences.

The introduction of the notion of a "democratic state ruled by law" into the Polish constitution was an intentional adoption of foreign, particularly German, patterns. Thereby, the authors of the December Amendment "invited" the practice and doctrine to seek more concrete substance in this general formula. Obviously, one can attribute many different meanings to the term a "state ruled by law". In the broadest sense, it is in fact tantamount to the sum of the characteristic features of the system of government of a modern democratic state. Therefore, the following attributes of the principle of a law state can be identified: constitutionalism, statutes as fundamental sources of the law (superiority and exclusiveness of statutes), separation of powers, constitutional regulation of

---

[4] In a judgment of 26th November 1997 (K 26/97), the Constitutional Tribunal held: "...basic substance of the principle of a democratic state ruled by law, expressed by Article 2 of the [new] Constitution may, and should, be understood in the same way, as it was understood in the previous constitutional order".

fundamental rights and freedoms of the individual along with mechanisms ensuring their effective protection (administrative courts, right of recourse, constitutional complaint), independence of judges[5]. Most of these principles and institutions are explicitly encompassed by separate constitutional provisions, nevertheless, sometimes they should be inferred directly from the principle of a democratic state ruled by law.

The principle of a state ruled by law in its formal aspect is expressed in Article 7 of the Constitution which requires that the State organs should "function on the basis of, and within the limits of, the law". From this it follows that the competence of a State organ cannot be assumed and, in case of a lack of expressly specified provisions conferring the competence (powers), we must deem that such powers have not been conferred[6]. This clearly contrasts with regulation of the position of a citizen who is allowed to do everything that has not been prohibited by the law (Article 31(1) and (2)).

2. In the practice of the Constitutional Tribunal there has developed a tendency to treat the clause of a democratic state ruled by law as a collective expression of several principles and rules of more precise character which, even if not explicitly written in the Constitution, emanates indirectly therefrom. Having "found" such coherent principles and giving them a constitutional form (and, hence, subjecting the ordinary legislator to their binding force), the Tribunal complemented — to a large extent — the text of the existing Constitution.

This was, in fact, an indispensable activity since the constitutional provisions existing before 1997 contained so many gaps and uncertainties that is was frequently necessary to use general clauses.

The Constitutional Tribunal has dealt especially comprehensively with the formal interpretation of a "state ruled by law". In its practice developed after 1986, the principle of exclusiveness of statutes and subsidiary nature of legal acts issued by the government has been accentuated. Since 1990, the Tribunal has particularly emphasized "the principle of citizen's confidence in the State" (resembling the German concept of *Vertrauens-*

---

[5] M. Wyrzykowski: *Zasada demokratycznego państwa prawnego [The Principle of a Democratic State Ruled by Law]*, (in:) *Zasady podstawowe...*, p. 68.

[6] See, in particular, Resolution of the Constitutional Tribunal of 10th May 1994, W 7/94, OTK 1994, part I, p. 211–212.

schutz). This principle results, inter alia, in the adoption of certain rules of law-making which are defined by the doctrine as "the rule of decent legislation". At this point, we should mention: the requirement of the definiteness of the law (enacting unclear or ambiguous provisions is regarded as violating the principle of a state ruled by law), the prohibition against ex post facto laws (relating to all provisions which alter the legal situation of a person to his disadvantage), the requirement to provide an appropriate adaptation period before a law comes into force (the *vacatio legis* principle, connected with the requirement to respect so-called "pending interests"), the protection of acquired rights (interference in vested rights acquired legally may be admissible only in extraordinary situations). The proportionality principle (also known as the prohibition of excessive intervention) should be mentioned separately. It concerns all domains of law, in practice — mostly administrative law[7]— and plays a special role in determining the scope of admissible limitations of an individual's rights. All these judicial considerations maintain their validity on the grounds of the Constitution of 1997.

The judgments of the Constitutional Tribunal have also found in the clause of a democratic state ruled by law certain material content, in particular some individual rights and freedoms. This resulted from the above-mentioned "constitutional deficit": since the text of the Constitution lacked certain fundamental rights and freedoms, the Tribunal inferred them from the law state clause. In this way, they "found" in the Constitution the right of access to courts (Judgment of 7th January 1992, K 8/91), the principle of dignity of the person (Resolution of 17th March 1993, W 16/92), the right to life (Judgment of 28th May 1997, K 26/96) and the right to privacy (Judgment of 24th June 1997, K 21/97). We must, however, note that the current Constitution comprehensively regulates all fundamental rights and freedoms of the individual and, therefore, there is no longer a need to infer them from the clause of a democratic state ruled by law.

3. The Constitution of 1997 also contains elaborate provisions dealing with the system of the sources of law (particularly Articles 87–94) which

---

[7] But on the basis on this principle, the Constitutional Tribunal also found (with three dissenting opinions) unconstitutional the provisions liberalizing abortion (judgment of 28th May 1997, K 26/96).

should be considered as a peculiar codification of previous judgments. The Constitution, in particular, distinguished the sources of universally binding law from the sources of internal law, stating that only the former may bind the citizen. The system of universally binding sources of law (a constitution — ratified international agreements — statutes — regulations) was given a closed character. Moreover, government legislation may only have an implementing nature. This issue is discussed elsewhere, however, we should not forget their direct connection with the clause of a democratic state ruled by law.

V. THE PRINCIPLE OF CIVIL SOCIETY

1. In Poland, the reasons for the existence of the concept of "civil society" appeared in the period of the so-called "first Solidarity" (i.e. 1980–81). It was used at that time as a slogan to oppose the existing situation, in which citizens were deprived of the possibility of influencing the process of governing, and to propose a situation where citizens would be able to participate in the process of transformation — and society would be an organization composed of individuals aware of their rights and goals and capable of implementing them. However, the conditions enabling the formation of such a defined civil society only appeared after 1989.

The Constitution of 1997 does not apply the notion of "civil society", but in numerous phrases it reveals basic elements of that concept. Above all, it assumes that a modern society has a pluralistic character and that freedom of expression of diverse views and interests is the essence of its functioning. Hence, everyone has the freedom to participate in the activity of organizations and structures of one's own choice, which enables one's self-realization as a citizen, a worker or a member of a local community.

The principle of political pluralism, with freedom for the creation and functioning of political parties as its central element, is of particular importance. A democratic state (at this point we come back round to the principles of the Nation's sovereignty and a democratic state ruled by law) is a state where there exists pluralism for political parties. This is one of the main differences from the model based on exclusive possession of power by one party. The freedom for the creation and functioning of political parties belongs to political freedoms of citizens. Its role is so essential that the authors of the Constitution decided to declare it in the first chapter, among the fundamental principles of the system of government. However, this freedom was further developed by the Act of 27th June 1997 on Political Parties.

Article 11 of the Constitution specifies three requirements which should be met by an organization to qualify as a political party: (1) it should be composed of at least 1000 Polish citizens; (2) members must associate on the principle of voluntariness and equality; (3) its purpose is to influence, by democratic means, the formulation of the policy of the State and the exercise of public authority.

However, freedom for the creation and functioning of political parties is not unlimited, since in Poland, similar to many other countries, historical experiences have led to certain restrictions in the enjoyment of this freedom. Pursuant to Article 13 of the Constitution, such prohibition relates to the programme and ideological character of a party (prohibiting those political parties: (1) whose programmes are based upon totalitarian methods and the modes of activity of nazism, fascism and communism, (2) whose programmes or activities sanction racial or national hatred), and also to methods and principles of party organization (prohibiting those political parties: (1) whose programmes or activities sanction the application of violence for the purpose of obtaining power or influencing State policy, or (2) provide for the secrecy of their own structure or membership).

Any organization whose characteristics correspond with at least one of the above mentioned features, cannot be recognized as a political party, but where existence of such features have been ascertained in relation to an already existing party, then its aims and activities may be declared not in conformity with the Constitution. Judgments in this respect may only be made by the Constitutional Tribunal.

2. Besides freedom for political parties, the Constitution also ensures freedom for the creation of other associations, societies and organizations (Article 12 and Article 58). They do not have to be composed of Polish citizens alone, but their programmes and activities are also subject to limitations and prohibitions imposed by Article 13 of the Constitution.

Social attention is paid in the Constitution to regulation of the status and duties of trade unions, which should be explained in the light of historical experience of "Solidarity" Trade Union. Article 59 ensures the freedom of association in trade unions, socio-occupational organizations of farmers, and in employers' organizations. These organizations and trade unions are entitled to bargain, to be a party in collective disputes, and to conclude collective labour agreements. The above-mentioned freedoms may be enjoyed by trade unions with such limitations as are permissible in accordance with international agreements to which the Republic of Poland is a party. The Constitution also guarantees the right to strike which is, however, "subject to limitations specified by statute". In order to protect the public interest, the conduct of strikes by specified categories of employees or in specific fields statutes may be forbidden.

Within certain professions self-regulatory bodies are created in order to safeguard the proper practice of such professions in accordance with, and for the purpose of protecting, the public interest (Article 17(1)).

3. Subjectivity of a citizen as an inhabitant of a particular territorial unit should guarantee the existence of local government, understood as a separation of certain domain of matters (due to their local character) and entrusting their independent solution to that social group which these matters mostly concern. The existence of local government is a prerequisite of a system of government in a democratic state. The Constitution of 1997 formulates an absolute requirement for the existence of local government and demands that it discharges a considerable part of public duties "in its own name and under its own responsibility" (Article 16). The basic role in this system of local government should be played by the commune [gmina] (Article 164(1) and (3)); however, the Constitution does not specify further levels of local government, but states that "other units of regional and/or local self-government shall be specified by statute" (Article 164(2)). As is already known, this provided a basis for the introduction, in 1998, of a three-stage structure of local government, composed of the commune, districts [powiat] and voivodship.

4. There are many other institutions and facilities indispensable for the actual functioning of civil society and of political pluralism as its basis. The first chapter of the Constitution identifies two basic institutions: means of mass communication as well as churches and religious organizations.

Freedom of the mass media (the press and other form of communication of printed matter, as well as the so-called electronic media, i.e.

radio and television) is a universally recognized prerequisite of political pluralism, and the prohibition against preventive censorship is the essence of that freedom. A general guarantee in this respect is formulated in Article 14 of the Constitution, as well as further found in the chapter on rights and freedoms of the individual (Article 54), whilst the status of radio and television is subject to further specific regulations (Article 213).

The role of churches and religious organizations is universally perceived in the context of the freedom of faith. However, Poland's specific historical experience requires the inclusion of churches and religious organizations in political deliberations about civil society. This fact is manifested in the Constitution in which individual guarantees of freedom of conscience and religion (Article 53) are accompanied by a general definition of the role of churches and religious organizations in Poland's system of government. Article 25 formulates four basic principles in this respect, including: (1) equality of rights enjoyed by churches and other religious organizations (though one should bear in mind that such equality of rights does not necessarily mean an absolute equality); (2) impartiality (neutrality) of the State in matters of personal conviction, whether religious or philosophical, or in relation to outlooks on life; (3) basing the relationship between the State and churches and other religious organizations on the principle of respect for their autonomy and the mutual independence of each in its own sphere, as well as on the principle of cooperation for the individual and the common good; (4) basing the form of relations between the Republic of Poland and other churches and religious organizations on statutes adopted pursuant to agreements concluded between their appropriate representatives and the Council of Ministers and, in respect of relations between the Republic of Poland and the Roman Catholic Church, on international treaty (a Concordat) concluded with the Holy See, and by statute.

VI. THE SEPARATION OF POWERS PRINCIPLE

1. This principle, one of the oldest fundaments of modern constitutionalism, has been contained in all Poland's democratic constitutions. It was, for the first time, outlined in the Constitution of 3rd May 1791 and continued in the March Constitution of 1921. It was then re-established,

almost 60 years after, in Article 1 of the Constitutional Act (the so-called Small Constitution) of 1992, and continued in Article 10(1) of the Constitution of 1997, which reads: "The system of government of the Republic of Poland shall be based on the separation of and balance between the legislative, executive and judicial powers".

Article 10(2) specifies subjects (constitutional organs) in which the exercise of the legislative, executive and judicial power is vested. However, only the holders of the legislative power (namely the Sejm and the Senate) are enumerated precisely and exhaustively — none of the State organs is entitled to adopt acts having the force of statute (with the exception provided for in Article 234 of the Constitution). Specification of holders of the executive power (the President of the Republic and the Council of Ministers) has only an illustrative character, indicating the main components of the executive, but omitting its other constitutional organs (e.g. the Prime Minister or ministers). Similarly, holders of the judicial power are generally defined as "courts and tribunals" and, therefore, specification of types and names of these organs are found in other chapters of the Constitution. In any case, this means that both tribunals (i.e. the Constitutional Tribunal and the Tribunal of State) are included among the elements of the judicial power, which definitely settles doctrinal disputes over this issue generated by the provisions of previous constitutions.

The purpose of Article 10(2) is not an exhaustive enumeration of constitutional organs of the State, but only to express a general principle. It should also be noted that certain constitutional organs of the State do not at all fall within the classic formula of separation of the three branches of power. These include the Supreme Chamber of Control, the Commissioner for Citizens' Rights, the National Council of Radio Broadcasting and Television and the National Council of the Judiciary.

2. The separation of power principle does not have an absolute character. Its main intent is to reject the possibility of accumulation of all power in one hand, but has never been understood as a prohibition against intersection or overlapping of powers of individual authorities. However, this cannot go too far. Against this background, the jurisprudence of the Constitutional Tribunal distinguished two detailed concepts: the concept of

presumed competencies and the concept of "essence" of individual authorities[8].

The former recognizes that competencies which might be relatively unequivocally specified from the point of view of their content — may be ascribed, by implication, to individual authorities. Such implication may, of course, be overthrown at any time by an explicit constitutional provision conferring the right to perform certain duties on an organ of another branch of power (cf. Article 92 of the Constitution conferring lawmaking powers to the executive). This is admissible, because all provisions of the Constitution have the same legal effect and, therefore, a specific provision may establish exceptions to the general principle expressed in Article 10. However, this requires an explicit constitutional regulation, since exceptions cannot be implied. This also means that each such specific provision is subject to literal (exact) interpretation and an extensive interpretation is inadmissible.

Implications concerning competencies, ensuing from the separation of powers principle, cannot be overthrown by provisions of ordinary statutes (not to speak of practice). In this context we should consider the concept of "the essence" of individual authorities. This concept assumes the existence of a specific "core" of competencies of the legislative, the executive and judicial powers, that cannot be interfered with by other branches, since this would mean elimination of the separation of power principle. Hence, ordinary statute may effect some transposition of particular competencies between branches of power; however, intervention in domains belonging to other branches cannot be too deep as such statutory regulation would violate the constitutional principle of separation of powers.

3. The Constitution of 2nd April 1997 establishes the parliamentary system of government in Poland, which corresponds with both the tradition of the Constitution of 1921 and the practice of life in Poland after 1989. Hence, organization of the executive power is based on the principle of dualism (the President of the Republic and the government headed by the Prime Minister) where the government (and individual ministers) are politically accountable to the Sejm and the President has no competencies enabling him to assume the supervision of governmental affairs. However,

---

[8] Cf. judgments of 21st November 1994, K 6/94 (OTK 1994, part II, p. 83 et seq.) and of 22nd November 1995, K 19/95 (OTK 1995, part II, p. 135 et seq.).

it is not a pure form of parliamentarism, since it still has one component typical of a presidential system, namely the election of a President in universal ballot and not by parliament. This is naturally far removed from the introduction of a presidential system, the more so as in the new constitution the actual powers of the head of state are substantially limited.

The system applied by the Constitution of 1997 may be defined as rationalized parliamentarism. The central place in the system of State organs is assigned to the Sejm; however, its decisions must often be taken by an absolute or qualified majority of votes and where there is a lack of such majority — the Sejm has to agree with the will of the Senate (e.g. Article 121(3)) or the President of the Republic (Article 122(5), Article 155). As I have already mentioned, a vote of no confidence in a government may only be passed with the appointment, at the same time, of a new Prime Minister (Article 158(1) — a constructive vote of no confidence).

Although Article 10(1) of the Constitution makes mutual balance a basis of relations between the legislative and the executive powers, other constitutional provisions ensure a considerably stronger position to parliament and, within its framework, to the Sejm. This is consistent with the tradition of Polish parliamentarism which has been characterized, in various periods of its evolution, by the peculiar preponderance of the Sejm[9]. It is, by no means, possible to speak about a full balance between the legislative and the executive, as it might be suggested by the formulations of Article 10(1). In this respect, it is also possible to speak about the unique nature of the present Polish model.

4. The position of the judicial power relies, however, on different principles, since it is based on the independence of the judicature from other branches[10].

---

[9] Cf. e.g. W. Sokolewicz: *Rozdzielone, lecz czy równe? Legislatywa i egzekutywa w Małej Konstytucji 1992 roku* [*Separated, but are they equal? The legislative and the executive in the Small Constitution of 1992*], „Przegląd Sejmowy" 1993, No. 1, p. 26–27; P. Sarnecki: Uwagi 10–12 do art. 1 Małej Konstytucji [Comments 10–12 to Article 1 of the Small Constitution], (in:) *Komentarz do Konstytucji Rzeczypospolitej Polskiej* [*Commentary to the Constitution of the Republic of Poland*], edited by L. Garlicki, Warszawa 1995. These comments have not lost their pertinence on grounds of the Constitution of 1997.

[10] It was repeatedly accentuated in the judgments of the Constitutional Tribunal — e.g. of 21st November 1994, K 6/94, OTK 1994, part II, p. 91; of 27th June 1995, K 4/94, OTK 1995, part I, p. 188.

The position of the judicature is based, to a large extent, on the principle of separation, or even isolation of this judicial power, as one of fundamental principles of a democratic state ruled by law in that only courts may administer justice. When interpreting the principle of separation of power in relation to the judicial branch, a strong stress is put on the principle of independence of courts and exclusive competence of the judicature to exercise the judicial power, and to finally decide about the rights and obligations of the individual or legal persons.

The basic means by which the legislative power may influence the activity of the judicature is making laws specifying the content of the law to be applied by the courts. According to the Continental tradition (including that of Poland), judges are subjected to statutes and, therefore, they have an obligation to respect the provisions contained therein. However, that situation has changed with the appearance of the constitutional courts, because their main purpose is to examine the conformity of statutes to the constitution, and to delete from the legal system those statutes that violate the constitution. Thus, this segment of the judicial branch of government constrains the powers of the legislative branch (a similar role in relation to the executive power is played by administrative courts). This enriches the present picture of the principle of separation of powers, even if it is not an easy task to accustom the common courts to observe the requirement that their decisions should be based not only on statutes, but also on the constitution and international agreements.

VII. THE PRINCIPLE OF SOCIAL MARKET ECONOMY

This principle provides a most general characteristic of Poland's economic system. Article 20 of the Constitution indicates that "a social market economy, ..., shall be the basis of the economic system of the Republic of Poland" and specifies basic components of that economy, including the freedom of economic activity, private ownership, and solidarity, dialogue and co-operation between social partners. Previously, only some of these principles and notions were known to constitutional law in our country. Hence, the assessment of its significance cannot always be made on the basis of established concepts of the doctrine and practice of court decisions.

The concept of "a social market economy" was applied following German doctrine. The Constitution of 1997 does not define this notion, instead, it identified three fundamentals of the system.

Firstly, it is the freedom of economic activity. This principle was formulated in Article 6 introduced to the constitutional provisions in 1989. This freedom finds additional confirmation in Article 22 which admits its limitation "only by means of statute and only" to protect an important public interest. This means that any limitation of the freedom of economic activity demands not only the satisfaction of a formal requirement, viz., including it in a statute (but not in a normative act of lower rank), but must also meet the substantive precondition of the existence of an "important interest of the State". A final decision on whether such requirement has actually been satisfied, or not, will be taken by the Constitutional Tribunal.

Secondly, it is private ownership that should be understood as any property belonging to subjects autonomous from the State and its sector of economic property. This formulation indicates a fundamental option on which the system of ownership relations should be based in Poland and rejects the possibility of return to a system based on the dominance of State property and State enterprises. Moreover, other provisions of the Constitution do not exclude the existence of State ownership and require that each category of ownership should receive equal legal protection (Article 64(2)). This does not, however, reverse the general tendency to accord an essential role to private ownership in the economic system which, in Poland's circumstances, means the requirement of continuing and completing the process of privatization. The role of ownership is also accentuated in other constitutional provisions which, inter alia, guarantees of its general protection (Article 21(1)), allowing any limitation thereof only by means of a statute and only to the extent that it does not violate the substance of that right (Article 64(3)), establishing special guarantees in respect of the procedure for expropriation (Article 21(2)) and referring protection of ownership also to other property rights and the right of succession (Article 21(1) and Article 64(1)).

Thirdly, these are "solidarity, dialogue and cooperation between social partners". These notions have no established tradition in our constitutional law. They seem to express a general concept that disputable matters should be settled by negotiation, which is separately formulated in Article 59 of the Constitution. This should be understood on the ground of the general rule of Article 1 which defines the Republic as the "common good", i.e. such a good as obliges everyone to sacrifice — to a certain degree — his/her own interest. The use of the notion of "social partners" by the Constitution, should be interpreted in the context of a dispute — accompanying its adoption — concerning the explicit regulation of the position and tasks of the so-called Tripartite Commission composed of representatives of the government, trade unions and employers organization, concerned primarily with wage negotiations. No such regulation can be found in the text of the Constitution; however, the fragment of Article 20 discussed above may be understood as a requirement to take into account the opinions of the cited "partners" in the course of resolving matters connected with the social consequences of the functioning of a social market economy.

The general principle of a social market economy relates to all economic sectors and areas, including the agricultural system. In this respect, however, an essential modification has been introduced by Article 23 which defines the family farm as a "basis of the agricultural system of the State". The functioning of market mechanisms cannot, therefore, lead to such structural changes in agricultural ownership as would deprive family farms of their constitutive role in the system. We shall see in the future whether the vision of the agricultural economy based on such model, will be attainable, especially in the light of necessary adjustment of Polish agriculture to the requirements of the European Union.

VIII. THE PRINCIPLE OF THE INHERENT DIGNITY OF THE PERSON

Both Article 30 of the Constitution, as well as the provisions of its preamble, identify "the inherent and inalienable dignity of the person" as the "source of human freedoms and rights". They confer upon it the attribute of inviolability and oblige public authorities to respect and protect it. Thereby, the principle of dignity of the person has been not only accepted as a basic regulation in the system of provisions concerning individual rights and freedoms, but should also be considered one of fundamental principles of the system of government in Poland.

Further analysis of this principle may be found in the chapter devoted to the constitutional status of the individual[11]. At this point, however, we should note that its legal significance is not confined to specification of the content of individual rights and freedoms. The whole system of constitutional norms is, indeed, subordinated to the realization of this principle (and also other principles of Poland's system of government). Hence, it also influence the substance and interpretation of provisions concerning the organization of the State apparatus and the manner of its functioning.

---

[11] Cf. J. Zajadło: *Godność i prawa człowieka* [*Dignity and rights of the person*], „Gdańskie Studia Prawnicze", vol. III, 1998, p. 53 et seq.

Kazimierz Działocha

Professor, University of Wrocław

LAW AND ITS SOURCES
IN THE CONSTITUTION OF THE REPUBLIC OF POLAND

1. A characteristic feature of Poland's Constitution is that it isolates the issue of the sources of law in a separate Chapter. In the course of work on the draft constitution in the Constitutional Committee of the National Assembly, as well as in jurisprudential discussions, doubts were raised about the aptness of such an arrangement. It has been argued that regulation of the sources of law in a single Chapter is problematic and cannot be exhaustive. Nevertheless, arguments for such treatment of the sources of law prevailed in principle. This occurred for the following, interrelated reasons:

a) a desire to arrange those matters which previously generated many disputes and confusion in legislative practice and which primarily resulted from permitting laws to be made in forms other than those specified in the Constitution;

b) attempts to enhance the role of law as a major regulator of relations between the state and individual, based on an awareness of the largely autonomous character of the issue of the sources of law — not constrained by the interests of the law-making body;

c) an intention to separate and codify certain general principles on which the system of sources of law is based (hierarchy and "closure" of the system, an obligation to promulgate acts of binding law, a clearly defined status for ratified international agreements and Community law within the domestic legal order), a task which would have been complicated by dispersal of the relevant provisions in various parts of the constitutional text and which would have reduced their significance[1].

---

[1] Compare: A. Bałaban: *Źródła prawa w polskiej Konstytucji z 2 kwietnia 1997 r.* [*The sources of law in the Polish Constitution of 2nd April 1997*], „Przegląd Sejmowy", 1997, No. 5, p. 34–35; E. Gdulewicz: *Konstytucyjny system źródeł prawa* [*Constitutional system of*

To a large degree, Chapter III of the Constitution fulfils the above-
-mentioned criteria. However, it does not contain a complete (exhaustive)
treatment of the issue of the sources of law, but does play a special role
(further discussed below) within the overall system of provisions dealing
with this topic.

The provisions specifying the competencies of organs of state authority
to issue normative acts are included in those Chapters devoted to particular
organs, also containing provisions specifying the procedures for their
issuance (this mostly relates to Chapter IV, titled "the Sejm and the
Senate", whose Articles 118–123 deal with the legislative process). The
specific principles of and procedures for financial statutes, including the
Budget, are specified in Chapter X — "Public finances" (particularly,
Articles 216–217 and 219–225). In Chapter XI — "Extraordinary measures" — Article 234 establishes a new, hitherto unknown to the basic
catalogue of normative acts contained in Chapter III, a category of
regulations having the force of statute ("decree laws") that may be issued
by the President of the Republic of Poland during any period of state of
siege. The status of the Constitution, which is generally considered
paramount in the catalogue of the sources of universally binding law
(Article 87(1)) is, in fact, defined by the provisions of Article 8 in Chapter I,
the provisions of Chapter XII on amending the Constitution, as well as the
provisions of Chapter VIII dealing with the competencies of the Constitutional Tribunal.

The partial departure from the problem of sources of law — and even
basic provisions about the notion of law outside Chapter III — can neither

---

the sources of law] (in:) *Polskie prawo konstytucyjne* [*Polish Constitutional Law*], edited by
W. Skrzydło, 1997, p. 193 et seq.; Konstytucja Rzeczypospolitej Polskiej z komentarzem
[The Constitution of the Republic of Poland with a commentary] edited by M. Kruk,
Warszawa 1997, p. 16; A. Gwiżdż: *Kilka uwag o tworzeniu prawa pod rządami nowej
Konstytucji* [*Some comments on the law-making under the rules of the new Constitution*],
„Gdańskie Studia Prawnicze", vol. III, 1998, p. 100–101; Z. Jarosz: *Parlament jako organ
władzy ustawodawczej* [*Parliament as an organ of the legislative power*], (in:) *Założenia
ustrojowe, struktura i funkcjonowanie parlamentu* [*Basic assumption of the organization,
structure and functioning of Parliament*], edited by A. Gwiżdż, p. 173–174; P. Winczorek:
Źródła prawa w projekcie Konstytucji Komisji Konstytucyjnej Zgromadzenia Narodowego
[*Sources of law in the Draft Constitution prepared by the Consitutional Committee of the
National Assembly*], „Przegląd Legislacyjny", 1996, No. 4, p. 17; S. Wronkowska, *ibid*, p. 32).

astonish nor provide reason for questioning the separation of that Chapter in the systematics of the Constitution. It can never be the case that "individual Chapters of the basic law (...) so completely cover refor- mulation of any particular sphere of matter that any other provisions dealing with the same subject could not appear in other Chapters of that same law"[2]. What is of more importance is that some "dispersion" of the issue of law and its sources in the text of the Constitution does not undermine the particular significance of the regulations contained in Chapter III. The Chapter establishes the basis for interpretation of all specific regulations of the Constitution within the sphere of law-making activity and is a basis for the settlement of conflicts and doubts which will obviously arise in the course of application of the new Constitution.

2. The Constitution does not contain an explicit definition of the notion of law. Its provisions, subject to the doctrine of law based on the continuity of notions typical of Polish legal culture, make it possible to identify which norms — on the grounds of the Constitution — are binding law within the Republic of Poland.

From the entirety of provisions of the Constitution dealing with the "law" (e.g. in Articles 7–9, Article 31(2), Article 32(1) and Articles 87–94) as norms binding in the Republic of Poland, with the obligation to observe the law (e.g. in Article 83), with various sources of law (particularly statutes), as compared with "rights" and "rights of a citizen (or everyone)", it follows that the law — according to the Constitution — consists of norms of behaviour having a general and abstract character, within the meaning of legal theory. Such an approach has also been taken for many years by legal science in Poland, notwithstanding all changes which have occurred in the field of the law[3]. A similar approach to the problem has

---

[2] A. Gwiżdż, *ibid.*, p. 100.

[3] Compare: S. Rozmaryn: *Ustawa w Polskiej Rzeczypospolitej Ludowej* [*A Statute in the Republic of Poland*], Warszawa 1964, p. 17, 54 et seq.; Konstytucyjny model tworzenia prawa w PRL [The constitutional model of making law in the Polish Peoples' Republic], edited by K. Działocha, Wrocław 1981, p. 122 et seq.; S. Wronkowska, M. Zieliński: *Pojęcie i zakres prawa w projektach Konstytucji RP* [*The notion and scope of law in the draft Constitutions of the Republic of Poland*] (in:) *Prawo, źródła prawa i gwarancje jego zgodności z ustawą zasadniczą w projektach Konstytucji RP* [*The law, sources of law and guarantees of its compatibility with the basic law in the draft Constitutions of the Republic of Poland*], edited by K. Działocha, A. Preisner, Wrocław 1995, s. 7 i n.

been observed, in general, in the practice of the Constitutional Tribunal (TK) which defines a normative act, in its material meaning, in close connection with the characteristic of law as a body of norms being general and abstract in nature (beginning with its judgment U 15/88[4]). The factor of generality and abstractness prevents a legal norm from being abrogated or "consumed" as a result of a single application (TK in the case U 5/94).

The view — known to previous literature concerning the Constitution of the People's Republic of Poland — that the notion of the law (in particular enacted by means of statute) may contain not only general and abstract, but also individual and concrete, norms, cannot be accepted on the grounds of the separation of powers principle (Article 10 of the Constitution), which requires an explicit specification of and distinction between the competencies of the legislative and executive bodies[5].

In light of the practice of the Constitutional Tribunal, particularly its decision U 5/94 — that sums up to some extent all its previous judgments in respect of the notion of a normative act — the view that under the notion of the law and among the sources of law (in a wider and rather indefinite meaning), the Constitution does not include "administrative provisions" (including police regulations) as a form of activity of public administrative authorities resulting from statutorily determined competencies of such authorities, is unjustifiable[6]. Administrative provisions, in the nature of things, do not belong to the scope of "law", but are acts of application thereof (general acts of application of the law) and are not, as such, a subject of constitutional regulation[7]. The author of the aforementioned

---

[4] Compare: J. Oniszczuk: *Orzecznictwo Trybunału Konstytucyjnego w latach 1986–1996 [Practice of the Constitutional Tribunal in 1986–1996]*, Warszawa 1998, p. 22–28; compare also K. Działocha: *Konstytucyjne cechy ustawy [Constitutional attributes of a statute]* (in:) *Postępowanie ustwodawcze w polskim prawie konstytucyjnym [Legislative procedure in Polish constitutional law]*, edited by J. Trzciński, Warszawa 1994, s. 26–28.

[5] Compare: L. Garlicki: *Polskie prawo konstytucyjne. Zarys wykładu [Polish Constitutional Law. Framework of lecture]*, Warszawa 1998, p. 194.

[6] Compare: M. Kulesza: *Źródła prawa i przepisy administracyjne w świetle nowej Konstytucji [Sources of law and administrative provisions in the light of the new Constitution]*, PiP 2/1998, p. 12–13; compare also comments by A. Bałaban: *Czy Konstytucja dotyczy przepisów administracyjnych [Does the Constitution applies to administrative regulations]*, PiP 5/1998, p. 94.

[7] This was stressed during the debate on the draft Constitution in the National Assembly — compare: Shorthand Report from the 3rd session of the National Assembly, part. I, p. 106.

view has also acknowledged this view, which makes the arguments against the Constitution incomprehensible.

Public power provides a basis for operation of the law, regarded as a body of rules governing the behaviour characterized by the above mentioned features. From the Constitution, it follows that the law is binding upon the Republic of Poland by whose institutions it is made (or considered as binding) and which sanction the observance thereof. That principle — accepted by the prevalent doctrine of the law — ensues, in relation to domestic law, from the following clauses: Article 8(1) which provides that "the Constitution shall be the supreme law of the Republic of Poland", Article 87 which specifies "the sources of universally binding law of the Republic of Poland" and, as regards a basis for operation of international law in Poland — from Article 9 ("The Republic of Poland shall respect international law binding upon it") and from relevant clauses introducing international agreements into the domestic legal system (Article 89, Article 92(2) and (3)). The law enacted by an international organization of an integrative character (Community law) finds the grounds for its applicability in Poland, expressed by her own will through the mechanism of adequate constitutional procedures specified in Articles 90 and 91(2).

From the above, it follows that the Constitution reflects a positivistic concept of law, according to which "the content of legal norms as binding norms of conduct, having the sanction of the State, is ultimately specified by means of adequate acts for their creation or recognition of some norms or facts as legal norms by the State. The body of norms of behaviour constructed in this way always emanates from the State [more strictly, according to the language of the Constitution — from the public power, including not only the power of the State and its organs, but also that of local government and its organs], in particular from constitutional organs of the State equipped with the law-making competence. This *ratio imperii* provides a basis for the binding force of the law and finally distinguishes between legal and moral norms"[8]. Such a view, voiced in the course of the debate on the draft constitution in the National Assembly, accentuates a general (model) orientation of the constitutional concept of law. This kind of approach prevailed in a discussion over attempts to back the

---

[8] Shorthand Report from the 3rd session of the National Assembly, part. I, p. 107.

Constitution on legal-normative concepts of law during the first sitting of the National Assembly and the 33rd sitting of the Sejm held on 21st October 1994[9]. Those attempts manifested themselves repeatedly during the discussion of the Constitutional Committee of the National Assembly and at the sitting of the National Assembly in the course of the second reading of the draft, when a proposal was offered to adopt a provision stating that "the Constitution is the highest enacted law of the Republic of Poland", which assumed the existence a higher law (superior to it) as well as the reliance — proposed in the draft prepared by the Solidarity Trade Union — on natural law found in the preamble to the Constitution[10].

The concept of law contained in the Constitution does not at all reflect a radical positivism based on an assumption that the content of law is shaped by the public authority or that the law is axiologically neutral, but — on the contrary — it is a "concept, typical of a democratic state ruled by law, largely oriented by axiological motives"[11] or an "enriched version of positivistic concept of law"[12]. Indeed, the Constitution does not regard moral norms (norms of natural law) as intrinsically having legally binding force, nor does it require them to form an indispensable basis (or condition) for the binding force of positive law. However, it notably restricts the independence of public power in shaping the content of law. In substance, it does so by introducing to the system of norms of the Constitution (binding upon the activity of law-making bodies) supreme (basic) principles which — more or less shaping their content — determine the activity of public authorities, including the foundations (outlines) of the tenor of law and its limits. These principles include, inter alia, those

---

[9] Compare, in particular, speeches of deputies A. Gaberle and A. Łuczak, opposing to speeches of deputies A. Dyrda and A. Grześkowiak: Spraw. Stenograf. z 1 posiedzenia ZN [Shorthand Report from the 1st session of the National Assembly] 21–23 Sept. 1994 r., p. 7, 31–32, 29 and „Diariusz Sejmowy", p. 31–32.

[10] Compare in particular speeches by Senator P.K. Andrzejewski and senator A. Grześkowiak: Sprawozdanie Stenograficzne z 3 posiedzenia Zgromadzenia Narodowego, [Shorthand Report from the 3rd session of the National Assembly] p. 38, 40, 21, 280.

[11] K. Działocha in the above: Sprawozdanie Stenograficzne z 3 posiedzenia Zgromadzenia Narodowego [Shorthand Report from the 3rd session of the National Assembly].

[12] R. Piotrowski: *Koncepcja prawa w projekcie Konstytucji RP* [*The concept of law in the draft Constitution of the Republic of Poland*] (in:) *Prawo i kontrola jego zgodności z Konstytucją* [*The law and control of its conformity to the Constitution*], edited by E. Zwierzchowski, Warszawa 1997, p. 8, 18.

having a nature of typical legal norms (constitutional rules of law) within the meaning assigned to them by the theory of law. They include most of principles implied from the provisions of Chapters I–II of the Constitution. They also comprise the principles which impose an obligation to act in a particular way in the sphere of legislation, referring to rules of a proto-legal character (and not positivistic) and requires the legislator to aim his endeavours at the "common good" (Article 1), "the principles of social justice" (Article 2), "the inherent and inalienable dignity of the person" (Article 30). In the meaning given to them in the practice of the Constitutional Tribunal, they should be treated as fundamental determinants of the content of law, which strongly reinforces the assumption that the Constitution is clearly axiologically oriented. As regards the principle referred to in Article 30, we have to deal with an absolute correlation, since the inherent and inalienable dignity of the person, referred to in this provision, is "inviolable, and protection thereof shall be the obligation of public authorities". It can be assumed — as is sometimes claimed — that Article 30 provides evidence for the application of the concept of natural law, if a directive ensuing from that provision would not have been narrowed to recognition of the inherent and inalienable dignity of the persons only as "a source of freedoms and rights of persons and citizens" but not as a whole law of the State and, what is more important, if we would have ignored an evident fact that the natural law concept, referred to in Article 30, indeed manifested itself in a positivistic construction of fundamental freedoms and rights in the provisions of Chapter II of the Constitution. In addition, the guarantees of freedoms and rights, even if dependent of an obligation to respect and protect the dignity of the person as a source of freedoms and rights, at last rest on the system of measures ensuring their protection contained in the Constitution and — still more — on specific reviewing clauses of Chapter I and II of the Constitution governed by Article 235(5) and (6). The lawmaker who has adopted these latter provisions, seems to guarantee — at the level of constitutional law — individual freedoms and rights based on recognition of the dignity of persons as their source.

The principle of a democratic state ruled by law has a distinct significance among constitutional principles shaping the content of law in a way limiting independence of public authorities. In its judgments made after the coming into force of the Constitution (compare: judgments K 26/97, U 11/97, published in OTK no. 5–6 , at pp. 441 and 470) the Constitutional Tribunal held that the content of that principle — specified in Article 2 — may, and should, be generally understood in the same manner as in the previously existing constitutional order. It assumes:

(a) a considerable degree of autonomy of the law from interference by public power, which ensures its "interior morality" manifested in such attributes of good law as: citizens' confidence in the law, protection of acquired rights, prohibition against *ex post facto* laws, requirement of clear and precise law (in respect the latter, see: judgment U 11/97, published in OTK no. 56, at p. 471);

(b) shaping of the content of law (this chiefly concerns the Constitution and statutes) under democratic procedures guaranteeing that citizens will exert a real influence on enacted law. This means, above all, the requirement that social viewpoints (as many as possible, including those of the minorities) be taken into account. The purpose of democratic procedures for the adoption of statutes is to contribute to making laws as the common good of all citizens (Article 1 of the Constitution), since "the laws of the Republic of Poland should unite its citizens in a State community, and should not divide them and confront one with another" (R. Piotrowski).

Autonomy of public authorities in the field of legislation (unlimited in extremely positivistic concepts of law) has also been restricted by the inclusion in the domestic legal system of the norms of international law, under Article 9, including — separately — ratified international agreements (Articles 89 and 91(1) and (2)). Analogous effects are obtained by incorporation of Community law into that system (Articles 90 and 91(3)). This, in each case, relates to norms which have not been unilaterally shaped by the institutions of the Republic of Poland and such norms which — provided their proper incorporation into the domestic legal system has been effected — are (according to Article 91) applied directly and have precedence over statutes in the event of a conflict of laws.

One should also remember that, among the norms of international law belonging to the domestic legal order, that there exist — in particular — the norms relating to the legal status of the individual in the State, beginning with the Universal Declaration of Fundamental Rights and

Freedoms, which accomplish a humanistic version of law based on universal ethical principles. This is an additional indication of an evident axiological orientation of the positivistic concept of law in the Constitution.

There is, however, no evidence justifying the assumption that the Constitution confers intrinsic legal binding force to moral norms (including natural-law norms)[13]. This, as has already been said, relates also to the content of Article 30. The correctness of this presumption is ultimately decided by the fact that no provision of the Constitution sets forth a norm envisaging any sanction — in the meaning of positive law — for a violation of any norm of natural law. Such sanction does not belong to the Constitutional Tribunal which adjudicates upon a law not to be in conformity to the Constitution and other normative acts of lower status, but not upon the nonconformity of acts of positive law to natural law. The Constitutional Tribunal's practice of adjudicating upon the constitutionality of the law on the basis of so-called constitutional values, even if well established on the grounds of the new Constitution, cannot exceed the foundation of its activity specified in Article 188 nor may it go beyond the limits of axiologically justified interpretation of the Constitution[14].

3. The notion of the sources of law, applied equivocally by the doctrine of law, in the title of Chapter III is used in its formal meaning. This does not, however, mean that the provisions of Chapter III specify all sources of law in formal meaning which, on the grounds of legal doctrine include unilateral acts of law-making, contracts, customary law. The provision of that Chapter deals only with the problem of enacting law by public authorities of the Republic of Poland (acts of domestic law) and the principles governing the incorporation of international agreements and acts of Community law into the domestic legal order, as well as certain principles of their operation. These issues form the main subject of regulation by the Constitution, pursuant to the expected reform of the system of the sources of law.

Nevertheless, the provisions of the Chapter do not govern the issue of concluding contracts as a source of internal (domestic) law, created by at

---

[13] No doubts in this respect have been raised to any of the draft Constitution by M. Zieliński and S. Wronkowska S., *ibid.*, p. 13.

[14] Compare: concurrent, in principle, attitude by R. Piotrowski, *ibid.*, p. 10, with exception as to the rightness of an opinion that, in a democratic state ruled by law, the Constitutional Tribunal "may be conducive to the positivisation of law-natural rules".

least two domestic subjects and containing general and abstract norms of behaviour as well as the principles of creation (emergence) of customary law. However, the Constitution does not exclude the possibility of existence of such sources of law in the domestic legal order. The admissibility of consensual law norms in labour law (Article 59(2)) may be inferred from the entirety of its provisions. Nor does the Constitution exclude the operation of customary law. In this respect, the Constitution — similar to other basic laws — simply remains silent. The Constitution has been written on the grounds of a particular doctrine of law, which recognizes the existence of customary law in the Polish legal system. In order to voice any different viewpoint on the issue of customary law it would have to exclude explicitly its operation under the rule of the new Constitution — however it did not do so. Such interpretation, in respect of the admissibility of both consensual and customary law, was applied in the course of work on a final version of the draft by the Legislative Council working for the Prime Minister[15]. Additionally, the principle of sub-sidiarity defined as a "fundament of laws" may be a premise for a belief that the draft admits recognition of the values of customary law to the extent that it functions in Polish law and allows for the possibility of the binding force of contractual forms of law-making.

A distinct role in regulation of the sources of law in the Constitution, particularly in respect of the meaning of the binding force of laws existing in the Republic of Poland, is played by the provisions of Article 9 (to be discussed below).

4. The basic construction of a system of sources of law, applied by the Constitution, is their (i.e. normative acts) division into sources of univer-sally binding law and sources of internally binding law. The former is expressly used in relation to acts specified in Article 87, the latter — indirectly, through determination (in Article 93) of features charac-terizing internally binding acts. Both appellations are compatible with the classification applied for years by Polish law theorists (e.g. S. Rozmaryn, H. Rot and many followers) and also in the practice of court decisions,

---

[15] Compare: Standpoint of the Legislative Council on the sources of law in the draft Constitution prepared by the Constitutional Committee of the National Assembly — version dated 19 June 1996, „Przegląd Legislacyjny" 4/96, s. 45 and articles by P. Winczorek and S. Wronkowska, contained therein.

where they find their definitions. It should be mentioned that the notion of internally binding acts have often been replaced by such terms as "intrinsic normative acts" or — less frequently — "acts with limited binding force".

The Constitution does not define the concept of sources (acts) of universally binding law, proceeding on the assumption that this notion has been sufficiently defined in the doctrine and practice of court judgments, and therefore confines itself to enumeration of these types of acts in Article 87. In the light of legal doctrine, this means such source of law that is intended to or may "potentially", in S. Rozmaryn words, be of use in the creation of legal norms binding upon all those to whom the law is addressed: legal subjects (organs, institutions, civil servants, citizens and legal persons as well as all other persons under the jurisdiction of the Republic of Poland). This is connected with the feature of regulating obligations and rights of citizens (individuals) and legal persons as well as the structure and scope of functioning of organs of public power. Such doctrinal characteristics of the sources of universally binding law was previously accompanied by a requirement of proclaiming a normative act as belonging to that type of sources of law. Even if, according to Article 83(1) and (3), the coming into force of an act rests upon such requirement, it is not a feature categorically distinguishing sources of universally binding law, because it mostly relates to all normative acts which are subject to proclamation in accordance with principles to be specified by a separate statute.

On the other hand, the constitutional characteristics of sources of internally binding law follow directly from the provisions of Article 93. It corresponds with the characteristics prevailing in the doctrine of law and, in a large degree, in the practice of courts. This law binds only entities organizationally subordinate to the organ which issues acts of that law (Article 93 *in fine*). This feature determines their binding force in the relation of superiority and subjection, and justifies calling them acts which "have an internal character". Secondly, they are issued on the basis of statute (first sentence of Article 93(2)), which means that they have — like in their counterparts in the legal system of the People's Republic of Poland — no autonomous character. Thirdly, in contrast to sources of universally binding law, they cannot provide a basis for making decisions relating to citizens, legal persons and other legal subjects (second sentence of Article

93(2)). Finally, acts of internally binding law are subject to scrutiny regarding their compliance with universally binding law (Article 93(3)) which gives them a status of lower legal force.

The aforementioned features of sources of internally binding law play a decisive role. Unlike universally binding law, their enumeration (specification), illustrative and not exhaustive (as is later shown), is less important.

5. The most important decision regarding the formation of the political system, consistent with a widely postulated reform of the sources of law, which has manifested itself in the provisions of Chapter III and in the whole Constitution is a "closure" of the system of universally binding sources of law. Such figurative, but usually accepted definition, may be considered in two aspects, subjective and objective.

"Closure" of the sources of universally binding law, in its objective aspect, means an exhaustive enumeration in the Constitution of the types of acts of such law. Here we mean chiefly, but not exclusively, acts of law decreed by the organs of the Republic of Poland. These are the acts specified explicitly in Article 87 (the Constitution, statutes, ratified international agreements, regulations and enactments of local law in the territory of the organ issuing such enactments). Additionally, there are also regulations having the force of statute ("decree laws"), issued during a period of state of siege by the President of the Republic (Article 234). The authors of the Constitution did not accept, despite a proposal made to this end in the initial work of the Constitutional Committee of the National Assembly, a proposal that regulations (decrees) having the force of statute be the second, apart from statutes, substitutional form of enacting norms at a time when parliament is in recess. Such decision finally resulted from the introduction of permanent style of debates of the legislative bodies and elimination of recesses between successive terms of office. There has been no approval for the concept of organic ("fundamental" or "cardinal") laws, offered in certain draft constitutions, mostly because of their complete novelty in the Polish tradition of government and the unnecessary complications which they would have caused in the organization of sources of the law. Finally, it has been decided not to introduce an expanded concept of acts implementing statutes, which would be reflected in the establishment — apart from regulations — of other forms of such type of acts (lacking precise definition) as acts of universally binding force — under the formula: "normative acts issued on the basis of, and in order to implement, a statute (Article 71 of the initial consolidated draft Constitution). Proposals of constitutional solutions, offered up almost until the end of the drafting process, aimed in this direction were definitively rejected. The representative of the Government in the Constitutional Committee was also against such an expanded category of acts implementing statutes in relation to acts of the Council of Ministers.

A regulation is, therefore, a single type of act implementing statutes, characterized in the provisions of Article 92(1). It is only within the scope of these characteristics that it is possible in practice to differentiate this category of act; practice to date seems to make such a possibility more likely. It should also be noted that the notion "regulation" — not as an act implementing a statute, but in the meaning of an act creating a particular extraordinary measure — is used by the Constitution in Articles 228(2) and 231. It is issued by the President of the Republic upon the basis of an appropriate statute on extraordinary measures and after satisfaction of other requirements specified by the Constitution. It is, in fact, an act of application of a statute in the circumstances thereby specified, though with far-reaching legal consequences.

Among the sources of universally binding law, the Constitution does not include the rules of procedure of the Sejm and those of the Senate, even if they obviously have the character of normative acts passed by means of a resolution. A lively discussion on the character of these rules of procedure held in the Constitutional Committee[16], in particular on the content of Article 112 of the Constitution and on subjecting of such rules to review exercised by the Constitutional Tribunal (which is finally reflected in Article 188(3)), may indicate the complex nature of the provisions of the rules of procedure, which include *inter alia* those having the character of universally binding law. These may be those of the rules of procedure, which govern "the manner of performance of obligations, both constitutional and statutory, by State organs in relation to the Sejm (a sentence from Article 112).

However — apart from acts enacted by unilateral decision of organs of public power — does the system of sources of universally binding law encompass other acts of law enacted in the Republic of Poland, particular-

---

[16] Compare: in particular Biuletyn KK ZN XIX, p. 46 et seq.

ly in accordance with contractual procedures? From the above comments it follows that the Constitution allows the existence of acts of law enacted upon the basis of contract between trade unions and employers as well as their organizations, having the form of collective agreements and other — rather indefinite — arrangements (Article 59(2)). We have grounds to consider collective agreements, even they are not mentioned in Article 87(1), as sources of universally binding law. Such position is justified by the prior character of collective agreements in jurisprudence and literature, while the modification of subjects (parties) to such contracts does not erase their significance as an "already existing" notion[17]. There are no compelling reasons to regard as acts of universally binding law another kind of consensual act which, according to the Constitution, are agreements concluded by the Council of Ministers with appropriate representatives of churches and religious organizations other than the Roman Catholic Church. Such agreements are not, indeed, intrinsic sources of law, but create only a "basis", or prerequisite, preceding the adoption of a statute specifying the relation between the Republic of Poland and other churches and religious organizations.

In respect of acts of international law, the principle of a "closed" system of sources of universally binding law includes, by virtue of Article 87(1), only ratified international agreements. However, a question arises how, from the point of view of this principle, we should understand the norm of Article 9 which states that "the Republic of Poland shall respect international law binding upon it". It is held that the sources of international law encompass rules of international law, international agreements and law-making resolutions of international organizations. The norm of Article 9, expressing the principle of general receptivity of the Polish legal system toward international law, at the same time establishes a "presumption of automatic — even if indirect — incorporation of international law norms into that order"[18]. It should therefore be assumed

---

[17] Compare: A. Gwiżdż: *Some comments...*, p. 102–104; L. Kaczyński: *Wpływ art. 87 Konstytucji na swoiste źródła prawa pracy* [*Impact of Article 87 of the Constitution on specific sources of labour law*], PiP 8/97, p. 61 et seq.

[18] R. Szafarz: *Międzynarodowy porządek prawny i jego odbicie w polskim prawie konstytucyjnym* [*International legal order and its reflection in Polish constitutional law*], (in:) *Prawo międzynarodowe i wspólnotowe w wewnętrznym porządku prawnym* [*International and Community law in the domestic legal order*], edited by M. Kruk, Warszawa 1997, p. 19.

that the above enumerated sources of law — except for ratified international agreements introduced into domestic legal order according to a different principle (transformation) — in particular universally accepted rules of international law, customary laws other than ratified international treaties as well as law-making resolutions of international organization should be applied in the Polish legal system. Due to the transfer, in large degree, of the content of principles of international and customary law (closely interrelated because of similar principles in their shaping) to international agreements, a catalogue of the sources of law, subject to application by virtue of Article 9 in internal relation of the State, has been actually reduced. However, this does not at all undermine the general principle of Article 9, in relation to the whole of international law, as a complex structure of norms. This is especially true when we consider that in the course of work on the Constitution that there long prevailed an attitude that — similar to the solutions applied by other countries — elements of such structure (and above all universally accepted rules of international law) should be enumerated in Article 9.

In view of the content of Article 9 of the Constitution, in the context of Article 87, it follows that the catalogue of the sources of universally binding law includes — apart from ratified international agreements specified in Article 87(1) — also other elements of the system of sources of international law. Different constitutional legal bases and different methods of their inclusion into the system of law applied in Poland should not pose any obstacle to such conclusion. The practice of application of Article 9 will show whether, and to what extent, this provision can provide, in the process of interpretation and application of the law, a basis for making reference to sources of law other than ratified international agreements.

However, there can be no doubt that — after realization of the stipulation of Article 90 of the Constitution (i.e. after Poland's accession to an international organization referred to in this provision) — legislative acts (which lack precise definition in the Constitution) of an international organization of an integrative character will be acts of universally binding law. Article 91(3), forming the legal fundament of their binding force in the domestic legal order, apparently has also a more extended meaning. It may provide a basis for the application in Poland of legal acts enacted from time to time by international organizations other than those referred to in Article 90(1). This follows from the wide scope of the clause contained in this provision and placing it beyond Article 90 which expresses an integrative option of Poland's policy.

The "closure" of the sources of universally binding law in its subjective aspect relates to acts of domestic law and is manifested in the specification in the provisions of the Constitution, in an exhaustive manner, of organs of public authority empowered with law-making competencies. In accordance with the provisions of the Constitution such powers belong to the Sejm and the Senate (the power to adopt a Constitution and statutes — Article 235 and Article 95(1)), to the President of the Republic (the power to issue regulations — Article 142(2) and regulations having the force of a statute — Article 234), to the Council of Ministers (the power to issue regulations — Article 146(3)(2)), the Prime Minister (the power to issue regulations — Article 148(3)), to ministers directing a branch of government administration (the power to issue regulations — Article 149(2)), to presidents of committees appointed to membership in the Council of Ministers (the power to issue regulations — Article 149(3)) and to the National Broadcasting Council (the power to issue regulations — Article 213(2)).

From the above, it follows that trade unions and employers and their organizations are empowered, by virtue of Article 59(2), to make law (by way of concluding collective labour agreements and other arrangements). Upon a general assumption of the "closure" of the system of the sources of law, explicit indication of subjects empowered to make law by way of consensual acts provides, indirectly, evidence of the inadmissibility of making — by such means — universally binding law by entities other than organs of public power, i.e. various voluntary organizations and associations (sometimes called "social holders of power"). From the same assumption one should derive a prohibition against law-making by organs of public power and other entities under the principle of a joint, equally possessed, competence that was a very common practice in the period of the Peoples' Republic of Poland (e.g. in the form of joint resolutions of the Government and the Central Council of Trade Unions). In the light of the Constitution which, in particular, bases the structure of public authorities on "social dialogue as well as the principle of subsidiarity in the strengthening the powers of citizens and their communities" [from the preamble to the Constitution], several forms (known to previous legislative practice) of making universally binding law by state organs with the participation of citizens' associations concerned are fully justified.

6. As has already been mentioned, the "closure" of the sources of binding law, in its subjective and objective aspects, was a deliberate assumption of the authors of the Constitution in shaping a new law-making system. It has been aimed at preventing, in practice, the issuance of several normative acts having no constitutional basis, lacking clear legal character or undermining the position of statute in the legislative system. Legal doctrine found such situation " threatening, from the point of view of both the accomplishment of the principle of a democratic state ruled by law, including in particular freedoms and rights of persons and citizens, and efficient functioning of the state"[19]. The establishing of the Constitutional Tribunal, despite its considerable impact on the reduction of negative consequences of "fuzziness" of the system of sources of law, particularly in the area of observance of citizens' rights, has not changed the situation for the better. This has been confirmed by annual information from the Constitutional Tribunal indicating repetition of bad practices in the field of law-making as a consequence of the present situation of constitutional law. Those who have accentuated in a specific manner the positive role of the Constitutional Tribunal in the area of improving the principles of law--making agree that the "fuzziness" of the system of sources of law posed "a substantial obstacle to the efficient functioning of the state, while the violation of principles of proper law-making came to be connected with considerable costs to be paid by the state"[20].

In the course of work on the Constitution, after the publication of the version (dated 16 January 1996) which contained a provision identical to Article 87 of the current Constitution, some authors claimed that full

---

[19] P. Winczorek: *Źródła prawa w projekcie Konstytucji...* [*Sources of law in the Draft Constitution...*], p. 20; and earlier: K. Działocha, *System źródeł prawa w Konstytucji PRL* [*System of the sources of law in the Constitution of the Polish Peoples' Republic*], (in:) *Problemy prawotwórstwa w nowej Konstytucji PRL* [*Law-making issues in the new Constitution of the Polish Peoples' Republic*], edited by A. Patrzałek, 1988.

[20] Compare: Z. Jarosz, *Parlament jako organ władzy ustawodawczej...* [*Parliament as an organ of the legislative power*], p. 175–176, S. Wronkowska, *Źródła prawa w projekcie Konstytucji...* [*Sources of law in the Draft Constitution*], p. 42.

"completion" of the sources of universally binding law is too restrictive. They drew attention to both the disputability of restricting the concept of executive acts implementing a statute only to regulations as a homogeneous institution and depriving numerous organs of central government administration and non-government bodies not subordinate to the executive authorities of the power to issue normative acts. If only such doubts had been justified more precisely, they could have been based on reference to "well-established practices" or to established arrangements for independence (from the Government or President) of specified subjects previously enjoying an opportunity to make laws. Their arguments ignored the fact that central offices (their heads) have never had any constitutional basis for enacting universally binding laws. In fact, this position meant an attempt to reach a compromise between the previous concept of "fuzzines of the system" sources of law (hitherto so much criticized) and a radical reform which had to be introduced by the Constitution. It might also be considered as indicating fear of such reform. The point, however, is that Poland's Constitution goes further: its provisions put a stop to that with which the Constitutional Tribunal had to cope with, seeking support in obscure constitutional provisions.

Bogusław Banaszak

Professor, University of Wrocław

THE CONCEPT OF INDIVIDUAL RIGHTS IN POLAND

1. THE CONCEPT OF INDIVIDUAL RIGHTS IN THE CONSTITUTION

Constitutional regulation of rights, freedoms and duties of an individual in every country does not form an accidental set of norms, but is rather determined by a particular concept of the status of the individual in the state. This does not necessarily mean that it must reflect such concept and that constitutions based on the same concept should be exactly alike. In fact, we must be mindful of the fact that any basic law does not come into existence in a vacuum and often applies institutions or solutions existing in a given country. On the other hand, despite widespread acceptance of one concept by the authors of an organic law, they may find it necessary to admit some elements typical of another (e.g. Declaration of Rights of Man and Citizen connected liberal ideas with elements of the natural-law concept). Moreover, concepts of the status of an individual themselves are not monolithic. They maintain only certain fundamental assumptions, but are subject to modification in respect of other questions and apply different approaches in resolving detailed issues. The result is that some — and sometimes far-reaching — differences can exist between individual countries, even those whose constitutional norms concerning rights, freedoms and duties of an individual have been based on the same concept.

Poland's constitution represents, above all, the concept of individual rights typical of the so-called social state ruled by law. The purpose of such state, in contrast to the liberal state, is to direct the processes of social development and to ensure impartial distribution of its fruits. In order to achieve its goals, it may apply not only the traditional means (i.e. commands and prohibitions) but also a wide spectrum of other measures designed to direct one's personal conduct (e.g. through taxation or subsidies). The state and society are not treated as mutually opposing forces, although they are not identical with each other. The social state ruled by law is separated from society, which guarantees freedom of the individual, but is also closely connected with it, thereby guaranteeing progress and social justice. This corresponds with the departure from regarding an individual as an isolated subject whose links with society are recognized. On the one hand, this makes it possible to emphasize individual responsibility for deciding the fate of the community and leads to re-evaluation of duties consigned to him/her, which, having received a wider social context, become instruments for implementing new tasks of the state. On the other hand, the state has been obliged to care for the subsistence of an individual and ensure the provision of opportunities for individual development as guaranteed in the constitution. This leads to a change in the character of individual rights that begin to function as an aim of the state's activities. Formal guarantees do not suffice, and the state is compelled to undertake political, environmental, social and other activities in order to carry out the programme formulated in provisions of the constitution relating to them. Rights and freedoms do not protect only the individual sphere of liberty of the person, but also play some social functions and, therefore, an enjoyment thereof should be socially oriented, i.e. when protecting interests of an individual they also serve the common good.

Confirming the significance of social rights, the social state ruled by law treats them in a different way from political or personal rights. They do not found any claims by an individual for a particular behaviour on the part of the state or any concrete performance, but are rather an imposition on the state of an obligation to undertake activity for their accomplishment.

The social state ruled by law, as compared to the liberal state, reverses the principles concerning the substantial scope of rights, freedoms and duties contained in the constitution. While under the liberal conception they relate, above all, to citizens, and only in exceptional situations — to non-citizens, under the concept of the social state ruled by law, it is assumed that provisions of the constitution specifying the status of an individual are addressed to all persons staying in the territory of a given state, except for the rights, freedoms and duties explicitly reserved for citizens.

The provisions of the constitution were set down taking into account some major assumptions of the concept of the status of an individual as formulated by the social thought of the Catholic Church. The most important of them are:

— the principle of personalism, which accepts the individuality and dignity of each person, and also emphasises the precedence of an individual over society (e.g. in Article 30);

— the principle of solidarity of all people, which means a rejection of the concept of class struggle (e.g. in Article 20);

— the principle of common good, based on the existence of a particular hierarchy of common goods; it declares that everybody has a right to enjoy material goods and that the state may interfere with the sphere of ownership relations, so that they contribute to the common good (Article 1);

— treating the person as a being which evolves in the society, which results in taking account of not only rights, but also emphasises the duties which are dealt with in a comprehensive manner and encompass a person's duties to oneself, to the family, to the state and human family; accepting a mutual connection between rights and duties, the Church notices that sometimes a right granted to an individual becomes the source of a duty.

2. CONSTITUTIONAL RIGHTS AND FREEDOMS

Using the aforementioned notion (in Article 31(3) and 79(1)), the Constitution of the Republic of Poland distinguishes the rights and freedoms guaranteed therein. Such distinction has certain consequences. First, the extent of enjoyment of constitutional rights and freedoms is subject to restriction only by statute, and only where it is necessary in a democratic state in order to protect goods fundamental for its functioning, including security, public order, environment, health and public morals or for the protection of the rights and freedoms of others. Second, everyone whose constitutional rights have been violated has the right to lodge a complaint [called a constitutional complaint] to the Constitutional Tribunal.

The provision of constitutional protection for a certain catalogue of rights and freedoms does not necessarily mean that other rights and freedoms should not exist. That principle is nowadays universally accepted in democratic states, even if not explicitly expressed in its constitution. It can also be derived from the provisions of the Polish Constitution (e.g. Article 80).

3. THE RIGHTS AND FREEDOMS OF PERSONS AND CITIZENS

When we contemporarily speak about civil rights we mean, in principle, rights of citizens of a given state resulting from law in its generic sense and aimed at the protection of interests of such citizens. A similar interpretation of "the rights of citizens" can be found in the provisions of Poland's constitution which reserves certain rights for persons being Polish citizens (for such purpose unequivocal phrases — e.g. "a citizen shall have the right" or "a Polish citizen shall have the right" — are applied).

The Polish Constitution also deals with "human rights and freedoms". In Article 37, this notion is understood as relating to the rights and freedoms contained in the Polish constitution and which belong to all individuals within its jurisdiction, hence to non-citizens. In such case, human rights are defined by their differentiation from civil rights. Moreover, the constitution in its provisions — mostly by adequate definition of their subject (e.g. "everyone shall have the right" or "everyone shall be entitled") — clearly indicates the rights which in Poland belong to non-citizens.

The Constitution of the Republic of Poland explicitly identifies the rights and freedoms reserved to citizens, declaring, in Article 37(1), a general principle that "Anyone, being under the authority of the Polish State, shall enjoy the freedoms and rights ensured by the Constitution." Exemptions from this principle, except for those specified explicitly in the constitution (civil rights and freedoms) may be made, according to Article 37(2), only by statute.

The wording of Article 37(1) and of other provisions of the constitution concerning the rights of an individual, undoubtedly show that they relate to natural persons already born. Such was also the intention of the authors of the constitution when rejecting the motion that life be protected from conception[1]. On 28 May 1997, just after the constitutional referen-

---

[1] 30 members (from amongst 43 participating in the vote) of the Constitutional Committee of the National Assembly voted for the wording lacking any phrase about the protection of life from conception (Biuletyn KKZN XII, Warszawa 1995, p. 92).

dum, the Constitutional Tribunal went beyond such position, adjudicating (on the basis of the then existing constitutional norms) that the imperative to guarantee "protection of the life of human being at each stage of its development"[2].

The constitution lacks any provision which would enable extension of the scope of constitutional rights and freedoms to include legal persons, as in the case of — for example — Article 19(3) of the Basic Law of the Federal Republic of Germany. Hence, the Polish constitution does not correspond with a trend observed in many democratic countries. In these countries, a view prevails that the extension of the scope of constitutional rights and freedoms to legal persons does not contribute to reinforcing the protection of such persons but rather to intensify the protection of individuals which compose it. Moreover, it is worth noting at this point that in situations where such extension has taken place, it does not relate to rights connected — by nature — with a natural person (i.e. the freedom of conscience, right to marriage, etc.).

4. PRINCIPLES UNDERLYING CONSTITUTIONAL REGULATION OF INDIVIDUAL RIGHTS AND FREEDOMS

General principles formulated in eight articles (Articles 30–37) precede detailed regulations concerning freedoms, rights and duties of persons and citizens contained in chapter II. The above principles include:

1) The principle of inviolability of human dignity. The constitution regards dignity as an inherent and inalienable good, being a source of freedoms and rights of persons and citizens. This means a reference to natural-law concepts, and leads to a prohibition against any action, taken by any person, which could breach or restrict it. Public authorities are not only obliged to respect it, but also to protect it against any violation or threat.

2) The principle of admissibility of restrictions in the enjoyment of constitutional freedoms and rights only in accordance with the law. The substantial scope of individual rights and freedoms cannot be unlimited. Every individual lives in society, and the law created by such society takes

---

[2] *Orzecznictwo Trybunału Konstytucyjnego. Zbiór Urzędowy [Judgments of the Constitutional Tribunal. An Official Collection]*, No. 2/1997, item 19.

into account not only his/her interests, but also the good of the public. This, in turn, produces the necessity to limit individual rights in order to prevent their real, or potential, collision with public interests. Links between particular freedoms and rights enjoyed by an individual as well as their mutual dependence, also imply a need for their delimitation. This prevents lawlessness, abuse of rights, etc. Hence, each legislative regulation of individual rights and freedoms must make it possible to determine such limits.

The Polish constitution contains (in Article 31(3)) a general clause relating to limitations of the rights and freedoms formulated therein. It states that such limitations "may be imposed only by statute, and only when necessary in a democratic state for the protection of its security or public order, or to protect the natural environment, health or public morals, or the freedoms and rights of other persons."

Therefore, the constitution accepts a principle, generally recognised by constitutional law in democratic states, which declares that fixing the limits of constitutional rights and freedoms is, primarily, the task of the legislator. The legislator is also responsible for the updating and specification of constitutional norms within the limits of existing social relations. He may determine the limits of such rights and freedoms in an exhaustive way by statute, or may foresee the necessity to issue appropriate implementing acts. He does so when he cannot specify in advance all cases in which such limitations should be imposed. Then, the legislator should indicate the direction and principles of sub-statutory regulation with such accuracy that the organ of executive power or a court could not have too much discretion to allow it to replace, in fact, the legislator.

Special limitations on constitutional freedoms and rights may be imposed by means of extraordinary measures. The Polish constitution distinguishes three of them, i.e. state of siege, a state of emergency and a state of natural disaster. In Article 228(2) it states that any of them may be introduced, upon the basis of statute, by regulations which require to be publicized. Statutes concerning particular measures determine the extent to which the freedoms and rights of persons and citizens may be limited, and also establish principles for the functioning of public authorities if any such measures have been introduced. They may also specify the principles, scope and manner of compensating for loss of property resulting from limitation of the individual freedoms and rights during a period requiring introduction of extraordinary measures.

The authors of the constitution assign to the legislator the task of specifying the detailed scope of limitations of constitutional rights and freedoms, however, they also formulate some general principles in this respect. From Article 228(5) it follows that they must be proportionate to the degree of threat and help to achieve the quickest restoration of normal functioning of the State. Article 233 specifies, by contrast, the rights and freedoms which cannot be subject to limitation, even if extraordinary measures have been introduced. Two methods are applied in this context. Paragraph 1 of this Article identifies the rights and freedoms which, in times of martial law and states of emergency, cannot be limited by the statute specifying the scope of limitation. These include: the dignity of the person, constitutional principles concerning the acquisition and loss of Polish citizenship, the right of citizens to protection by the Polish state during their stay abroad, protection of life, the freedom from being subjected to scientific experimentation without one's voluntary consent, from torture and inhuman treatment or punishment as well as corporal punishment, the principle of *nullum poena sine lege* (applied both to statutory norms and norms of international law), the right of counsel, the right to be presumed innocent until one's guilt is determined by the final judgment of a court, the right of access to a court, the right to legal protection of one's private and personal rights, freedom of conscience and religion, the right of petition, the right of parents to rear their children in accordance with their own convictions and taking into account the degree of maturity of a child and his/her convictions, as well as protection of the rights of the child.

Whereas, paragraph 3 enumerates the rights and freedoms which may be limited during states of natural disaster, thereby prohibiting any limitation of other constitutional rights and freedoms. The aforementioned group of rights and freedoms subjected to limitation includes: the freedom of economic activity, personal freedom, inviolability of the home, the freedom of movement and sojourn on the territory of the Republic of Poland, the right to strike, the right of ownership, the freedom to work, the right to safe and hygienic conditions of work, the right to rest.

Article 233(2) of the Constitution contains additional restrictions imposed on any possible limitation of rights and freedoms during a period requiring introduction of extraordinary measures. It states that any limitation of such rights and freedoms "only by reason of race, gender, language, faith or lack of it, social origin or property" shall be disallowed. This norm, in fact, repeats — though in a slightly modified wording — the appropriate provisions of treaties binding on Poland (Article 4(1) of the International Covenant on Civil and Political Rights and should be understood as *lex specialis* to the principle of equality declared in Article 32).

To sum up this comment on limitations to constitutional rights and freedoms, it should be said that the constitution does not determine the limits of all rights and freedoms guaranteed by it, nor does it do so in respect of any particular right or freedom. These limits are fixed, as a rule, for a particular case, to which the principle *in dubio pro libertate* should be applied, as it ensures the highest possible effectiveness of the constitutional rights and freedoms.

The constitution and laws developing its provisions guarantee to an individual a definite extent of a freedom to enjoy his/her rights and liberties. Where his/her behaviour does not exceed the limits defined by the law, an individual may demand protection of the rights and freedoms belonging to him/her, even if it would be inconsistent with universally accepted moral, ethical or other principles.

3) The principle of inviolability of the essence of freedoms and rights. The constitution does not give to the legislator a full discretion to fix the limits of rights and freedoms guaranteed therein. Its Article 31(1) provides *in fine* that such limitations "shall not violate the essence of freedoms and rights" (inviolability of the substance of a particular right is also dealt with in Article 64(3), however, it is a needless repetition of a general principle). Nevertheless, it does not determine how such essence should be understood.

Generally speaking, it should be assumed that the essence of a right or freedom is violated when legal provisions — without abolishing that right or freedom — have made the exercise of that right practically impossible (e.g. when imposition of high tax rate on privately owned means of production makes their use unprofitable).

In addition to that general clause, several provisions of the constitution contain phrases excluding any limitations or allowing for imposition of limitations by means of a statute. The former category includes Article 30 which states that the dignity of the person is "inviolable". The latter group is more numerous (see, e.g. Article 41(1) *in fine*); and the fact that the authors of the constitution additionally allow for limitations upon a given right by statute implies that their intention was to set limits for reasons other than those enumerated in the general clause.

4) The principle of equality before the law. This relates not only to Polish citizens, but to all persons within the jurisdiction of the Polish state. The formula of equality before the law, adopted by the constitution, corresponds with a general, descriptive notion of equality as an attachment of a given object to the same class, which we can distinguish from the point of view of a feature considered as essential, and is not analogous with the notion of identity. It is supplemented by everyone's right to equal treatment by public authorities. Approach to this principle in the provisions of the new constitution do not depart, in essence, from that applied by the previous constitution. We may also expect that the position established in the practice of the Constitutional Tribunal in this respect will not be changed. Such position declares that equality before the law should be understood as a situation wherein all subjects who are characterised to the same degree by a given substantial feature should be treated equally, i.e. on even terms, without any favourable or unfavourable distinction. However, the Tribunal allowed for a so-called positive discrimination, i.e. active preferential treatment of certain groups, where this is necessary for obtaining a real equality (e.g. favoured treatment in social insurance of an insured who has become disabled due to injury at work, where the law does not entitle him/her to special compensation)[3]. This principle is *lex generalis* for other constitutional norms dealing with, and precisely defining, equality. They include:

— prohibition of discrimination against anyone in political, social or economic life for any reasons whatsoever (Article 32(2));

— equal rights for women and men in family, political, social and economic life, and particularly equal rights to education, employment, the right to equal compensation for work of similar value, to social security, to hold offices and to receive public honours and decorations (Article 33);

---

[3] See, e.g. *Orzecznictwo Trybunału Konstytucyjnego w 1992 roku* — cz. I. [*Judgments of the Constitutional Tribunal in 1992*, part I], Warszawa 1992, p. 133.

— citizens' right of access to public functions, based on the principle of equality (Article 60);

— the principle of equal suffrage (we discuss this issue in a separate part dedicated to electoral rights);

— equal access to cultural goods (Article 6);

— equal rights of churches and other religious organizations (Article 25);

— equal access of citizens to health care services financed from public funds (Article 68(2));

— equal access of citizens to education (Article 70(4)).

5) The principle of ensuring the rights of national and ethnic minorities. According to it, the freedom of Polish citizens belonging to national or ethnic minorities to maintain and develop their own language, to maintain customs and traditions, and to develop their own culture is ensured. Such minorities have the right to establish educational and cultural institutions, institutions designed to protect religious identity, as well as to participate in the resolution of matters connected with their cultural identity.

While formulating the principle of protecting national and ethnic minorities, the constitution, does not, however, define the notion of these minorities. We can assume that these are groups of persons who share common culture, religion and/or language. It should, however, be recognized after the Human Rights' Committee's interpretation of Article 27 of the International Covenant on Civil and Political Rights dealing with minority rights, that a guarantee of the rights of national and ethnic minorities has no "collective" dimension, nor does it relate to group rights, but rather deals with the rights of persons belonging to minorities[4]. It may justify reasonable differentiation of rights of these persons if the measures undertaken are intended to improve conditions of enjoyment of the rights granted to them. In this context, a state is obliged not only to protect the rights of minorities against any breach or denial, but also to undertake positive actions designed to protect the identity of minorities and the rights

---

[4] *Komentarz Komitetu Praw Człowieka dotyczący osób należących do mniejszości chronionych* [A Commentary by the Human Rights Committee on Persons Belonging to Protected Minorities], (in:) „Toruński Rocznik Praw Człowieka i Pokoju 1994–1995", vol. 3, Toruń 1996, 117–122.

of their members. The Committee, in contrast to Poland's constitution, held that members of minorities do not have to be citizens or, even, permanent residents. "Hence, migrant workers or even visitors in the State Party, also constituting a minority are entitled to enjoy — without any challenge — the rights" available to persons belonging to minorities[5].

Article 35 of the constitution concentrates itself on the cultural rights of minorities, but are not confined to them. They also include, inter alia, the right to participate, to an appropriate extent, in the process of political decision-making. Even if the constitution is silent in this case, such right is guaranteed at a statutory level and, therefore, prior to the coming into force of the constitution, representatives of minorities (8 in the 1st term of office of the Sejm and 4 in the 2nd term of Sejm, as well as 1 — in the 1st and 2nd terms of office of the Senate) held seats in Polish Parliament (due, inter alia, to the fact that in accordance with Articles 3–5 of the Act of 1993 on the Elections to the Sejm, the requisite thresholds are not applied to election committees of registered organizations of national minorities during the allocation of seats among constituency lists and national lists of candidates — this issue is discussed in detail in a subchapter dedicated to electoral rights). So the legislator goes beyond the literal boundaries specified in Article 35, nevertheless fulfilling a principle set down in that Article. It is also respected by certain statutes adopted before the coming into force of the constitution. In this respect, we can mention, as an example, Article 21(4) of the Act of 22 December 1992 on Broadcasting, which states that "programmes of public radio broadcasting and television should take into account the needs of national and ethnic minorities". Nevertheless, one can show examples to the contrary; such as, for instance, the lack of possibility of using their own language in official actions before central or local government administration by a language minority, even if in the area where they live and constitute a majority. In Poland, in contrast to many other democratic states, there is no single law regulating comprehensively the situation of minorities, and different issues are dealt with by several laws. By the way, it should be mentioned that protection of minority rights has been improved as a consequence of 13 bilateral agreements concluded by Poland with other states after 1989. Such agreements contain provisions concerning minority rights.

---

[5] *Ibidem*, p. 119.

There is lack of reliable statistical data which would make it possible to determine the number of persons belonging to different national and ethnic minorities. The latest available data concerning national minorities in Poland dates back to 1947. Now, according to different sources, it can be assumed that 1–1.3 million persons residing on the territory of the Republic of Poland (or 3–4% of its total population) belong to national minorities[6]. The national minorities include Germans (around 500,000), Ukrainians (250,000–300,000), Byelorussians 250,000–350,000), Lithuanians (15,000–20,000), Jews (8,000–10,000), Ruthenians (13,000–15,000), Romanies (up to 25,000), Czechs (up to 10,000) as well as Russians, Armenians, Greeks, Macedonians, Tatars, Palestinians, Vietnamese, Kurds (around 2,000 each).

6) The rights of Polish citizens to protection by the Polish state during their stay abroad.

7) The principle of enjoyment of constitutional rights and freedoms by all persons within the jurisdiction of the Republic of Poland, and the admissibility of statutory exemption therefrom. The issue has already been discussed in a point dedicated to the substantial scope of constitutional rights and freedoms.

8) The principle of direct application of provisions of the constitution, set down in Article 8(2), is of major importance from the point of view of an individual whose intention is to exercise his/her constitutional rights and freedoms. Such approach to them impacts on the determination of their normative character and position in the system of law. On the basis of that principle, one should assume that statutes do not have to define rights and freedoms guaranteed in the constitution, and that constitutional norms

---

[6] There are considerable disparities between particular data. The German minority is an example. When we take into account all persons belonging to various organizations of this minority, we can obtain a figure of around 300,000 as compared with 350,000–500,000 persons supporting representatives of this minority in parliamentary or local government elections (after J. Szeliga, *Obecna sytuacja mniejszości narodowych w Polsce* [*Current situation of national minorities in Poland*] (in:) W. Lesiuk (ed.) *Mniejszości na Górnym Śląsku. Pomost czy przeszkoda w stosunkach polsko-niemieckich* [*Minorities in Upper Silesia: a bridge or obstacle to Polish-German relations?*], Opole 1994, p. 52). According to leaders of the German minority organizations their number amounts to 800,000 (see, P. Mohlek, M. Hoskowa, *Der Minderheitenschuty in der Republik Polen, in der Tschechischen und der Slowakischen Republik*, Bonn 1994, p. 23).

related to them will be applied spontaneously. Such approach is, after all, generally accepted in the constitutional systems of democratic states.

At this point, it should be noted that the Constitution of the Republic of Poland belongs to that group of basic laws of democratic states that do not recognise the third-party effect of rights and freedoms.

5. CONSTITUTIONAL REGULATION OF FREEDOMS AND RIGHTS OF INDIVIDUAL

The catalogue of constitutional rights and freedoms includes three groups, among which two categories (rights and freedoms of persons and rights and freedoms of citizens) may be distinguished:

1) Personal freedoms and rights:

— that may be enjoyed by any person within the territory of the Republic of Poland, including: the right to protection of life, freedoms from being subjected to medical experimentation without one's consent, freedom from torture and inhuman or degrading treatment and from corporal punishment, the right to personal inviolability (i.e. prohibition against unlawful deprivation of liberty, the principle of judicial control of the legality of deprivation of liberty, the *nullum crimen sine lege* principle), the right of an accused to a defence, the right to a fair and public hearing without undue delay by a competent, independent and impartial court, freedom from arbitrary deprivation of property (which may be forfeited only in cases specifeid by statute and only by virtue of a judgment of a court, the right to privacy and protection of one's honour and good reputation, the right of parents to rear their children in accordance with their own convictions (taking into account the degree of maturiy of the child as well as his/her freedom of conscience and belief and also his/her convictions), freedom and privacy of communication, the inviolability of the home, the right to protection of personal data, freedom of movement as well as the choice of place of residence and sojourn within (and to leave) the territory of the Republic of Poland, freedom of conscience and religion, freedom to express opinions and also to acquire and disseminate information, freedom from extradition of a foreigner suspected of the commission of a crime for political reasons but without the use of force, the right of foreigners to be granted asylum in the Republic of Poland.

— that may be enjoyed by Polish citizens only, including: freedom from being expelled from the country and the right to return to it, freedom from acquisition, collecting and making accessible of information on citizens other than necessary in a democratic state ruled by law, freedom from extradition.

2) Political freedoms and rights:

— that may be enjoyed by any person within the territory of the Republic of Poland, including: the freedom of peaceful assembly, the freedom of association, the right to submit petitions, proposals and complaints.

— that may be enjoyed by Polish citizens only, including: the right of access to public service [public functions], the right to obtain information on the activities of organs of public authority as well as persons discharging public functions, the right to participate in a referendum, the right to vote and to run for office in the election of parliament, president and local government bodies.

3) Economic, social and cultural freedoms and rights:

— that may be enjoyed by any person within the territory of the Republic of Poland, including: the right to ownership, other property rights and the right of succession, the freedom to choose and to pursue one's occupation and to choose one's place of work, the right to safe and hygienic conditions of work, the right to protection of one's health, the right of the disabled persons to assistance from public authorities to ensure their subsistence, adaptation to work and social communication, the right to education, the right of the family to protection, the right of a mother to special assistance from public authorities, the right of the child to protection and to care and assistance provided by public authorities, the freedom of artistic creation and scientific research as well as dissemination of the fruits thereof, the freedom to teach and to enjoy the products of culture, the right to environmental protection and undertake actions to protect the environment as well as to be informed of the quality of the environment and its protection, the protection of the rights of tenants, rights protecting consumers, customers, hirers or lessees against activities threatening their health, privacy and safety as well as against dishonest market practices.

— that may be enjoyed by Polish citizens only, including: the right to social security whenever incapacitated for work or being without work, equal access to health care services financed from public funds, the right to establish schools of any level, equal access to education.

Generally speaking, constitutional regulation of individual freedoms and rights takes into account, both in the catalogue of such rights and freedoms and specific provisions concerning them, norms of international law binding on Poland as well as constitutional standards existing in democratic states. Nevertheless, the authors of the constitution have not avoided some defects which, sometimes, considerably depreciate the legal merit of the adopted solutions and which in the future may make constitutional provisions difficult to interpret and apply.

Despite the fact that the constitution contains a separate chapter (chapter II) dedicated to freedoms, rights and obligations of persons and citizens, norms relating to this matter can also be found in other parts of the basic law. Such an attitude leads, on the one hand, to redundancies and differences in a normative approach to the same right (e.g. the rights contained in chapter I and the same rights contained in chapter II), which fact may have serious consequences for the interpretation of particular provisions. On the other hand, the right of suffrage, one of the fundamental political rights of citizens is governed, in detail, in chapters other than I and II. This means that the protection it receives is somewhat weaker, since any amendment of the provisions of chapters I, II and XII of the constitution require more complicated procedure for enactment.

In this context, it is worth considering whether it is reasonable to put the elements of four freedoms (of association, of the press and other means of social communication, of economic activity, of conscience and religion) together with the right to ownership outside the "bracket" of regulations of chapter II, and include them, among general principles of the system, in chapter I. Undoubtedly, provisions of chapter I contain interpretative rules for normalization of constitutional rights and freedoms (e.g. the principle of a democratic state ruled by law). One may, however doubt whether it is also true in respect of those of them which establish certain elements of rights and freedoms. Let us illustrate this with the example of some elements of the freedom of association. Article 12, under chapter I, provides that the Republic of Poland "shall ensure freedom for the creation and functioning of trade unions, socio-occupational organizations of farmers, societies, citizens' movements, other voluntary associations and foundations". Article 58(1) under chapter II contains a more general formula, which follows: "the freedom of association shall be guaranteed to everyone". It is accompanied by the provisions of Article 59(1) which ensures "the freedom of association in trade unions, socio-occupational organizations of farmers and in employers' organizations". Articles 58 and 59, in contrast to Article 12, define the limits of the freedom of association. Hence, the freedom of association is governed inconsistently in different articles, instead of being included in one part of the constitution, in one article or — at least — in a series of consecutive articles. The situation is much better in respect of a special type of association, i.e. political parties. An article governing the freedom of their creation and functioning (Art. 11) is included in chapter I. Besides the above-mentioned article, the issue of political parties appears in the constitution in two additional instances, though in a strictly specified context. These include Article 13, in chapter I, which specifies categories of political parties and other organisations (including, inter alia, associations, foundations, etc. referred to in the aforementioned Article 12) forbidden by law, as well as Article 188 establishing the competence of the Constitutional Tribunal to adjudicate regarding the conformity to the constitution of the purposes or activities of political parties.

Therefore, this element of the freedom of association is governed coherently, even if included, almost entirely, in chapter I dealing with the general principles of the State system, rather than in that part dedicated to freedoms and rights. On the other hand, however, for that reason the regulation of the freedom of association included in chapter II is incomplete, so that in order to get a relatively complete view you have to combine provisions dispersed in five articles spread over two chapters. Such fragmentation of legislative regulation of certain rights and freedoms is disadvantageous not only for the ordinary citizen, but also for the bodies administering the law.

Many defects may also be found in the constitutional regulation of electoral rights : it is not uniform. Its principles were specified separately for particular types of election, which is additionally stressed by the fact that provisions concerning elections to a particular body (bodies) are included in the chapters dealing with a given body (bodies). Article 96(2) of the constitution establishes principles for the election of the Sejm, including the requirements of being universal, equal, direct, and proportional, and being conducted by secret ballot. In respect of the election to the Senate, the list of principles, set forth by Article 97(2), is shorter and includes the requirements of being universal, direct and being conducted by secret ballot. According to Article 127, the President of the Republic is elected in universal, equal and direct election, conducted by secret ballot. Constitutional principles of the election to local councils (contained in Article 169(2)) include universality, equality and directness and the requirement of being conducted by secret ballot. Additionally, Article 62 of the constitution, contained in that part of chapter II which deals with political freedoms and rights, includes provisions on the principle of universality of suffrage. This Article determines the age limit (18 years attained no later than on the day of the vote) for taking part in referenda as well as presidential and parliamentary elections and also in elections of representatives to organs of local government. It also applies a principle which states that only a court may deprive a person of the right to vote in elections or to participate in a referendum, adjudicating his/her legal incapacity or deprivation of public or electoral rights. Provisions specifying the age qualification for candidates running in elections are included in further parts of the constitution. They are: 21 years of age in respect of candidates for Deputies to the Sejm (Article 99(1)), 30 — candidates for Senators (Article 99(2)), and 35 — candidates for a President of the Republic. The age limits for candidates, in respect of any of the above mentioned offices, is specified as to be attained no later than on the day of vote. The constitution is silent in relation to the age limit for persons running for membership of local councils.

The constitution does not establish any catalogue of principles, common to all types of election, whereas regulations related to them are dispersed in its text. This means a regression in comparison to the scheme applied in the constitution of 1952 which included the principles of election within a single chapter (9)[7]. A backward movement is also evident in one additional instance. The new constitution eliminates the free election principle from the list of constitutional principles (previously, the constitution applied it only in relation to the election of Senators). By

---

[7] Its scope of regulation was not complete. For more on this subject, see B. Banaszak, *Prawo wyborcze obywateli* [*Electoral rights of citizens*], Warszawa 1996, p. 23–24.

ignoring the principle of equality, it maintains a different approach to elections to the Senate, which is difficult to justify.

Constitutional regulation of the principles of electoral rights may be used as a source of diverse interpretation, and its defects may have practical significance (e.g. allowing an excessive instrumentation of electoral rights in electoral laws). At this point we face questions of such importance for the entire system of individual rights and the functioning of a democratic state, that the solutions adopted by the constitution should not have engendered any doubts. This matter may, obviously, be resolved in electoral laws (e.g. by introducing therein the principle of free election), but ordinary laws should not substitute for a constitutional minimum, which — in modern times — contains a coherent catalogue of principles of electoral law.

The constitutional provisions concerning economic, social and cultural freedoms and rights have their weak points. Such is the delegation of power to adopt specific legislation to the ordinary legislator without specifying directions and frameworks for his lawmaking activities. Let us examine its consequences by example of Article 68(2) which provides citizens with "equal access to health care services, financed from public funds" stating at the same time that "the conditions for, and scope of, the provision of services shall be established by statute". Here, there is no guarantee of the gratuitous nature of at least basic services, and the notion of "access" is not unambiguous in its contents. Moreover, the provision envisaging specification by statute of conditions for the provision of health services leaves too wide a discretion to the legislator and, in practice, may limit the accessibility of health care by the introduction of paid services.

Deciding to include this group of rights and freedoms in the constitution, its authors attempted to meet emerging aspirations of the public, but were at the same aware of the limited financial capabilities of the State. Therefore, in Article 81, they distinguish two categories of economic, social and cultural freedoms and rights depending on the criterion of protection:

1) The rights and freedoms that may be exercised directly on the basis of constitutional norms, i.e. those in respect of which the content of their guarantees has a real character, including a judicial protection. However, even in order to determine their scope the constitution often assigns

a decisive role to statutes extending its provisions (e.g. Article 67). Such type of rights and freedoms include: the right to ownership, other property rights and the right of succession; the freedom to choose and to pursue one's profession and to choose one's place of work; the right to social security in whenever incapacitated for work or without work; the right to have one's health protected; the right to education; the right of the child to be protected and the right to care and assistance provided by public authorities; the freedom of artistic creation and scientific research as well as dissemination of the fruits thereof, the freedom to teach and enjoy the products of culture.

2) The rights and freedoms that may be asserted exclusively within the limits specified by statute. They include all remaining economic, social and cultural rights and freedoms. Provisions of the constitution relating to them often impose on public authorities an obligation to pursue a specified policy, such as, e.g. Article 75(1), which states that: "Public authorities shall pursue policies conducive to satisfying the housing needs of citizens...". Such formulation makes it possible to vindicate exercise of that category of rights not only by individuals, but also collectively by organized groups of citizens applying means of political action (e.g. a motion of no confidence in the government, submitted by Deputies representing one of the political parties).

Proponents of constitutional regulation of economic, social and cultural freedoms and rights hold that it corresponds with international standards specified in agreements concerning human rights. However, they ignore the fact that such acts do not require that group of rights and freedoms be included in the constitution, but only impose particular obligations on organs of individual countries and allow their realization by means of ordinary laws. At this point, it should be mentioned that the constitutions of many democratic states (e.g. Austria, Germany or Switzerland) contain regulation of social, economic and cultural rights and freedoms less extensive than those set forth in Poland's constitution. This, however, does not determine equal social effects of state actions. Moreover, a typical feature of West European states and the European system of protection of individual rights is the different treatment in the sphere of potential realization of social, cultural and economic freedoms and rights on the one hand, and political and personal rights and freedoms on the other hand.

Nevertheless, the viewpoint that social rights should not be included in a constitution has many proponents in the doctrine of constitutional law in several developed democracies. It is held that such rights have a programmatic nature and that in this respect the state must implement whole social programmes. Personal and political rights and freedoms require that the state creates adequate institutional guarantees or only refrains from interfering with the legally protected autonomy of the individual. They may be accomplished more easily and quickly, and state activity is in this respect determined to a smaller degree by economic factors.

At this point, it might be said that "even in most advanced democratic systems of government, there have been observed permanent or occasional departures from the proclaimed principles. This mostly relates to social and cultural rights whose extent, and, particularly, level of realisation is very often determined by the stage of the business cycle, depending on place and time. Any instances of international or domestic recession result in trends towards the reduction of social benefits"[8].

---

[8] E. Zwierzchowski, *Wprowadzenie do nauki prawa konstytucyjnego państw demokratycznych* [*An introduction to the teaching of constitutional law of democratic states*], Katowice 1992, p. 22.

Zbigniew Witkowski

Professor, Nicholas Copernicus University, Toruń

PRINCIPLE OF THE SOCIAL MARKET ECONOMY IN THE NEW CONSTITUTION OF THE REPUBLIC OF POLAND

The problem of admissibility of regulation regarding the social and economic issues in constitutions has been the basis for discussion between theoreticians and pragmatists over a long period. The opposition of Max Weber to the idea of the complex regulation of social issues in basic laws is especially well-known[1]. This opposition seems to be appropriate as regards the wish to regulate economic issues in a more complex way in a situation when this sphere has an obviously labile character. There are three possible approaches to the manner of regulating the economic system that can be encountered in constitutional practice[2].

Firstly, there is the type of regulation that emphasizes the principles of the free market economy in respect to which the state should establish only the general frames of order without making any attempts to specify social and economic aims, but which does not simultaneously eliminate the possibility of the realization of these aims when the common good requires it. Secondly, there is a type of regulation based on the social market economy which allows for the activity of the state called liberal interventionism; however, the state interference in market mechanisms should be in conformity with the principles regarding these mechanisms and be treated as exceptional measures. Thirdly, there are also regulations that allow for a broader interference of the state in market mechanisms and authorization for such interference is granted in the ordinary legislation[3]. The problem is to choose such a solution as makes possible the preservation of significant flexibility for state activities within the economy and,

---

[1] K. Sobczak discusses this subject (in:) *Wolność gospodarcza w kręgu problemów konstytucyjnych* [*Economic Freedom Within the Sphere of Constitutional Problems*] „Przegląd Ustawodawstwa Gospodarczego" 1996, No. 3, p. 5.

[2] They are reconstructed on the basis of the work of K. Sobczak, *op.cit.*, p. 5.

[3] Compare the above.

at the same time, allows for the comprehensive protection of economic rights and freedoms of citizens.

As the thesis about the need for state neutrality within the economy was rejected during the constitutional debate on the role of the state, it became clear that the new constitution would have to take a position regarding this issue[4]. The opinion has been emphasized that "the state's tasks, connected with the transition to a new type of economic system, provide for making choice of the type of the economy accepted by the whole society"[5]. However, it was difficult to reach a decision regarding the law-making process in this sphere. This can be easily observed as regards Article 20 of the new constitution which has a fundamental significance for the character of the economic system of the Republic of Poland. It defines our economy as "a social market economy" and is the result of a far-reaching compromise regarding economic issues. This article was incorporated into the text of the basic law only during the second reading of the bill in the Constitutional Committee of the National Assembly[6]. In consequence, the principle of "the social market economy" as a feature of the system of government (i.e., the second type of possible solution) gained the status of one of the most basic constitutional principles pursuant to the decision of the legislator[7].

It should be also noticed that the discussed principle stands today in contrast to the model of the so-called socialist planned economy discussed

---

[4] Compare materials from report on the discussion on the: *Rola prawa w procesie reform gospodarczych w Polsce na posiedzeniu Komitetu Nauk Prawniczych PAN [Role of the Law in the Process of the Economic Reforms in Poland Discussed at the Meeting of the Committee of the Legal Sciences of the Polish Academy of Science]* „Państwo i Prawo" 1994, Vol. 11–12, p. 116.

[5] Compare above work and remarks by J. Jaskiernia: *Przemiany społeczno-polityczne i gospodarcze a treść nowej Konstytucji RP [Social, Political and Economic Changes and the Contents of the New Constitution of the Republic of Poland]* (in:) *Konstytucja stabilizatorem III Rzeczypospolitej [Constitution as the Stabilizer of the Third Republic of Poland]*, Warszawa 1998, p. 27 and the following.

[6] Compare W. Skrzydło, *Konstytucja Rzeczypospolitej Polskiej. Komentarz. [The Constitution of the Republic of Poland. A Commentary]*, Kraków 1998, p. 24.

[7] Compare comment to the Article 20 of the Constitution (in:) *Konstytucje Rzeczyspospolitej oraz komentarz do Konstytucji RP z 1997, [Constitutions of the Republic of Poland and Commentary to the Constitution of the Republic of Poland of 1997]* edited by J. Boć, Wrocław 1998, p. 51.

in the previous Constitution of the People's Republic of Poland of 22nd July 1952. Therefore, it means that the features constituting the new model of the market economy desired by the legislator, as regards the Constitution of 1997, are as follows: freedom of market activity, private property, solidarity, dialogue and cooperation between social partners. These features remain in opposition to the features constituting the hitherto--existing model of the planned economy based on the significant dominance of state property, ruled by an extensive and inefficient machinery of state administration and significant interference by a ubiquitous party economic apparatus, as well as based on the principle of strict limitations on the activity of non-state economic subjects. The approval given in the new constitution for an economy, whose main driving force is market mechanisms, means that the legislator of the constitution limits in advance the common legislator in his attempts to choose the appropriate economic model for the state[8]. The common legislator will, in the future, have to approve a structure of the market based on the principle of free competition and in which all participants have equal rights and chances. Certainly, the state has not been deprived of the possibility of exerting influence on market mechanisms since it still enjoys the competence of law-making. This thesis has been justified by the use of the adjective "social" preceding the category "market economy" by the legislator. It has been rightly stated in the literature that this qualification proves that the traditional liberal meaning of the definition has been rejected i.e., the definition which assumed as inadmissible any interference of the state in the functioning of market mechanisms[9]. It is also unquestionable that such interference cannot be unlimited although it should not mean the right of the state to substitute such mechanisms by means of its own decisions. Thus, we may conclude that due to an increasing threat to free action in the modern economy and due to imperfections of market mechanisms, the state may or sometimes must shoulder the role of independent arbitrator[10].

---

[8] Compare Z. Witkowski (in:) *Prawo konstytucyjne [Constitutional Law]*, edited by Z. Witkowski, Toruń 1998, p. 74 and compare comments on this subject by L. Garlicki (in:) *Polskie prawo konstytucyjne. Zarys wykładu [Polish Constitutional Law. Outline of a Lecture]*, 2nd edition, Warszawa 1998, p. 79.

[9] See above mentioned, p. 79.

[10] Compare B. Polszakiewicz: *Systemowe odmiany gospodarki rynkowej [Systemic Variants of the Market Economy]* „Życie i Myśl" 1996, No. 4, p. 13.

Since the weaknesses of the market economy, demonstrated in practice, tend to establish excessive disproportions and social inequalities, as well as risking destruction of the social security system, then so-called "shock absorbers" interacting within emerging tensions and dangers should be established and introduced to the socio-economic system.

According to the above arrangements, the main theoreticians of the so-called ordoliberal model of the economy[11], introduced after World War II in the Federal Republic of Germany and called there the social market economy (*Soziale Marktwirtschaft*), like A. Muller-Armack, W. Eucken, L. Erhard and W. Ropke[12], allowed for the possibility of state interference that facilitated the adaptation processes by easing the tensions connected with them. This interference remained (and should remain at present) in conformity with the market system functioning today; however, structural policy should be conducive to decentralization processes, equalization of inter-regional differences and giving preference to the attitude called "economic humanism". To put it another way, state interference was to be aimed at counteracting the problems regarding the functioning of the economy, controlling the unemployment rate, making the required changes in certain spheres of the economy, as well as stimulating the development of social benefit systems.

These guidelines also seem to be valid under the principles of the governmental and economic system established by the provisions of the new Constitution of 1997. The Polish legislator has not opted for an extreme liberal model of the state economy but rather for a state of so-called sensitive social orientation guided by economic processes. These arrangements, in comparison with provisions of the Article 20 of the new constitution, are to be achieved under Polish conditions by, among others: the obligation of the state to take steps aimed at mitigating the social effects of market mechanisms, as well as showing respect for those mechanisms and the rights associated with them. The Polish legislator

---

[11] Compare the above mentioned.

[12] Professor A. Muller-Armack is regarded as the author of the definition of the social market economy whose principles explained in his work: *Kierowanie gospodarką a gospodarka rynkowa* [*Economy Management and the Market Economy*], published in 1946 — see C. Kosikowski, *Prawo gospodarcze publiczne* [*Public Business Law*], Warszawa 1994, p. 8. The concept of the social market economy in the Federal Republic of Germany appeared within the so-called Ahlen's Program of the CDU in 1974.

included in the provisions of the new constitution many directives regarding requested state activities in this respect. These directives result directly from the provisions of the Article 24 of the constitution which protect work (thought this does not necessarily mean that the constitution guarantees the right to work since it is a so-called unclaimable right), as well as from many other detailed social rights and tasks discussed in Articles 65–76 of the new constitution (i.e. pursuing policies aiming at full, productive employment, ensuring the right to safe and hygienic conditions of work, the right to social security whenever incapacitated for work by reason of sickness or invalidity as well as having attained the retirement age, the right to health protection, the right to equal access to health care services financed from public funds, the right to education, pursuing policies conducive to satisfying the housing needs of citizens and policies ensuring the protection of consumers, customers, hirers or lessees against activities threatening their health, privacy and safety, as well as against dishonest market practices).

As previously remarked before, the new constitution makes the provisions of Article 20: a. freedom of economic activity, b. private ownership and c. solidarity, dialogue and cooperation between social partners, the fundamental canons of the social market economy.

Freedom of economic activity is a category that signifies both freedom to undertake economic activity whose basic aim is to make profit, as well as freedom to undertake this activity in the objective and subjective context. It can be noticed that Article 22 of the new constitution states at the same time that freedom to undertake economic activity is not an absolute principle (this provision is in conformity with the judgment of the Constitutional Tribunal)[13]. Imposition of such limitations or barriers on this activity is admissible, however exceptional, provided there are justified reasons for it[14]. It is also important that only statutes, not acts of lower significance, should constitute the basis of such barriers or limitations and that such limitations are justified e.g. by a social interest of particular significance. The limitations discussed above may not be discretionary. The Constitutional Tribunal stated in one of its judgments

---

[13] See e.g. judgment of the Constitutional Tribunal No. K. 5/89 of 6th March 1990.

[14] The Constitutional Tribunal expressed this opinion in its judgment No. K. 4/92 of 20th August 1992.

that these limitations cannot lead to general exclusions forbidding certain categories of persons from undertaking economic activity[15]. The limitations may and should pertain to specific fields of activity and may be justified by the protection of human life and health[16]. It has also been emphasized in many comments that the principle of freedom of economic activity guarantees freedom of activity from the point of view of an individual. In this context it means that economic activity can be performed by anyone on an equal rights basis[17]. It is not possible to disagree with the statement frequently found in the literature, that the provisions of Article 22 of the new constitution containing limitations on economic freedom are directed, above all, to the Parliament and to the Constitutional Tribunal i.e., to the law-making organs and organs ensuring its conformity with the Constitution and that the constitutional principle of economic freedom should be realized regardless of the form of property since the basic law principle regarding private property specified in Article 20 of the new constitution, being only a constitutional signpost, should not be treated as "one excluding economic freedom from economic activity that is not based on private property"[18].

For a long time, private property has constituted a driving force in the development of human civilization, so it is not surprising that it has today become the canon of the social market economy in the Republic of Poland. It unambiguously follows from Article 20 of the new constitution that the definition of "private property" refers to any type of property which belongs to any other person or entity than the state and remains within the non-state property sector. Therefore, considering the problem in the context of the constitutional provisions, it is not important whether the basis for the property law is introduced by means of the provisions of the

---

[15] See judgment of the Constitutional Tribunal No. U.9/90 of 9th April 1991.

[16] See above. It would be inadmissible to lead economic activity forbidden by provisions of the criminal and misdemeanor law e.g., falsification of products, counterfeiting of currency or excise signs, drug trafficking, illegal arms trade and trade in munitions — compare J. Boć (editor) *Konstytucje Rzeczypospolitej [Constitutions of the Republic of Poland]* p. 51 and following.

[17] Compare K. Kruczalak, *Wolność gospodarcza i jej ograniczenia w świetle Konstytucji RP [Economic Freedom and its Limitations in the Light of the Constitution of the Republic of Poland]*, „Gdańskie Studia Prawnicze". Also: A. Szmyt (editor) *Wybrane zagadnienia nowej Konstytucji [Selected Issues of the New Constitution]*, Gdańsk 1998, Vol. 3, p. 45.

[18] See the above, p. 46.

civil code or provisions of any other statute[19]. Provisions of Article 218 of the constitution refer to state property represented by the State Treasury as well as to the property of other state legal persons. The provisions of Article 165 (1) of the new constitution refer to communal property, i.e., property of units of local government and other communal legal persons.

The contents of Article 20 include a clear directive from the legislator forbidding taking any activities (among them, those of a law-making character) which are aimed at the restoration of a system based on state property and subjects representing the state as functioned in the former People's Republic of Poland. The provisions of Article 20 of the new constitution also include another clear directive aimed at the common legislator, i.e., an order to continue and to conclude the existing process of privatization of state property.

The principle of protection of property and the right to succession [Article 21 (1)] supplements the above-mentioned directives. It is worth stressing that the protection guaranteed here by the constitution clearly refers to **every form of property** regardless of the type of the criterion[20]. This arrangement has not been changed by the fact that the issue of private property takes priority in the new economic system. We may also learn from the provisions of the Article 21 (1) of the new constitution that the property right is not treated by the legislator as an absolute right. The Constitutional Tribunal has expressed its opinion regarding this matter[21]. Both the legislator and the Tribunal allow, exceptionally, for expropriation of property. This may happen on condition that such expropriation is made in order to take over the expropriated property for public use regardless of the form of the expropriation; and that this expropriation is made for so-called just compensation. Such just compensation, in the light of the judgment of the Constitutional Tribunal, constitutes a lawful compensation that is appropriate and so does not detract from the idea of compensation for the property taken[22].

---

[19] See the judgement of the Constitutional Tribunal No. K.3/88.

[20] It has been regretted in certain comments that the issue of any form of property has not been specially emphasized in Article 21 (1) of the new constitution but it refers only to the problem of the private property see: J. Boć (editor) *Konstytucje... [Constitutions...]*, p. 52.

[21] See judgment of the Constitutional Tribunal No. K.1/91.

[22] See judgments of the Constitutional Tribunal: K.1/90 and K.2/90.

The significance of the property issue is emphasized by other provisions of the new constitution, among them the provisions of Article 64 (1–3) which acknowledge the right of anyone to ownership and other property rights through the right to succession. They acknowledge also equal protection of any form of ownership, other property rights and the right to succession as well as admissibility of limitation of ownership only by virtue of a statute (never by virtue of acts of lower significance) and to the extent to which this statute does not violate the essence of the property right.

The third canon of the social market economy in the Republic of Poland provides for: solidarity, dialogue and cooperation between social partners. These are new elements in Polish constitutional law but they play a significant role as regards the system of government and especially as regards the continuation of important social processes initiated in our country. The principle of solidarity is of an exceptional significance in Poland since it refers to the social doctrine of the Catholic Church[23]. Rooting of this principle in the legal provisions should proceed carefully considering the fact that possible negative effects may also appear[24].

It seems that the above concepts constitute an integrative principle of the constitution which states that any consensus that may be reached during negotiations in spheres of conflict are, or at least should be, the basis for social cooperation. A constitution in a pluralistic society must anticipate and permit the existence of mechanisms enabling solution to perennial social tensions and conflicts, harmonization of social and economic relations, easing of emerging disproportions or preventing economic hardship not only amongst economic subjects but also groups of workers. A basic law permitting the existence of such mechanisms makes the integration and identification of the citizens with the state easy. It

---

[23] Compare encyclicals of the Pope John Paul II: *Laborem exercens* of 1981 and *Centesimus annus* of 1991.

[24] Authors of the comment *Konstytucje Rzeczypospolitej* [*Constitutions of the Republic of Poland*] edited by J. Boć observe that: "The principle of solidarity cannot be imposed by virtue of legal provisions. It is also not possible to oblige the partners of the social dialogue to be ruled by general not particular interest. Consensus reached in such a dialogue may have other than positive significance. It may also signify stiffening of the economic adjustments mechanisms e.g., on the employment market, in the restructuring process of the mining industry or in the transformation process of the agrarian structure" p. 52.

seems that the provisions of Article 59 (2) of the new constitution should be perceived in this light since they provide for the right of trade unions, employers and especially their organizations to negotiate in order to solve collective disputes and to conclude collective labour agreements as well as agreements of other types.

The new constitution generally prefers dialogue and cooperation between social partners. Therefore, the principle of cooperation, not confrontation, in situations requiring cooperation results from its provisions. To put it otherwise, the new constitution prefers mechanisms aimed at establishing systematic organizational steps in this area, not instruments and procedures applied temporarily. It means that the principles of solidarity, dialogue and cooperation between social partners should not be presently understood as meaning approval for exceptional "anti-crisis" measures — by definition often temporary or ad hoc, in the case of any conflicts or threats of such conflicts. Such dialogue and cooperation are to be a normal and stable element of mechanisms for the functioning of public authority in its relations with all possible social partners.

At the same time, these partners while solving existing social and economic problems and conflicts, and taking into account the rights they enjoy such as the right to strike and right to other forms of protest, guaranteed to them by law, should always keep in mind the contents of Article 1 of the constitution which states: "The Republic of Poland shall be the common good of all its citizens". The important principle of putting the common good above the good of an individual or a group results from the provisions of this Article.

The third pillar resulting from the provisions of Article 20 and the values it emphasizes (i.e. solidarity, dialogue and cooperation between the social partners) are also guiding principles that are given by the constitutional legislator to the common legislator. The latter should recall, during the law-making process, the necessity of following these principles when establishing legal mechanisms that allow for overcoming the tensions and conflicts which cannot be avoided in a modern pluralistic society. The presence in our national legislation of such institutions as, for example, the Tripartite Committee and their work are good examples of such a tendency.

It should be stated at the end of this analysis of the significance of the principle of the social market economy that a detailed description of the economic model adopted as the market economy can be found in the provisions of Paragraph 9 of the consolidated text of the Hungarian Constitution of 1990. The description of the features of this model, without however giving their detailed definitions, can be found in Article 46 (1) and the following of the Lithuanian Constitution of 1992. Different methods and forms of cooperation and dialogue as well as amicable solutions of the social and economic tensions and conflicts are included in the constitutions of many countries, particularly members of the European Union[25].

---

[25] For example: there should be mentioned the Dutch Social and Economic Council, mechanism of the so-called social partnership in Austria and the so-called joint action in Germany.

Andrzej Szmyt

Professor, University of Gdańsk

REPRESENTATION — ELECTIONS — DEMOCRACY

REPRESENTATION

The new Constitution of 1997 declares in Article 4(2) that "The Nation shall exercise [supreme] power directly or through its representatives". Hence, apart from the exercise of power by the sovereign (the Nation), the constitutional formula provides a basis for the principle of representation (indirect) or representative democracy. The essence of such manner of exercising power consists, obviously, of making decisions on behalf of the sovereign particularly by parliament (the Sejm and the Senate) whose composition is determined in elections. The provisions of Article 104, closely related to the above, states that "Deputies shall be representatives of the Nation" (the first sentence of paragraph 1); this provision also applies to Senators (Article 108), which ensures the same status to members of both houses. While the constitutional phrase regarding the Deputies and Senators as representatives of the Nation raises no doubts, one may notice that the wording of Article 4(2) is not precise. The exercise of power in its representative form is not actually exercised through representatives (Deputies and Senators) but rather through the legislature (the Sejm and the Senate) to which they have been elected and in which they sit. These are the legislative bodies, and not individual representatives, to whom the exercise of power has been conferred. Nevertheless, the way in which the principle has been expressed does not affect its essence as a formula establishing the exercise of power by the Nation[1]. Moreover, it is somewhat unfortunate that the text of Article 4(2) lacks any explicit mention that it concerns "State" power. The constitutional wording sometimes leads to the conclusion that the sequence in which both forms of democracy are enumerated determines accepting representative

---

[1] See, Z. Witkowski (ed.): *Prawo konstytucyjne* [*Constitutional Law*], Toruń 1998, p. 69.

democracy as fundamental method of government of the State[2]. However, such sequence should rather be perceived as only a declarative act in relation to reality, in a situation where the modern state allows for treating the forms of direct democracy as both specific and legally equal.

The constitutional provision concerning forms of the realization of power of the Nation is logically as well as legislative-technically associated with the principle of supremacy (sovereignty) expressed in Article 4(1) which says that "supreme power in the Republic of Poland shall be vested in the Nation". This formula is of significance for the principle of representation — most expressly manifested in the wording of the provision — since it emphasizes that supreme power "is vested" in the Nation and not only "emanates" therefrom. This highlights the permanent nature of such supremacy and shows that realization of representative democracy does not exclude the possibility of simultaneous realization of direct democracy in its various forms.

The correlation between the principle of representation and the principle of sovereignty of the Nation also has other dimensions as the existence of parliament is not sufficient for the real presence of representative democracy. The form of electoral procedures, based on the manner of understanding the [notion of the] sovereign, is of significance. At this place, the principle appears as a link connecting the principle of sovereignty with the principle of political pluralism. When we recognize the use of such notions as the "nation", "people" and "working people of towns and villages" in the constitutional theory of the 19th and 20th centuries, we cannot ignore the fact of their different meanings, and their widespread influence on other constitutional provisions. The interpretation of these notions contributed, in varying degrees, to the accentuation of the class character of the State, or a role played by a particular political party[3] in the system of government. For example, one could find a constitutional formula stating that "the Polish United Workers' Party shall be the leading

---

[2] See, L. Garlicki: *Polskie prawo konstytucyjne. Zarys wykładu* [*Polish Constitutional Law. Draft lecture*], Warszawa 1998, p. 55.

[3] From preamble to the Constitution of the People's Republic of Poland, of 1952 (repealed by the Amendment of 29th December 1989): "The current people's power in Poland shall be based on the alliance between the working class and working peasants. The principal role in this alliance shall belong to the working class, as a leading class in society, based on the revolutionary heritage of the Polish and international working movement (...)".

political force in society aimed at building socialism"[4]. A definition of the sovereign which enables its perception without the use of a class approach better corresponds with the assumption of abandonment of one-party hegemony. The formula of the sovereign as a type of politico-legal community is better expressed by the classic notion of the "Nation". Such formula is contained in Article 4(1) of the Constitution. Hence, it is a concept of sovereignty, established in European doctrine at the turn of 18th century, which rejects the possibility of both accepting one social class or group as a holder of power or leaving it beyond the definition of the Nation. This, of course, does not mean that the sovereign should be treated, in all aspects, as a monolith. The constitutional principle of political pluralism, determining democratic nature of election of the representatives of the Nation (Article 11) is harmonized with internal socio-political diversification.

Interdependence of a series of principles "supremacy — pluralism — representation" is further defined in other provisions of the Constitution and by doctrinal analysis. Undoubtedly, the authors of the Constitution employ the term of the "Nation" in its political, and not ethnic, meaning. The notion used in Article 4 should also be referred to such terms as "community of all citizens" (Article 1), "We, the Polish Nation — all citizens of the Republic" (from the preamble) or "Poles living abroad", mentioned in Article 6(2). On the other hand, power in fact emanates from the decisions of citizens with the right to vote (the so-called electoral body). This process cannot occur — in the modern understanding of representation — until an authentic version of representation has been established through selection of representatives only by the electoral body and by procedures recognized as democratic.

Moreover, the concept of representation is given substantive content by the way a representative's mandate is understood. The relation between Deputies and electors is factually clear; in the theory of representation it is expressed by model approaches such as the concept of imperative mandate or the concept of free mandate. A distinctive feature of the imperative mandate is that Deputie's are legally constrained by their dependence on their electors who may give them binding instructions and to whom they

---

[4] Article 3(1) of the Constitution of 1952, in the wording after the amendment of 10th February 1976, in force until 29th December 1989.

are accountable, and by whom they may even be recalled. The free mandate is its opposite, which means that Deputies represent the whole Nation, hence any "orders" given to them by electors will have no binding force. Moreover, Deputies cannot be recalled during their term of office. The present Constitution explicitly accepts the concept of the free mandate in Article 104(1): this states that "Deputies shall be representatives of the Nation. They shall not be bound by any instructions of the electorate". Since the Deputies represent the Nation as a whole, no legal links appear between them and the sovereign defined "partially" in any manner, nor in any political party dimension[5]. In accordance with the Constitution (Article 11(1)), the purpose of political parties is "to influence the formulation of the policy of the State by democratic means". However, the law does not permit political parties to "participate" in the relations specified by Article 104 of the Constitution. Parties nominate their candidates for representatives, conduct election campaigns and exercise control over decision-making processes in parliament, but their interests in the sphere of representation are not protected and any violation thereof cannot be claimed on grounds of public law.

Before the changes, the constitutional provisions said that the Nation exercises its power "through its representatives elected to the Sejm and the Senate". Such phrase raised doubts as to whether the President, chosen in universal election, had the status of a representative of the Nation. The new Constitution similarly does not name the President a representative of the Nation, even if he/she is chosen in an election (Article 127) that has the same democratic credentials as the parliamentary election. Thereby, the constitutional provisions emphasise the special position of parliament; however, this is not inconsistent with the fact that the President also has at his/her disposal a direct legitimization based on the will of the Nation. This allows us argue that, from the "substantive" point of view, the President is also a representative of the Nation, which differentiates his/her position compared to other systems where presidents are elected by parliaments or a similar body[6]. Any recognition of the President as a representative body

---

[5] More on this subject, A. Szmyt: *Partie polityczne a parlament* [*Political parties and Parliament*] (in:) A. Gwiżdż: *Założenia ustrojowe, struktura i funkcjonowanie parlamentu* [*Assumptions for Organization and Structure of Government and the Functioning of Parliament*], Warszawa 1997, p. 141.

[6] See in L. Garlicki: *Polskie prawo konstytucyjne...*, p. 55.

would mean that such classification has not been impaired even though the Constitution (Article 126) explicitly recognizes the President as "the supreme representative of the Republic of Poland", hence the representative of the "State", not the Nation. If the President were considered the representative of the Nation, then the character of his/her "mandate" would be uniform with the mandate of a Deputy or Senator. However, the provisions of the Constitution are sometimes interpreted in a way explicitly rejecting the President's status of a representative of the Nation[7], based on the assumption that representative character of a body in relation to the Nation cannot be decided only by the fact of being chosen in universal elections. The concept of two representative bodies — parliament and president — would lead to an increased significance of the referendum as a form enabling the resolving of disputes between them in relation to important State issues[8].

ELECTIONS

The phrase contained in Article 4(4) of the Constitution, stating that the Nation exercises power through its representatives necessarily requires organizing the election of representative bodies. Additionally, in the study of constitutional law it is stressed that "elections understood as regular, repeated renewals of the composition of parliament, as a result of decisions taken under specific procedures by all citizens having full civil rights, are an inseparable part of any democratic political system"[9]. Hence, elections are the result of the principle of sovereignty of the Nation and they constitute the main form by which supervision of the rulers by the ruled is accomplished. The existence and observance of election procedures is today a basic standard whose European dimension is included in the essence of the provision stating that states "undertake to hold free elections at reasonable intervals by secret ballot, under conditions which will ensure

---

[7] See, Z. Witkowski (ed.): *Prawo konstytucyjne...*, p. 259, or W. Skrzydło (ed.): *Polskie prawo konstytucyjne [Polish Constitutional Law]*, Lublin 1998, p. 211.

[8] M. Pietrzak: *Demokracja reprezentacyjna i bezpośrednia w Konstytucji Rzeczypospolitej Polskiej [Representative and Direct Democracy in the Constitution of the Republic of Poland]* (in:) M. Staszewski (ed.): *Referendum konstytucyjne w Polsce [Constitutional Referendum in Poland]*, Warszawa 1997, p. 24.

[9] See e.g. (in:) L. Garlicki: *Polskie prawo konstytucyjne...*, p. 117.

the free expression of the opinion of the people in the choice of the legislature"[10].

The Constitution of 1952 had a separate chapter devoted to electoral issues. In the new Constitution elections are dealt with in several places. These include, in sequence, the following provisions: (1) Article 62 (Chapter II — The freedoms, rights and obligations of persons and citizens); (2) Articles 96–101 (Chapter IV The Sejm and the Senate; subchapter — Elections and the term of office); (3) Articles 127–129 (Chapter V — the President of the Republic of Poland) and (4) Article 169 (Chapter VII — Local Self-Government). The constitutional foundations of electoral law are complemented by special statutes, traditionally called in Polish "*ordynacja wyborcza*" [election ordinance]. In this respect, the following acts now exist in Poland: (1) the Act of 28th May 1993 on Elections to the Sejm of the Republic of Poland[11], (2) the Act of 10th May 1991 on Elections to the Senate of the Republic of Poland2[12], (3) the Act of 27th September 1990 on Elections to the Presidency of the Republic of Poland[13] and (4) the Act of 16 July 1998 on Elections to councils of communes, councils of districts and voivodship assemblies[14].

More precise regulations of electoral law are based on the so-called fundamental principles, developed in the past and, today, indicating concrete standards, particularly in relation to the first house of parliament (the Sejm). Fundamental principles are sometimes traditionally called "electoral adjectives", and therefore we use such terms as a "four — or five — adjective electoral system". In accordance with the Constitution of 1997, the elections to the Sejm are five-adjective — universal, equal, direct and proportional and are conducted by secret ballot (Article 96(2)). The Constitution specifies that elections to the Senate are universal, direct and are conducted by secret ballot (Article 96(2)). This means that not only the principle of proportionality, but also the principle of equality, has been

---

[10] Article 3 of Protocol No. 1 of the European Convention for the Protection of Human Rights and Fundamental Freedoms signed in Paris on 29th March 1952 (Dziennik Ustaw of 4th April 1995, No. 36, item 175).

[11] Dziennik Ustaw of 2nd June 1993, No. 45, item 205, as amended.

[12] The consolidated text: Dziennik Ustaw of 1994, No. 54, item 224, as amended.

[13] Dziennik Ustaw of 2nd October 1990, No. 67, item 398, as amended.

[14] Dziennik Ustaw, No. 95, item 602.

omitted. The fact that the Constitution is silent in this respect allows the legislator to determine the shape of elections to the Senate at his own discretion — either as proportional or as based on a majority principle and — in respect of the principle of equality — taking it into account or ignoring it. The President of the Republic of Poland is elected by the Nation, in universal, equal and direct elections, conducted by secret ballot (Article 127(1)). It is obvious, in the nature of things, that the principle of proportionality cannot be applied where only one mandate is to be taken. Hence, the Constitution explicitly employs the majority principle (Article 127(4) and (6)). In Article 169(2) the Constitution states that elections to the local councils are to be universal, direct, equal and by secret ballot. The choosing of the proportional representation or the majority system has been left to the decision of the legislator.

It should be noted that the new Constitution does not expressly formulate the principle of "free" elections, though such principle was proclaimed in 1992 by the so-called Small Constitution in respect of elections to the Senate; it was also contained in the previous (1991) Act on Elections to the Senate. Departure from this norm can be explained by the lesser need, in today's circumstances, to emphasise this characteristic of the elections as compared to the initial period of transformations. More-over, this norm made manifest the presumption, now seemingly self--evident, that the provisions of electoral law should guarantee solutions implementing the principle of political pluralism[15].

The principle of universal suffrage, specifying the range of subjects to whom electoral rights are conferred, is regulated by Article 62(1) and (2) of the Constitution in the area of the voting rights (so-called in Poland active electoral rights). Such right is granted to a Polish citizen who, no later than on the day of vote, has attained 18 years of age. Persons who, by a final judgment of a court, have been subjected to legal incapacitation or deprived of public or electoral rights, have no right to vote. Hence, the

---

[15] One should, however, bear in mind that the new Constitution contains, in Article 13, the prohibition of "Political parties and other organizations whose programmes are based upon totalitarian methods and the modes of activity of nazism, fascism and communism, as well as those whose programmes or activities sanction racial or national hatred, the application of violence for the purpose of obtaining power or to influence the State policy, or provide for the secrecy of their own structure or membership".

Constitution uniformly governs the rights of citizens to participate in elections to all the above-mentioned bodies. The imposition of the requirement of citizenship is explained by the character of electoral rights as political rights. The age limit has a natural character, so it is not a discrimination.

Qualifications for membership (a so-called passive electoral right) is formed in a different manner, depending on the kind of elections, particularly as regards the age limit. The possessing of the right to vote (the so-called active electoral right) is a common prerequisite of all kinds of elections. There are the following minimum age limits for candidates in particular elections: (1) 18 years of age (the same as for the voting right) — for elections to local councils; (2) 21 years of age — for elections to the Sejm (Article 99(1)) — which is Poland's traditionally established limit; (3) 30 years of age — for elections to the Senate — which means a considerable rise in comparison with 1989, the year of restoration of the Senate, when this limit was 21 years for both houses of Polish Parliament, but is a reference-back to the inter-war regulations; (4) 35 years of age — for presidential elections (Article 127(3)). In the previous constitutional provisions (Article 96), there existed a qualification of domicile (permanent residence) which was not continued in the new Constitution[16].

The principle of equal suffrage in its formal meaning ("one person, one vote") today seems self-evident. However, in its material meaning, the principle consists of a requirement that each vote has the same force, what would be fulfilled when the same number of voters could elect the same number of representatives. The provisions of the Act on Elections to the Senate have not yet taken this into account, since two candidates (Senators) are, in general, elected in each voivodship also being a constituency, even if those voivodships differ considerably in respect of the number of their inhabitants. Such situation justifies the lack of this principle in the Constitution, in the catalogue of "electoral adjectives" listed in relation to elections to the Senate.

The constitutional principle of direct suffrage compels the legislator to shape the manner of elections of representatives as one-stage only, without

---

[16] Such constitutional departure makes the domicile requirement, contained in the Act on Elections, groundless.

any intermediate elements (levels or stages). Thus, it is the voter who is to decide on the composition of a representative body[17].

The principle of secret ballot concerns only the act of voting and guarantees that the content of a voter's decision cannot be identified or disclosed. For that reason, secrecy of voting should be treated as an obligation, not a right of the voter, and election authorities should provide condition enabling voters to cast their votes in circumstances ensuring secrecy.

The majority principle, used to establish the results of elections, are envisaged by the Constitution only in relation to presidential elections. A candidate who has received more than half of the valid votes cast is to be elected President of the Republic (the first sentence of Article 127(4)); this is the principle of absolute majority. If, however, none of the candidates has received the required majority of votes in the first round of voting, then a repeat ballot shall be held on the 14th day after the first vote. So, this is a two-stage system. The two candidates who have received the largest number of votes in the first ballot participate in the second. If one of the two such candidates withdraws his consent to candidacy, forfeits his electoral rights or duties, he shall be replaced in the repeat ballot by the candidate who received the next highest consecutive number of votes in the first ballot. In such case, the date of the repeat ballot shall be extended by a further 14 days. The candidate who receives the higher number of votes in the repeat ballot shall be elected President of the Republic (Article 127(6)). Hence, a relative majority is required in the second round. It might be added that — given the silence of the Constitution — the legislator applied, in election laws, the majority rule also in relation to election to the Senate and to the councils of communes whose number of inhabitants does not exceed 20 thousand. The system, statutorily introduced, is based on the relative majority rule, where it is sufficient to obtain such majority in the first vote, a two-round system is not necessary. But these are not constitutional requirements.

---

[17] From the point of view of the directness rule, the existence of a nationwide list (the so-called national list of candidates) in the election to the Sejm, may raise doubts. This solution maintains only certain elements of exerting influence of voters' will on the results of election; in legal context, however, the voter has not opportunity to cast his/her vote on a candidate obtaining the mandate from such list.

In Poland, the proportional representation is applied for elections to the Sejm (Article 96(2)) and — by virtue of the election Act, and silence of the Constitution — in elections to voivodship assemblies [*sejmiks*], councils of districts and council of those communes whose number of inhabitants exceeds twenty thousand. The Constitution, based on the principle applied for the conduct of elections to the Sejm, does not specify the method of distribution of mandates, either by preferring stronger parties or supporting weaker parties, it is silent about the admissibility of "threshold clauses", the institution of the so-called "State list", preferences for lists of national minorities. Such regulations have been introduced by statutory provisions. The issue of election campaigns are, in general, outside constitutional regulation.

In accordance with the Constitution, elections to the Sejm and the Senate are ordered by the President of the Republic (Article 98(2)), and election of the President of the Republic shall be ordered by the Speaker of the Sejm (Article 128(2)). Candidates for Deputies and Senators may be nominated by political parties or voters, but no one may stand for election to the Sejm and the Senate at the same time (Article 100 (1) and (2)), while a candidate for the Presidency must be nominated by at least 100,000 citizens having the right to vote in elections to the Sejm (Article 127(3) *in fine*). The validity of the elections to the Sejm and the Senate and the validity of the election of the President of the Republic is adjudicated upon by the Supreme Court, and a voter has — in accordance with principles specified by statute — the right to submit a complaint to the Supreme Court against the validity of the elections. The Constitution also contains a reference to statutes, in which the principles of and procedures for the nomination of candidates and the conduct of the elections, as well as the requirements for validity of the elections and submission of any complaints (Articles 100–101 and 127–128) are dealt with. Such statutes (Acts on Elections) form — apart from the Constitution — a widely developed electoral law which could be beneficially consolidated in one electoral code, fully adapted to the assumptions of the new Constitution.

DIRECT DEMOCRACY

Poland's new Constitution, unlike all its predecessors, contains a relatively wide range of provisions concerning direct democracy, to be found in nine articles. Article 4(2), states that supreme power in the Republic is vested in the Nation, and such Nation exercising its powers "directly or through its representatives" provides, obviously, a starting point in this respect. At this point, no concrete form of direct democracy is mentioned, however, there is a positive solution in respect of the principle itself.

This fact is worth stressing, especially as such solutions are rare in the Polish legislative tradition. The institution of direct democracy was unknown to the Constitution of 1921, the Constitution of 1935 and the Constitution of 1952 in its original wording. In 1987, Article 2 the Constitution, establishing the representative form of power of the people, was amended by adding paragraph 3 in the following wording "The exercise of State power by working people may also be implemented by means of a referendum [...][18]. Hence, this was not a declaration of a complete "principle", but rather an incidental introduction of one well-known institution of direct democracy. The Small Constitution of 1992 specified the issue of referendum in a separate provision, although it maintained the above-mentioned provision of Article 2 of the Constitution of 1952[19]. During these years, an increase of interest in the issue of direct democracy has been evident, especially in the perspective of State organization meeting the requirements of civic society. Notwithstanding the threats posed by its different forms, this reflected the attractiveness of democratic values contained in the idea of direct democracy and its relevant institutions. A review of drafts submitted in the course of many years spent on work on the new Constitution, shows that the idea (or principle) of direct democracy has been manifested in these drafts with such a force that — whilst maintaining representation as the major form of exercise of the Nation's sovereignty — direct democracy should have been treated as a fully recognized element in the future Constitution. We should add that, in the meantime, a separate Act on the Procedure for Preparing and Enacting a Constitution for the Republic of Poland provided explicitly, for the first time in Poland[20], the obligatory holding of a constitutional

---

[18] Dziennik Ustaw, No. 14, item 82.

[19] Articles 19 and 77 of the so-called Small Constitution of 1992 (Dziennik Ustaw of 1992, No. 84, item 426).

[20] Dziennik Ustaw, No. 67, item 336.

referendum, and its amendment in 1994 admitted the people's initiative in the field of submission of a draft Constitution[21].

Hence, in comparison with the previous provisions, the new Constitution considerably strengthens the concept of direct democracy, declaring it as a principle plainly equivalent to representative democracy (Article 4(2)), and also making reference to it in its numerous provisions. Direct democracy does not propose, given the realities of the system of government, a competitive alternative to representative democracy, although it may be treated as a significant counterbalance to its dominance. The Constitution, accepting the principle, provides the widest base for the direct accomplishment of the sovereignty of the Nation.

Chapter II of the Constitution (The freedoms, rights and obligations of persons and citizens) confirms the right of citizens to participate in a referendum (Article 62(1) and (2)), while the origin of the provision indicates the legislator's attempts to stress the "active" status of a citizen in the State, the citizen evidently participating in the exercise of power[22]. Other provisions of the Constitution, concerning direct democracy, deal with two concrete institution thereof, i.e. citizen's legislative initiative and referendums.

The issue of citizen's legislative initiative is governed by Article 118(2) contained in Chapter IV of the Constitution, devoted to the Sejm and the Senate. This institution deserves a separate consideration even on grounds of those legal systems which envisage the accomplishment of direct democracy, since — as a rule — they confine themselves to a referendum. According to the Constitution, the right to introduce legislation shall also belong — apart from Deputies, the Senate, and the President of the Republic and the Council of Ministers — "also to a group of at least 100,000 citizens having the right to vote in elections to the Sejm. The procedure in such matter shall be specified by statute".

It is difficult to argue that this institution is well established in the tradition of the Polish system of government. It was hitherto unknown to

---

[21] Dziennik Ustaw, No. 61, item 251.

[22] W. Kraluk: *O rozumieniu i regulacji normatywnej demokracji bezpośredniej w nowej Konstytucji* [*On the understanding and normative regulation of direct democracy in the new Constitution*], (in:) A. Szmyt (ed.): *Wybrane zagadnienia nowej Konstytucji* [*Selected issues of the new Constitution*], „Gdańskie Studia Prawnicze", vol. III, Gdańsk 1998, p. 26.

all the Constitutions, including the Small Constitution of 1992. Attitudes taken by constitutional law doctrine have oscillated from initial explicit objection to it, through scepticism about the practical value of the institution, to support for granting such right to citizens[23]. As reference is made in the Constitution (Article 118(2) *in fine*) to statute, it is evident that the institution may obtain its concrete shape by means of statute, and cannot function in practice without the adoption of an appropriate statute. Such statute should confine itself to the sphere of "procedure of conduct"; in particular it cannot restrict the scope of people's initiatives beyond the limits explicitly resulting from the Constitution. We can indicate several provisions of the Constitution that limit such citizen's initiative: Article 221, establishing xclusive power of the Council of Ministers in the area of financial statutes specified by this provision; and Article 235 which prohibits submitting draft amendments to the Constitution under this procedure. The constitutional requirement for the submission of "bills" means that the authors of the Constitution decided to apply the so-called "formulated" initiative, which means the requirement for submission of a draft in the form required by the principles of legislative technique. It should also be noted that the Constitution distinguishes the right of citizen's legislative initiative (Article 118(2)) from the right to submit petitions (Article 63). It also draws attention to the fact that the Constitution does not envisage that a bill submitted under this procedure should be submitted to initial (prior) control as to its conformity to the Constitution.

The second institution of direct democracy, namely a referendum, is accepted by the new Constitution, but it also appeared in Poland's government system under the rule of previous Constitution since 1987. The Referendum was also accepted by the Small Constitution of 1992. The new Constitution provides for both nation-wide and local referenda. According to Article 125 of the Constitution, a nation-wide referendum may be held in respect of matters of particular importance to the State. Members of a self-governing community may decide, by means of a referendum, on matters concerning their community, including the dismissal of a local council established by direct election. The principles of

---

[23] See also A. Szmyt: *Obywatelska inicjatywa ustawodawcza* [*Citizens' legislative initiative*] (in:) A. Szmyt (ed.): *Wybrane zagadnienia nowej Konstytucji...*, p. 145.

and procedures for conducting a local referendum shall be specified by statute (Article 170). Hence, both types of referendum — nation-wide and local — are of facultative nature, because no obligation compelling their use results from the legal provisions. A separate provision of the Constitution states that a nation-wide referendum cannot be held during a period of introduction of extraordinary measures (a state of siege, a state of emergency or a state of natural disaster) as well as within the period of 90 days following its termination (Article 228(7)).

Pursuant to general principles contained in Article 125 of the Constitution, the right to order a nation-wide referendum is vested in the Sejm, to be taken by an absolute majority of votes in the presence of at least half of the constitutional number of Deputies, or by the President of the Republic with the consent of the Senate given by an absolute majority vote taken in the presence of at least half of the statutory number of Senators. A result of a nationwide referendum is binding, if more than half of the number of those having the right to vote have participated in it. The validity of a nationwide referendum is determined by the Supreme Court. The principles of and procedures for the holding of a referendum shall be specified by statute.

The subject of a nationwide referendum, constitutionally defined as in respect of "matters of particular importance to the State", should rather be perceived in the context of the interests of the State taken as a whole, and not in a particular, fragmentary way; however, this is a matter of assessment, falling within the competence of referendum management authorities. In any case, the Constitution does not recognise a procedure for questioning the admissibility of a referendum on grounds of a claim that the "case has had no particular importance to the State". The decision on a given case cannot mean that by means of a referendum it would be possible to proceed to violate the legal competencies of other subjects, e.g. to adopt a statute in a referendum instead of using a constitutionally prescribed legislative path in parliament. On the other hand, given the lack of other constitutional limitations in relation to the matter, parliament cannot specify — by means of a statute — cases excluded from a referendum.

A decision by the President of the Republic, taken with the consent of the Senate, may be an alternative to the action, or lack thereof, by the Sejm in respect of ordering the holding of a referendum. Such solution was designed as an element of balancing, with a simultaneous cooperation, between the branches of government. It also provides a guarantee to the Sejm, since it excludes the possibility of the head of state ordering a referendum against the will of both houses of Parliament. Pursuant to the Constitution (Article 144(3)(5), proclaiming the holding of a nationwide referendum is not subject to the requirement of a countersignature by the Prime Minister. Nevertheless, the consent of the Senate may be an instrument of support for the head of state in the face of erroneous, or particularly controversial, actions taken by the Sejm.

The constitutional provisions also distinguish two specific situations and govern them in a different way. First, Article 90(3) states that granting consent for ratification of such international agreements, by virtue of which the Republic of Poland delegates to an international organization or international institution the competence of organs of State authority in relation to certain matters, may also be passed by a nationwide referendum in accordance with the provisions of Article 125. The method of referendum is an alternative to a legislative process, while the Sejm is an appropriate body to decide which way is chosen. The characteristic feature of the legislative way is — in this case — a requirement to obtain (an increased) two-thirds majority support in both houses of parliament. Second, Article 235(6) provides that if a bill to amend the Constitution relates to the provisions of its Chapters I (The Republic), II (The freedoms, rights and obligations of persons and citizens) or XII (Amending the Constitution), the subjects legally empowered to submit a bill to amend the Constitution may require, within 45 days of the adoption of the bill by the Senate, the holding of a confirmatory referendum. Such subjects shall make application in the matter to the Speaker of the Sejm, who shall order the holding of a referendum within 60 days of the day of receipt of the application. The amendment to the Constitution shall be deemed accepted if the majority of those voting express support for such amendment. Hence, in this situation, the demand for referendum may be a form of opposition against an amendment to the Constitution adopted by parliament.

Marian Grzybowski

Professor, Jagiellonian University, Cracow

THE SYSTEM OF GOVERNMENT
IN THE CONSTITUTION OF THE REPUBLIC OF POLAND
OF 2ND APRIL 1997

1. INTRODUCTORY REMARKS

Establishing the organizational and functional relations between the fundamental institutions of public power in the state is one of central dilemmas of any system of government. The choice of solutions in this area determines the manner of the exercise of power in the state, in other words: the system of government. In legal literature on systems of government, these relations determine — in both legal (normative) and practical-political (factual) aspects — the system of government existing in a given state.

In the doctrinal approach, involving a developed concept of the system of government, as in the constitutional approach, that is, the normative definition of the rules of required and legally enforceable functioning of the fundamental institutions of public power, a system of government chiefly remains a theoretical construct, a specific model (type) of ideal mechanism of the exercise power in the state[1].

In the practical-political approach, the notion of a system of government and its characteristics limits itself to observation of fundamental attributes of mutual relations between the main institutions of public power existing in practice.

Both normative and practical (behavioural) levels of examination of the systems of government are interrelated. Provisions of constitutional law determine the scope (framework) and principles of the functioning of public power institutions. They also specify the means and legal forms of interrelation of these institutions. However, they do not constitute a sole or — often — the most influential factor determining their practical status,

---

[1] Cf. St. Gebethner: *System rządów parlamentarno-gabinetowych, system rządów prezydenckich oraz rozwiązania pośrednie* [*Parliamentary and Presidential Systems of Government as well as intermediate solutions*] (in:) A. Domagała (ed.): *Konstytucyjne systemy rządów* [*Constitutional Forms of Government*], Warszawa 1997, p. 77.

significance and principles of functioning. Hence, in order to fully elucidate and characterize a system of government, it is necessary — and justified — to take into account both legal (constitutional) and practical- -political (behavioural) aspects.

Developing a model for the system of government in the course of work on a new Constitution for the Republic of Poland, the following patterns of government remained "typical": "parliamentary government", "parliamentary-presidential government" (however, also ambiguously called "intermediate system") and "presidential government"[2]. At this point one should bear in mind the differences in interpretation of any of the above-mentioned models and, above all, distinctions accentuating their essential elements, as well unpredictable practices in fact modifying the model constructions of government.

Fundamental difference between the premises of parliamentary and the presidential government can be discerned. The former resolves the question of practical legitimisation and political accountability of the Government (Cabinet) and its members. A common feature of all parliamentary systems (with considerable differentiation in its types) remains that the authorization to undertake and accomplish the function of current government (management) is based on the composition of political forces represented in parliament and — more precisely on the support (or at least tolerance) shown by the current parliamentary majority. In the system of presidential government, grant of powers to the organs of executive power emanate from the authority of an elected president to whom a sovereign community of citizens (voters) transfer their authorization to exercise the executive power, directly or indirectly. The functionaries of the executive derive their authorizations from the authorization ("power") of the President. They are also politically accountable to the President.

In the practices of the system of government and, partly — in constitutional solutions — boundaries between types of ideal systems of government became obliterated by reception of halfway solutions associating both the elements of classical parliamentary and presidential

---

[2] W. Sokolewicz: *Korzystanie z obcych wzorów przy projektowaniu nowej konstytucji: konieczność czy możliwość* [*Application of foreign patterns in the course of drafting a new constitution: a necessity or opportunity*], (in:) *Zagadnienia współczesnego prawa konstytucyjnego* [*The questions of modern constitutional law*], Gdańsk 1993, p. 36 et seq.

systems. In particular, solutions are found linking the direct election of a president by all citizens (inhabitants) with the right to vote to the separate election of parliament and appointment of a government with normatively required support and accountability to parliament (its majority). In constitutional law literature, the system of government of such a type is defined as "mixed", "intermediate" or — more accurately — as "presidential-parliamentary" ("semi-presidential") government[3].

Other approaches, both of a legal and political-scientific nature, focus their attention on the dualistic structure of the executive. The scope of its concerns and powers includes the subsystem of the president's powers (who possesses, as a rule, legitimacy independent of parliament) and that of the government's powers whose authorizations — in the political sense — derive from a parliamentary majority[4]. The political-scientific approach particularly stresses the dualism of the function of government and leadership of the executive, exercised by president and government, respectively.

Another attribute of parliamentary government remains the possibility of forming and recalling governments by an effective parliamentary majority. Thus, both the formation of a government and its further existence depends on the composition of forces in parliament and, in particular, on the parliamentary majority's attitude to the government. Such dependence does not exist in a presidential system.

Mixed systems, as mentioned, are characterised by a combination of certain features typical of both parliamentary and presidential systems. Opinions on the precise character of such systems of mixed government are divided. According to Jean Blondel[5] and others, they have an unstable (temporary) nature and evolve either towards a model of parliamentary government or to a pattern of presidential government. Another view, supported also by the practice of governments (e.g. in Finland, Iceland or

---

[3] M. Duverger: *A New Political System Model — Semi-presidential Government*, (in:) *Parliamentary versus Presidential Government*, edited by A. Liphardt, New York 1992.

[4] S. Lindman: *The "Dualistic" Conception of Parliamentary Government in the Finnish Constitution*, (in:) *Democracy in Finland. Studies in Politics and Government*, Helsinki 1960, pp. 44, 46–49.

[5] Cf. J. Blondel: *Dual Leaderships in the Contemporary World*, (in:) *Semi-presidential Government*, (in:) *Parliamentary versus Presidential Government*, edited by A. Liphardt, New York 1992.

— to some extent — the Fifth French Republic) regards mixed systems as a specific and relatively permanent form of government[6].

In his study on constitutional models of government, Stanisław Gebethner attempts to identify distinctive elements of typical models and, particularly, to establish criteria of existence of a given model.

He argues, in particular, that meeting the following four criteria is requisite for the model of parliamentary government:

a) the bipartite nature (dualism) of the executive power, where the head of a state (monarch or president) does not directly exercise the function of government-management; this function is entrusted to a Cabinet, i.e. a Council of Ministers presided over by the chief executive (Prime Minister);

b) political accountability of the Cabinet and its members to parliament (its first house chosen in direct election);

c) existence of political accountability of the Cabinet of collective character, as well as of individual accountability of particular ministers;

d) providing the executive (the head of state with actual influence exerted by the Cabinet) with a guarantee of powers "balancing" political accountability of Cabinet (including the right to dissolve parliament before the expiry of its term).

In the opinion of Gebethner, the following constructions and solutions are necessary for existence of the system of presidential government:

a) the President has full executive power and directly exercises the function of government-management;

b) the President is not politically accountable to parliament and functionaries of the executive are "exclusively or principally" accountable to the President[7],

c) the President is chosen in universal election, direct or indirect, by which a sovereign nation decides to charge a particular person with

---

[6] J. Nousiainen: *The Finnish Political System*, Cambridge, Mass 1971, p. 277–281; H. Paloheino: *Governments in Democratic Capitalist States*, Helsinki 1984, p. 92; W. Skrzydło: *Ustrój polityczny Francji* [*The French Political System*], Warszawa 1992, p. 244–246 (Pointing out the elasticity of the constitutional system of the 5th Republic); M. Grzybowski: *Systemy konstytucyjne państw skandynawskich* [*The Constitutional Systems of the Scandinavian States*], Warszawa 1998, p. 76, 78–82.

[7] St. Gebethner, *op cit.*, p. 81.

the function of a president thereby legitimizing his/her exercise of full executive power.

Additionally, Gebethner distinguishes a system, though slightly too comprehensively perceived, of the "semi-presidential, premier-presidential, presidential-parliamentary or, simply, mixed" governments[8] whose essential distinctive features are — in his view — three elements;

a) existence of a dualistic (bipartite) executive, where president, not being politically accountable to parliament, directly performs some functions of government independently without any need assent of ministers and prime minister, constituting a collective body i.e. a Cabinet;

b) the office of president is assumed by means of universal election (direct or indirect) by which his/her exercise of power in the name of the nation is legitimized;

c) apart from political accountability of members of government to parliament, there exist political accountability to the President.

Opinions about the attributes of fundamental models of systems of government are generally differentiated. Relatively common, but not lacking some traces of superficiality, there remains a belief that a presidential system conduces to consolidation and — as a result — strengthening of the executive power. Such opinion relates mostly to presidentialism with an "uplifted" (strengthened) position of the President, and to a lesser degree (if only) to a model system with full separation and — at the same time — balance of "powers".

A dominant belief, rather more justified, is that the presidential government really functions only in circumstances of stabilized bipartisanship or a stable, two-bloc nature of party structure. In the circumstances of a dispersed party system, with lack of a dominant party, the presidential system does not function with adequate efficiency in a situation where different parties (party blocs) exert political control over the executive and the legislative, and the latter lacks a politically uniform majority.

---

[8] *Ibid.* p. 81; M. Duverger and (after him) W. Skrzydło prefer the use of the phrase "semi-presidential system". Cf. M. Duverger: *Systeme presidentiel et systeme semi-presidentiel*, (in:) *La Presidence en France et aux Etats Unis* edited by J.L. Seurin, Paris 1986, p. 347; W. Skrzydło: *Ustrój...*, p. 244. J. Robert proposes a notion of "parliamentary presidentialism". Cf. J. Robert: *Le President de la Republique*, (in:) *La Presidence...*, p. 333.

The parliamentary model remains, to a larger degree, open to cleavages existing in society as well as socio-political and ideological diversities. It also contributes to resolution of social conflicts in the framework of institutions composing a system of government of the state.

The presidential system, in its turn, stabilizes the executive by immunising it against the influences of regular regrouping amongst the political parties. It seems to be more favourable to plebiscites as a form of expression of the will and political preferences of citizens.

Mixed systems are a specific (but often distinguisable) amalgam of elements typical of presidential and parliamentary systems. Their common feature is still the bipartite nature of the executive, encompassing institutions of the head of state and a government. Any of these institutions has its own competence and scope of powers as well as a separate political legitimization.

Apart from possessing a direct mandate from the nation (majority of electors), the president can perform — depending on concrete constitutional regulations, and also on the political context — different roles in the system of government.

While the Constitution does not provide for (nor does the practice evolve in the direction of) dominance of the president over the whole executive, the role of president is to be an arbiter in relations between the government and parliament and, sometimes (owing to basing his/her mandate on the nation's confidence) between parliament, government and the nation. So understood, presidential arbitration includes, in particular, such powers as the president's right to dissolve parliament (discretionary or applied only in circumstances specified by the Constitution), the right to order a nationwide referendum, the right to veto legislation (veto of a suspensive character), as well as the right to apply to the constitutional court (tribunal) for its adjudication regarding the constitutionality of acts of the parliament (above all — statutes). A wider (and more strongly) defined role of arbiter also contains dynamic actions taken by the president in order to avoid government crises and during the formation of a government (especially after parliamentary elections). The powers and actions of the mentioned categories may be interconnected. Dissolution of parliament and proclamation of a new parliamentary election may be, in particular, applied when steps taken to resolve conflicts within the government or between the government and a current parliamentary majority have failed.

At the political level, the position of the president and the scope of his/her influence on the functioning of government institutions depends not only on the constitutional catalogue of presidential powers, but also on the extent of support given to the government by parliamentary majority and on the consolidation of such majority. A consolidated and overwhelming pro-government majority constitutes a peculiar limitation of a president's position.

At the level of constitutional law, vital for mutual relations are the powers of parliament in relation to president, particularly the limitations of choice (discretion) in the exercise of competencies of the president, as well as the powers enabling parliament to assess a president's actions and to exert political or constitutional (legal) control thereof. Apart from constitutional norms and practice, the influence (impact) of the president is determined by: the style of exercise of powers, his/her personal capabilities and political individuality as well as a concrete political context (current composition of political forces and institutions). Sometimes, considerable disparity may occur between the assumed normative model and the practice of a given system of government.

2. CONDITIONS FOR FORMING A SYSTEM OF GOVERNMENT IN THE CONSTITUTION OF THE REPUBLIC OF POLAND OF 2ND APRIL 1997

The parliamentary government remains the unquestioned base of constitutional work and adopted solutions. Reference to this model resulted not only from the democratic tradition of Polish government from the period of existence of the March (1921) Constitution, but also from its tendency to refer to the European model of parliamentary democracy, as the dominant system of government in most West European countries. The countries of Central and South-Eastern Europe, including those with previous parliamentary constitutional experience (e.g. Czechoslovakia and Estonia with the constitutions of 1920 and those lacking such antecedents (e.g. Albania, Bulgaria, Latvia or Lithuania) have also turned to the parliamentary system.

The tendency to remain in the circle parliamentary-based solutions has been accompanied by an attempt to guarantee — both at legal and political level — the balance of the legislative, executive and judicial powers, and — in any case — to diminish the dependence of the executive upon parliament (and its dominance) typical of a classical parliamentary system.

The peaceful and evolutionary nature of the political transformations — i.e. the transition from "real socialism" to a market economy and taking of power by a new political class — has favoured the continuation of the system of government, gaining experience from previously applied principles, institutions and procedures. Difficulties with economic transformation, and the resulting atmosphere of discontent and destabilization have led to criticism of many institutions and procedures of parliamentary democracy and have given inspiration — even if indirectly — to a strengthening of the position of the executive bodies: the president and Cabinet and to equip them with extraordinary competencies conducive to their efficient functioning.

On the other hand, pluralization in and far-reaching fragmentation of the political system, impeding the establishment of a consolidated and permanent parliamentary majority and, consequentially, the creation of a stable government, has aroused criticism of the parliamentary system and parliament itself. It has also led to attempts to rationalize the classical parliamentary system (e.g. through complicating the procedures for dismissing the Cabinet and replacing an "ordinary" vote of no confidence with a "constructive vote", as well as a modification of the system of elections to parliament, which prevent extensive atomization of its party composition[9].

The Constitution of the Republic of Poland adopts — as the main structural basis of the system of state organs — the principles of (1) separation of powers and (2) balance between the legislative, executive and judicial powers. Formulation of these principles together in one provision (Article 10(1)) seems to confirm the assumption of equality between the two above mentioned principles and, moreover, as W. Skrzy-

---

[9] P. Winczorek: *Uwarunkowania prac nad nową Konstytucją RP [Circumstances of the work on a new Constitution for the Republic of Poland]*, „Państwo i Prawo" 1997, No. 11–12; M. Kruk: *Parlament–prezydent–rząd: wybór modelu rządów [Parliament––President–Government: A Choice of a Government Model]*, (in:) *Prawo w okresie przemian ustrojowych w Polsce [Law in the period of transition in Poland]*, Warszawa 1995.

dło defines it[10], is the "introduction of this principle [or these principles — my remark] in its classical form". However, an analysis of other provisions of the Constitution of 2nd April 1997 leads to certain modification of such interpretation which is still based on the precedence of the legislature over other branches of government.

The most essential change as compared to the constitutional provisions existing before 1989, consists of the departure from the principle of unity of the state power which — even if treated *de facto* declaratively — has enabled parliament to be regarded as the holder of full state power, and not only a legislative body. As a result of the constitutional shift of 1989 and the coming into force of the Small Constitution dated 17th October 1992, followed by the adoption of the Constitution of the Republic of Poland of 2nd April 1997, the role of parliament has been confined to making laws and — beyond a strictly legislative functions — the performance of particular powers of control and appointment to State offices specified by the constitution and statutes. There are, however, no grounds to attribute to parliament other competencies or functions in the government system, in particular drawing up the outlines of state policy by extra-statutory means as well as the "creation" i.e. establishing and appointment of other (top) state organs[11].

Confining the scope of authority of parliament (namely, the Sejm and Senate) to the legislative power is accompanied by attempts to prevent diminution of its legislative powers by restricting the participation in legislative acts of other state organs. The Constitution of 2nd April 1997 makes only one departure from the exclusiveness of the legislative powers of the Sejm and the Senate, which empower the President of the Republic with the right to issue regulations having the force of statute in circumstances (and periods) of emergencies.

The guarantee of full legislative powers to parliament (except for the above mentioned powers of the President of the Republic) means widening

---

[10] W. Skrzydło: *Konstytucja Rzeczypospolitej Polskiej. Komentarz* [*The Constitution of the Republic of Poland. A Commentary*], Kraków 1998, p. 17.

[11] Z. Jarosz: *Parlament jako organ władzy ustawodawczej* [*Parliament as a legislative body*], (in:) *Założenia ustrojowe, struktura i funkcjonowanie parlamentu* [*Structural and Political Assumptions and Functioning of Parliament*], edited by A. Gwiżdż, Warszawa 1997, p. 162–163.

of its competence as compared to its legal status of 1992–97. At that time, the government was able — though under parliament's control — to exercise the right to issue regulations having the force of statute. Thus, in this respect, the Polish legal system remains, in general, more favourable to parliament than that of many other East European countries.

However, a common feature of most constitutional provisions in this region is that they depart from assigning to parliament the function of general direction of state policy and leave to its competence, apart from lawmaking, political control over the government in constitutionally determined forms, as well as participation in appointments to particular state offices.

The situation in certain former Soviet republics — today independent states — is more complicated. On the one hand, presidential competencies in these countries have been constitutionally reinforced to determine the main directions of domestic and foreign policy of the state (e.g. in Russia or Belarus) whilst, on the other hand, parliament remains the principal (even if not exclusive) legislative body.

In accordance with Article 10(2) of Poland's Constitution of 2nd April 1997, "legislative power shall be vested in the Sejm and the Senate". Thus the Constitution distinguishes two separate, if interrelated, legislative bodies by reason of their organization and competencies. Such an attitude calls in question the use of the collective notion of parliament, which — in the juridical sense — remains an extra-constitutional concept. Article 95(1) repeats the provision (relating to competencies) which confers legislative powers on the Sejm and the Senate. This norm does not specify the scope of participation of each of them in making laws. Nor does it resolve the question of their equality, or lack thereof, in this respect. However, it does not allow the allocation of the whole legislative power to one of these bodies.

The provisions of Article 95(2) are of the utmost significance. It states that "the Sejm shall exercise control over the activities of the Council of Ministers within the scope specified by the provisions of the Constitution and statutes". The interpretation of this paragraph leads to the unequivocal conclusion that the function of control over the government "within the scope specified by the provisions of the Constitution and statutes" (hence: legally limited) remains a function of the Sejm — being only one of the legislative bodies. The second legislative body, the Senate, does not participate in the exercise of control over the activity of the Council of Ministers.

As regards determining the composition of State organs, the Constitution of 2nd April 1997 guarantees certain powers to both the Sejm and the Senate, but the scope and gravity of the Sejm's competencies to appoint or recall are wider and higher.

Despite the bicameral character of the legislature, the Sejm remains the chief legislative partner of the Executive (also dualistic) with an evident marginalization of the function and competencies of the Senate. In this situation, the relation — Legislature/Executive — should be analysed taking into account that the Sejm is the dominant arena for conflict between political parties and coalitions in the parliamentary forum because of the very proportionality of its elections.

In the sphere of executive power, the Constitution of 2nd April 1997 advocates a dualism in structure and competency. In particular, it divides the functions and powers of the Executive between the President of the Republic and the Council of Ministers (Government) directed by the Prime Minister. The Council of Ministers maintains the character and status of a collective body. Nevertheless, the Prime Minister with his/her strengthened position and powers, has been treated as an independent organ of the State with a separate competency.

As compared to the opportunities available under the previous Constitutional Act of 17th October 1992, the present Constitution minimizes the possibility of interference by the President of the Republic, chosen in universal election, within the sphere of current direction of the work of the Council of Ministers. Under the provisions of the 1992 Constitutional Act, the President of the Republic could convene sittings of the Council of Ministers, presided over by himself, and to demand information about the work of the Government (and thereby to assess and inspire assessment by the public). He might also exert a non-binding influence on the appointment to important government positions of a competence parallel to that of President of the Republic (i.e. Ministry of Defence, Ministry of Internal Affairs and Ministry of Foreign Affairs) and to administrative posts — as well as to introduce and veto laws. Currently, his/her prerogatives (e.g. giving opinions on nomination of candidates to the above mentioned ministries) have been considerably limited (e.g. limitations on power only to convening a Cabinet Council which cannot constitutionally undertake the activities of the Council of Ministers).

Whilst upholding the position of the President strengthened by direct and universal election, the 1997 Constitution simultaneously limits his/her powers to influence the functioning of the government. This means maintaining the principal features of the parliamentary model. Unlike the Constitution of the Russian Federation, the prerogatives of the President relating to the appointment of the Prime Minister and members of government, and to their recall[12], as well as making partial "regroupings" within its composition, are narrowed.

The inclusion of the Constitutional Tribunal and the Tribunal of State, along with courts, among the institutions of the judicial power considerably strengthens the role of this branch in the system of government. This mostly relates to the Constitutional Tribunal as empowered to finally resolve the constitutionality of statutes and, particularly, to settle disputes concerning the competence of constitutional organs of the State. This is of utmost importance in the initial period of the interpretation of a newly adopted Constitution and its application. Moreover, the Constitutional Tribunal may exert influence, even if indirectly, on state finances and government policy in this respect. It finally adjudicates, within the time limit not exceeding 18 months, the binding force of acts whose implementation is inseparably connected with financial outlays.

3. THE CHARACTERISTICS OF THE SYSTEM OF GOVERNMENT UNDER THE CONSTITUTION OF THE REPUBLIC OF POLAND OF 2 APRIL 1997

The period of political reform, 1989–92, and the practice of application of the Constitutional Act delivered useful experience relevant for the

---

[12] Cf. comments on the activities of the President of the Russian Federation, (in:) M. Kruk: *System rządów w Konstytucji Rzeczpospolitej Polskiej z 2 kwietnia 1997 r.* [*System of Government in the Constitution of the Republic of Poland, dated 2nd April 1997*], (in:) XL Ogólnopolska Konferencja Katedr i Zakładów Prawa Konstytucyjnego [The 40th Polish National Conference of Constitutional Law Faculties], Kazimierz Dolny n. Wisłą, 4–6 June 1998. p. 12.

selection of a model of government to be included in the basic law finally adopted.

In the light of that experience, a choice has been made — often *per facta concludentia* — from among the many available and suggested solutions. The most important decisions in this respect include:

A. A decision not to introduce the presidential government;
B. Maintenance of universal and direct election for the Presidency;
C. Maintenance of bicameral structure of the Legislature, composed of the Sejm and Senate, and diversification of the procedures for elections to those bodies;
D. Adoption of a parliamentary system in its rationalized version;
E. Strengthening of the position of the Prime Minister in the system of government;
F. Strict separation of the functions and competencies of the President and Government.

A.

The presidential government has no antecedent in the Polish tradition of government. The European versions of democratic systems, whose experiences formed the basis for the work on the constitution, combining parliamentary and extraparliamentary groups, also remains distant from the model of presidential government. In the course of work preceding the final stage of preparations of a new constitution (1993–97), the concept of a presidential system was most evident in the draft proposed by the Constitutional Committee of the Senate of the 1st Term. Even the draft submitted by President Lech Wałęsa departed from a presidential model.

In Polish political practice developed after 1989, there was no political infrastructure conducive to a presidential model. In particular, it lacked a stable bipartisan or two-bloc party system. Persons aspiring to the office of President (including Lech Wałęsa) had no unquestionable support from the electoral majority of parties or party coalitions. Additionally, the manner of discharging the presidential duties in the testing periods of 1989–90 and 1990–95 did not greatly contribute to consolidation of a pro-presidential attitude amongst electors or political groups (for reasons — we stress — that varied between individual populations or socio--political formations).

B.

It is a characteristic — and to some degree, surprising — fact that even with the lack of a political majority favouring a presidential system, the option to maintain a plebiscitary principle of direct and universal election of the president by the nation (introduced in 1990) continued to predominate. Given the previous "cession" of the right to elect a president to the nation, any attempt to alter the situation to the advantage of the National Assembly had become "inconvenient" for most political groups (because it might possibly profit their opponents). Nevertheless, Polish historical tradition in this respect is different. In the tradition of March Constitution (1921), and in the years 1947–1952, presidents were elected by the National Assembly.

The presidential elections of 1990 and 1995 were characterized by a great number of candidates in the first round, and a lack of support by a consolidated electoral majority for most candidates for office. There have been no coherent majority forming a political base for the main contestants in the second round of elections. In such situation, candidates (including the elected president) should have been rather more moderate in formulating electoral promises. They, indeed, lacked an adequate political base for the realization of a more resolutely formulated electoral programme, particularly as the profile and political programme of the government originated — in the circumstances of a peculiar cohabitation — in a politically separate parliamentary majority.

In consequence of the diverse political aspirations and concepts of governmental systems, the scope of presidential powers became the resultant of legitimisation of his/her authority through a nationwide universal election coupled with a trend to deprive him/her of actual influence on the process of governing the State. The President was deprived of his/her powers enabling him/her to exercise control of the government. In areas concurrent with his/her own competence — namely, defence, protection of external and internal security, protection of the Constitution and ensuring the stability and harmonious co-operation between state organs, the President may apply legal and political instruments to exert influence on the government and, to a constitutionally limited extent, on the Sejm and the Senate.

C.

Despite doubts raised as to the usefulness of the continued existence of the Senate, or to the organizational concept of the Senate, as adopted by the April (1989) Amendment and fixed in the provisions of the Constitutional Act of 17 October 1992, as well as proposals for a unicameral legislature (or local government house[13] — as proposed in a draft submitted by the Polish Peasant Party (PPS) and the Labour Union (Unia Pracy)), the Constitution of 2 April 1997 maintains the existing concept of a Polish Senate.

The very method of electing the Sejm — as well as delineating its powers — differs from that of the Senate. In accordance with Article 96(2) of the Constitution of 2 April 1997, "elections to the Sejm shall be universal, equal, direct and proportional and shall be conducted by secret ballot". However, Article 96(7) of the Constitution states that "elections to the Senate shall be universal, direct and shall be conducted by secret ballot". Thus, the one substantial difference — from the point of view of the political system of government — is that the composition of the Sejm is determined in accordance with the principle of proportional representation, where the choice is made from among candidates (entered in the lists of candidates) nominated by political parties and electoral groups (coalitions). This makes the Sejm a major body of representation of political parties and decides its position in relation to the President of the Republic and government. Elections to the Senate are conducted according to the majority system which not only discloses the political affiliation of candidates, but also allows for a personal factor (i.e. the personality of candidates and their individual electoral popularity).

---

[13] Cf. *Dyskusja nad rolą drugiej izby parlamentu* [*Discussion on the Role of a Second House of Parliament*], Biuro Studiów i Analiz Kancelarii Senatu, Series: *Materiały i opracowania*, M-203, November 1993, p. 1–5; B. Banaszak: *Czy Polsce potrzebna jest druga izba* [*Does Poland Need a Second House*], (in:) *Problem zasadności istnienia dwuizbowego parlamentu w Polsce* [*The Reasons for the Existence of a Bicameral Parliament in Poland*], Biuro Studiów i Analiz Kancelarii Senatu, Series: *Opracowania tematyczne*, OT-83, in particular p. 6–15; Z. Witkowski: *Druga izba parlamentu w przyszłej Konstytucji RP. Czy izba niepotrzebna?* [*The Second House of Parliament in a future Constitution of the Republic of Poland. Is it Unnecessary?*], ibid., p. 16–21; Z. Jarosz *Problem dwuizbowości parlamentu w przyszłej Konstytucji RP* [*The Issue of Bicameralism in a Future Constitution of the Republic of Poland*], „Przegląd Sejmowy", No. 1(9)/95, p. 10–20.

Apart from establishing a "five-adjective" electoral right — including the principle of proportionality of elections to the Sejm — the Constitution does not precisely determine the system of elections to the Sejm and the Senate. It provides the legislator with a considerable discretion in its shaping. Notwithstanding the structural discrepancies of each legislative body, different principles concerning election, functions and scope of competencies, the authors of the constitution have decided to closely connect the periods of authority (terms of office) of the Sejm and the Senate. These terms of office are identical as regards their duration (covering four years beginning on the day on which one of these bodies, namely the Sejm, assembles for its first sitting after an election. Any shortening of the term of office of the Sejm by its own resolution, or as a consequence of the President's decision to that effect in the instances specified by the Constitution, results in an unqualified and automatic shortening of the term of office of the Senate (even if the preconditions for shortening of the term of office relate exclusively to the Sejm)[14]. Effectively, this means that the fate of the Senate and Senators of a given term is determined by decisions and circumstances taken by, or relating to, the Sejm (which decides on the shortening of its own term of office and, consequently, that of the Senate by a resolution passed by a majority of at least two-thirds of the constitutional number of Deputies); and there is no possibility of adverse reactions. A resolution on the shortening of the term of the Sejm (and, as a result, the Senate) may result from a political crisis within the Sejm. This may also be a consequence of a conflict between the Sejm and government or the Sejm and the President. In all such cases, the Senate becomes a "victim" of circumstances with no opportunity to directly influence them.

Situations in which the President of the Republic may order the shortening of the term of office of the Sejm (and, hence, the Senate) are limited to two circumstances determined by the provisions of two articles. These concern the situation (Article 155(2)) of the failure to appoint the Council of Ministers pursuant to Article 155(1), i.e. as a result of failure to give a vote of confidence (taken by a simple majority of the Deputies to the Sejm) to the government designated by the President of the Republic,

[14] P. Sarnecki: *Senat RP i jego relacje z Sejmem (lata 1989–1993)[The Senate of the Republic of Poland and its Relations with the Sejm (1989–1993)]*, Warszawa 1995, p. 16.

and in the event that within 4 months of the day of submission of its draft to the Sejm, the Budget Bill has not been presented to the President of the Republic for signature.

In the first instance, the Constitution introduces an obligation to shorten the term of office of the Sejm and the Senate. In the second instance, it leaves the decision to the discretion of the President of the Republic. Hence, only in the second instance (failure to pass the Budget within a 4-month time limit), does the President retain some discretion in the exercise of the powers vested in him.

The powers of the Senate, as compared with those of the Sejm, in respect of making laws, including the Budget Act, as well as influencing appointments to State posts, are considerably more limited. Apart from submitting a bill to the Sejm in accordance with the procedure specified for legislative initiative (with the possibility of discretionary rejection of the bill by the Sejm), the Senate, within 30 days of submission of a bill passed by the Sejm, may adopt it without amendment, introduce amendments or reject it as a whole. Any failure to adopt an appropriate bill within the above-mentioned time limit should be interpreted (pursuant to Article 121(2) of the Constitution of 2nd April 1997) as adoption of the bill according to the wording submitted by the Sejm. Moreover, the Sejm may reject, by an absolute majority vote in the presence of at least half of the constitutional number of Deputies, a resolution of the Senate proposing amendments to a bill or rejecting it. Hence, it is the Sejm that finally decides the adoption or rejection of a particular text of a statute.

D.

The assessment of the system of government established by the Constitution of 2nd April 1997, is based on the finding that its constitutive elements are typical of particular models of a governmental system. The issue is to identify the fundamental constructs of the constitution concerning the system of government, and to appraise the latter's extent and powers under the basic law of 1997.

The Polish constitutional model of 2nd April 1997, undoubtedly corresponds — in its most substantial aspects — to the parliamentary government. It is characterized by a dualistic Executive, composed of a President of the Republic, chosen in universal and direct elections, and a Council of Ministers in which a parliamentary majority reposes its confidence. Each of these bodies has its independent competencies and functions (even if several acts of the President require countersigning by the Prime Minister). Article 144(2) provides that "official acts of the President [...] shall require, for their validity, the signature of the Prime Minister who, by such signature, accepts responsibility therefor to the Sejm"[15].

The requirement for countersignature reflects the parliamentary nature of the system of government (as it serves to control and enforce parliamentary accountability, borne — in this case — by the Prime Minister). Its purpose is to limit the discretionary powers of the President, along with requiring co-operation with the Prime Minister and the appropriate minister in respect of foreign policy.

Similar limitations relate to certain aspects of presidential control of the armed forces. In accordance with Article 134(2), "The President of the Republic, in times of peace, shall exercise command over the Armed Forces through the Minister of National Defence". In a period of war, the President of the Republic shall, pursuant to Article 134(4), appoint — and dismiss — the Commander-in-Chief of the Armed Forces on request of the Prime Minister. The President of the Republic, on request of the Minister of National Defence, confers military ranks as specified by statute. All the above requirements distinctly illustrate the lack of full autonomy of the President, even if his function in relation to the armed forces has been defined as the "supreme command".

Provisions of importance for any characterization of the functions of the President and government are also contained in Article 146(1) of the Constitution, which reads: "The Council of Ministers shall conduct the internal affairs and foreign policy of the Republic of Poland", as well as in the second paragraph of that Article, stating that "The Council of Ministers shall conduct the affairs of State not reserved to other State organs or local government". This does not, however, indicate a monopolistic position of

---

[15] Article 144, paragraph 3, enumerates exceptions to the requirement of countersigning the acts of the President. Cf. comments by P. Sarnecki concerning disputes about the scope of official acts issued by the President and subject to the requirement of countersignature, (in:) *Kontrasygnata aktów prawnych Prezydenta RP [Countersigning of Legal Acts of the President of the Republic of Poland]*, „Przegląd Sejmowy", No. 2(14)/96, p. 24–29.

the government in shaping and directing the pursuit of internal and foreign policy. Nevertheless, the presumption of competence requires that the jurisdiction of other state bodies, including the President or the Sejm, must ensue from concrete constitutional provisions. The jurisdiction of the Council of Ministers is based on a permanent (namely constitutional) presumption of competence.

Direct election of the Presidency provides a factor which somewhat balances the numerous limitations on the independence of its activities. This also prevents situations in which a new parliamentary majority determining the political profile of government would be confronted with a President whose legitimacy derived from a parliamentary majority present in a previous term of office.

The creation of a Council of Ministers completely corresponds with the construction of the parliamentary government. Formally, the initiative of designating a Prime Minister originates with the President of the Republic who, on request of the Prime Minister, appoints a Council of Ministers headed by the Prime Minister, and accepts the oath of office of their members. The government so appointed submits a programme of its activity, together with a motion requiring a vote of confidence. The Sejm passes such vote of confidence by an absolute majority of votes within the constitutional time limit of 14 days following the taking of oath by the government. In the event that a government has not been appointed in accordance with this procedure, or has failed to obtain a vote of confidence by an absolute majority of votes, a repeat attempt to appoint a Prime Minister and select the composition of the government will be made by the Sejm. If such an attempt has also failed, the initiative returns to the President; however, the requirement for an absolute majority of votes for passing a vote of confidence is replaced by the requirement for a simple majority of votes. Only in the event of failure of such an attempt, should the President shorten the term of office of the Sejm (and the Senate) and order a new, early election.

It is worth noting that the authors of the Constitution do not allow further stages in the formation of a government, including the repeated initiative of the Sejm with vote of confidence granted by a simple majority of votes and, particularly, they do not admit the formula of presidential government, based only on the confidence of the head of state, with

153

a "tested" lack of confidence obtained even from a simple parliamentary majority. This means the strengthening of the "parliamentary" element and — to a certain degree — departure from semi-presidential models.

The requirement of obtaining an absolute, or at least simple, majority of votes during a vote of confidence limits the powers of the President of the Republic, both in designation of a Prime Minister and in the course of forming the government. The President must take into account the results of parliamentary election and the position of any Sejm majority, rather than his own political or personal preferences.

The existence of many political parties, and the dispersion of their parliamentary representation in the III Republic has led the authors of the Constitutional Act of 17th October 1992, followed by the authors of the Constitution of 2nd April 1997 — to introduce provisions securing the stability of a government. In this context, the most important decision seems to be the replacement of a simple vote of no confidence by a constructive vote of no confidence which was, to a large degree, based on the provisions of the Bonn Grundgesetz of 1949. Nevertheless, this solution did not prove useful in May 1993 when the Sejm succeeded in passing a vote of no confidence in the government of Hanna Suchocka[16]. Such situation along with the political significance of the institution of a constructive vote of no confidence in the government (a motion to recall the existing government is tantamount to a motion to appoint a new Prime Minister) has encouraged the authors of the new Constitution to "expand" it by adding several regulations (a motion may be moved by at least 1/10 of the constitutional number of Deputies, and put to a vote no sooner than 7 days after it has been submitted, a subsequent motion of a like kind may be submitted before the end of 3 months if such motion is submitted by at least 115 Deputies). All these details are aimed at limitation of a "spontaneous" use of a constructive vote of no confidence and to promote the stability of a government. Analogous *ratio legis* justifies impediments to passing a vote of no confidence in individual ministers[17]. Such a motion

---

[16] President Lech Wałęsa responded by refusing to accept the resignation of government, dissolving the Sejm and Senate, and ordering an early election.

[17] L. Garlicki: *Parlament a rząd: powoływanie–kontrola–odpowiedzialność [Parliament versus Governement: Appointment–Control–Accountability]*, (in:) A. Gwiżdż (ed.): *Założenia ustrojowe, struktura i funkcjonowanie parlamentu...*, p. 213 et seq.

requires the support of 69 (i.e. 15% of constitutional number of) Deputies. However, such method of enforcement of the accountability of members of government has not been established in the practices of Polish tradition, even if there exist conditions for their use in the circumstances of coalition government and programmatic disparities between parties forming the government. One factor diminishing the above institution is an alternative form of partial "reconstruction" of government, namely, the dismissal of a government by the President on the request of the Prime Minister. Currently, Article 161 of the Constitution which states that "The President of the Republic, on request of the Prime Minister, shall effect changes in the composition of the Council of Ministers", is mostly interpreted as a peculiar constitutional obligation dependent on the submission of appropriate request by the Prime Minister. It also limits President's powers to dismiss only to the offices of members of government *strictu sensu*, excluding the office of a Prime Minister (whose change — pursuant to Article 162 — is treated as a change of government and requires compliance with the procedures specified in Articles 154 and 155 of the Constitution)[18].

However, from the point of view of a government's stability, the provisions of the Article, pursuant to which "The Prime Minister may submit to the Sejm a motion requiring a vote of confidence in the Council of Ministers", are not unequivocal. Such decision enables the Sejm to initiate controlling activities in relation to the government, though on the government's initiative and mostly in its own interest. It is the Prime Minister who may be particularly interested in confirmation of the support for his/her government or in manifesting the range of support from a parliamentary majority.

A motion requiring a vote of confidence in the government is a double-edged weapon. Any failure of passing a vote of confidence in the Council of Ministers (by a simple majority of votes in the presence of at least half of the constitutional number of Deputies) would indicate that the government policy has not won the support of the Sejm majority, which in turn compels the Prime Minister to submit his/her resignation to the President of the Republic. The use of a motion requiring a vote of confidence is therefore accompanied with some risk, both by the govern-

---

[18] W. Skrzydło: *Konstytucja Rzeczypospolitej Polskiej. Komentarz...*, p. 170.

ment and Prime Minister. Moreover, it is not quite clear whether this is a form of applying for a renewed confidence, as is suggested by W. So-kolewicz[19], or rather an instrument of exerting pressure on parliament in order to obtain its support in the course of taking decisions on legislation proposed by the government[20].

E.

The system of government established under the provisions of the Constitution of the Republic of Poland (of 2nd April 1997), in comparison to the classical model of a parliamentary system or the tradition of Poland's government in 1921–35 and 1989–92, is characterized by the strengthened position of the Council of Ministers as an element of such system of government.

The Constitution contains a series of regulations confirming the above-mentioned trend[21]. The constitutional procedures for appointing a Council of Ministers (Articles 154–155) distinguish the act of appointment (Article 154(1) and Article 155(1)) or election (by the Sejm — Article 154(3)) of the Prime Minister from the act of appointment of other members of the Council of Ministers. The Prime Minister submits a programme of activity of the Council of Ministers to the Sejm and a motion requiring a vote of confidence (Article 154(2) and Article 160) in the Council of Ministers. The motion requiring a constructive vote of confidence contains the indication of a new Prime Minister (but not a new government). It is personally the Prime Minister to whom the voting in the Sejm concerning this motion actually refers (Article 158). Any change in the office of Prime Minister means a dismissal of the previously existing Council of Ministers as well as the appointment and taking the oath of a new Council of Ministers (the second sentence of Article 158(1)).

The Prime Minister, designated by the President of the Republic (or elected by the Sejm) proposes to the President — on the principle of exclusiveness — the appointment of particular persons to concrete offices in the Council of Ministers. In the circumstances of existence of two

¹⁹ W. Sokolewicz.: *Odpowiedzialność parlamentarna rządu RP [Parliamentary Accountability of the Government of the Republic of Poland]*, Warszawa 1993, p. 29.

²⁰ L. Garlicki: *Parlament a rząd...*, p. 222.

²¹ W. Skrzydło: *Konstytucja...*, p. 156.

categories of ministers, i.e. (a) those directing statutorily specified branches of government administration and (b) those performing tasks allocated to them by the Prime Minister (the first sentence of Article 149(1)), it is the Prime Minister who specifies the competence of ministers belonging to the latter group[22].

The Prime Minister possesses several independent competencies and official functions. He/she represents the Council of Ministers in its relations with other bodies and manages its work. The Prime Minister "[shall] ensure the implementation of the policies adopted by the Council of Ministers and" — what is of particularly note — "specify the manner of their implementation" (Article 148(4) *in fine*). The Constitution ascribes to the Prime Minister an official function (and — as we would imply — appropriate competencies) in the area of co-ordination and control over work of members of the Council of Ministers. It also accords the PM with an official superiority in relation to employees of the government administration (Article 148(7)) and of the corps of civil servants (Article 153(2)). Moreover, the Prime Minister exercises supervision (mostly from the point of view of the observance of provisions of universally binding law) over local government. The scope and forms of the exercise of such supervision are specified by the Constitution and statutes. The Prime Minister (together with the Minister for Foreign Affairs) is a partner of the President of the Republic in a constitutionally required co-operation in the conduct of foreign policy. It is also the Prime Minister (and not appropriate ministers) who countersigns those official Acts of the President which require the countersignature by a member of the Council of Ministers (Article 144(2)). He also requests the appointment, for the period of duration of war, of the Commander-in-Chief of the Armed Forces (Article 134(4)).

F.

As it concerns executive power, the constitutional construction of the system of government attempts to draw a precise distinction between the

---

[22] W. Skrzydło speaks about establishing "the detailed scope of activity of a minister", indicating that the tasks so fixed are binding only in the period of existence of a given Council of Ministers and cease to have effect from the moment of the appointment of a new government, and — in respect of a given ministry — with the change in the office of minister. The latter part of this opinion may raise doubts, but the solution depends on the legal meaning of "conferring of tasks".

scope of activity, responsibility and competencies (powers and obligations) of the President of the Republic and the government (the Council of Ministers). This trend also manifests a praiseworthy and more exacting attitude by the authors when approaching the apportionment of tasks and areas of competence of the State;s constitutional organs. Partly, it also results from examination and assessment of ambiguous interpretation and application of relevant provisions of the Constitutional Act of 17th October 1992[23].

The Constitution does not expressly envisage the participation of the President of the Republic, or his representative, in the sittings or work of the Council of Ministers. In this situation, the government appointed in 1997, and its Prime Minister (J. Buzek), has refused its consent for permanent participation of the President's representative in the sittings of the Council of Ministers. The Cabinet Council introduced — after the example of such institution known in the years 1921–35 and 1947–52 (though not functioning in practice) — pursuant to Article 141 of the Constitution, is limited to "particular matters". Even if the selection of such matters and, as a consequence, the convening of the Cabinet Council, is decided by the President of the Republic, the Constitution clearly attempts to prevent the Cabinet Council from taking over the powers of the Council of Ministers. Pursuant to Article 141(2) of the Constitution, " The Cabinet Council shall not possess the competence of the Council of Ministers".

Hence, sittings of the Cabinet Council may serve as a forum for presentation of viewpoints of both the President and the government on major problems of State policy or for the exchange of opinions or mutual explanation of reasons for taking particular actions. This, however, does not allow the President to overtake the direction of administration, or internal or foreign policy. The implementation of an agreed initiative or arrangement, provided that it will be effected by use of the government's competence, requires separate decisions taken at a "normal" sitting of the Council of Ministers (i.e. presided over by the Prime Minister).

The rules of division of competence (and powers) of the President of the Republic and that of government have also been spelt out. The above-mentioned provisions of Article 146(2) of the Constitution, stating

---

[23] Cf. M. Kruk: *System rządów...*, p. 23.

that "The Council of Ministers shall conduct the affairs of State not reserved to other State organs", generate a legal situation where the President performs the competence conferred to him in respect of matters falling within his jurisdiction on the basis of expressly formulated provisions of the law. The remaining area of executive power exercised on an all-State scale belongs — as an implied competence — to the government and government administration.

The Constitution of 2nd April 1997 departs from regulations applied by the Constitutional Act of 17th October 1992, which allowed for a peculiar coincidence of jurisdiction and accountability between President and the Council of Ministers. This relates, especially, to provisions of Article 32(4) and Article 51 of the Constitutional Act of 1992. Pursuant to Article 32(4), the President exercised "general supervision in the field of international relations", while under Article 51 "the Council of Ministers shall conduct the internal affairs and the foreign policy of the Republic". The provisions of the current Constitution do not contain the presidential function (competence) of "general supervision in the field of international relations", which is difficult to distinguish from "conduct of foreign policy" falling within the jurisdiction of the Council of Ministers. The provision empowering the President to exercise "general supervision with respect to the external and internal security of the State"[24] was also discontinued because of the difficulty in precise and unequivocal distinction from the jurisdiction of the Council of Ministers in respect of "the conduct of the internal and foreign policy of the Republic" and of ensuring "the external and internal security of the State"[25].

The requirement of Article 61 of the Constitutional Act of 17th October 1992 that any motion to appoint the Ministers of Foreign Affairs, of National Defence and of Internal Affairs should have been presented by the Prime Minister after consultation with the President, was repealed. Hence, currently, the President does not share the responsibility (whether of a political nature and to public opinion) for personal appointments to the top offices in these significant government ministries. There is no equivalent in the Constitution of 2nd April 1997 to the provisions of Article 38(1) of the Constitutional Act of 17th October 1992, pursuant to which the

---

[24] Article 34 of the Constitutional Act of 17th October 1992.
[25] Cf. Article 51(1) and Article 52(2)(8) of the Constitutional Act of 17th October 1992.

Prime Minister was obliged to inform the President about fundamental matters concerning the activity of the Council of Ministers". This does not exclude the possibility of meetings of the chief of government with the President of the Republic (which actually take place in practice); but rather means that they have lost their institutional character and constitutional basis. The President has also lost his right "in matters of particular importance to the State"[26], to summon sittings of the Council of Ministers and preside over them. Such powers have found a paler equivalent in the President's prerogative to convene the Cabinet Council. Under the previous regulations, some decision-making attributes of the Council of Ministers *in pleno* might have been ascribed to sittings of the Council of Ministers presided over by the President of the Republic. However, the Constitution of 2nd April 1997 states that "The Cabinet Council shall not possess the competence of the Council of Ministers". Moreover, the Cabinet Council does not possess any decision-making powers and serves only as an institutionalized forum for contact and exchange of information between two mutually "autonomous" holders of executive power.

4. CONSTITUTIONAL REGULATIONS AND PRACTICE.
THE IMPACT OF INTERPRETATION AND CONSTITUTIONAL PRACTICE ON DEVELOPMENT OF THE SYSTEM OF GOVERNMENT IN THE REPUBLIC OF POLAND

Legal interpretation of constitutional provisions and the practice of their application is of utmost importance for assessing the system of government contained in the Constitution. This is true, in particular, of those provisions that authorise the supreme organs of State to undertake action without specifying the circumstances and frequency of the use of appropriate powers.

This group, first of all, includes the right to introduce legislation, the right of suspensive veto by the President, and the right to initiate control of the constitutionality of statutes.

As concerns the use of legislative initiative, the Constitution does not determine the substantive scope and the extent of the right to introduce bills by the Deputies, the Senate and — especially important — the

---

[26] Cf. Article 38(2) of the Constitutional Act of 17th October 1992.

Council of Ministers and the President of the Republic. In these latter instances, there can be alternative sources of legislative initiative originating with two separate, sometimes political, centres of executive power. A view can be found in the literature according to which "in the context of separation of competencies between the government and President of the Republic", the legislative initiative of the President "should be used sparingly", in particular in relation to matters expressly conferred on the government. One should, however, bear in mind that this postulate has only a doctrinal character and does not follow directly from the literal wording of constitutional norms. The phrase "matters expressly conferred on the government"[27] has no unequivocal meaning either.

An analogous issue may be the use by the President of the right (pursuant to Article 122(5)) to refer a bill, with reason given, to the Sejm for its reconsideration (i.e. the so-called presidential suspensive veto). This also relates to the President's right to apply to the Constitutional Tribunal for examination of the conformity of such bill to the Constitution (Article 122(3)). The conditions in which the President may "launch" the use of these powers — and whether he does so on his own initiative or is prompted by certain political circles or by a segment of the public opinion — and for what reasons, obviously remain unspecified.

Under the new Constitution, the powers to shorten the term of office of the Sejm and Senate (or dissolution thereof before the expiry of their terms) are restricted as compared to provisions of the Constitution of the People's Republic of Poland as amended in 1989 and the Constitutional Act of 17th October 1992. The provisions enabling the dissolution of parliament as a consequence of the adoption by the Sejm of a resolution "disqualifying the President from the performance of his constitutional powers". This phrase provided President with autonomy, or even arbitrariness, in the use of the right to shorten the term of office of the legislatures, because it was the President himself who could determine whether the resolution adopted by the Sejm had incapacitated his performance of constitutional powers.

Under the Constitution of 2nd April 1997, the President may shorten the term of office of the Sejm and Senate only in two relatively definitely specified circumstances: (a) the failure of the government to obtain a vote

[27] Cf. M. Kruk: *System rządów*..., p. 26.

of confidence under the third constitutional variant of forming a government, (b) the failure to adopt the State Budget within 4 months following the receipt of its draft by the Sejm. In the former instance, the shortening of the term of office of the Sejm and Senate is obligatory by virtue of the Constitution, in the latter — it is left to the President's discretion.

One can easily note that both the above conditions are designed by the authors of the Constitution to help in the creation of a government and in the adoption of the Budget Act proposed by the government. In the latter case, the President acts as a peculiar arbitrator in the relations between the government and parliament (parliamentary majority), but it depends on the President whether to engage or not. Nevertheless, in both situations the President exercises his powers to shorten the terms of office of the Sejm and the Senate independently, without seeking a countersignature by the Prime Minister.

Due to its flexible regulation by the Constitution, the power of the Prime Minister to countersign official acts of the President is a power whose application in practice will determine the shape of the system of government. The formulations of the Constitution of 2nd April 1997 concerning countersignature demonstrate an attempt to reconcile two tendencies. On the one hand, the general clause contained in paragraph 2 of this Article introduces a requirement of countersigning by the Prime Minister of official acts of the President, explaining that through such signature he accepts responsibility to the Sejm for the content of such act and for its consequences. On the other hand, numerous exceptions from such requirement, enumerated in paragraph 3 of this Article manifest a tendency to make the President (chosen by the Nation in universal election) an independent decision-making body, free from the requirement to seek countersignature of the Prime Minister, and bearing only constitutional responsibility for the exercise of powers freed from such requirement, i.e. his prerogatives. Presidential prerogatives, enumerated in Article 144(3) of the Constitution, are the substrate of the real power of the President elected by the Nation and implying a political responsibility to it. They also form a class of official activities "excluded" from the area of current haggling over the power, and therefore, to a certain extent, apolitical. The fact that these prerogatives encompass the appointment of judges, the Presidents of the Constitutional Tribunal and the Supreme

Court, as well as requesting the Sejm to appoint the President of the National Bank of Poland and members of the Council for Monetary Policy or the National Broadcasting Council seems intended to free these bodies from direct involvement in political divisions and controversies.

The Constitution of 2nd April 1997 vests a monopolistic power in Parliament to make laws. However, there are some requirements attached to universally binding legal acts issued by the executive power. These relate to those regulations issued by the government, the Prime Minister and ministers on the basis of specific statutory authorization (with the possibility of formulating directives on the content of the regulation and with a requirement — specified by the rules — that the bills should be submitted together with drafts of envisaged implementing regulations). They justify the exercise by parliament of a substantial, preliminary control over the law-making activity of organs of the executive power. The Sejm and the Senate are also empowered to give consent — by means of a statute — for ratification of international agreements in matters whose regulation requires — pursuant to the Constitution — a statutory method.

The admissible scope of "interference" by the executive in the sphere of legislation remains therefore considerably restricted. The right to order parliamentary elections (at a time and on conditions determined by the Constitution), to convene first sittings, to sign and promulgate statutes at constitutionally specified time limits, and even to participate in the sittings of the Sejm and Senate and to offer amendments to their own bills, still remain within the limits of the parliamentary model of government.

This model includes parliamentary control of the government, even if limited to a scope "specified by the provisions of the Constitution and statutes". The power for its exercise — despite the dualistic nature of executive power — has been concentrated in the Sejm. A vote of confidence for the government and a (constructive) vote of no confidence are both a subject of Sejm sittings. The instruments of parliamentary control (typical of all parliamentary systems of government) such as plenary debate on government policy (in general outlines or individual areas), controlling activities of permanent or ad hoc committees and, finally, interpellations and Deputies' questions, are of importance for the fate of the government or its members, to the extent to which they influence the confidence of the Sejm majority in the government. It is, however, important that the scope of parliamentary (Sejm) control exercised over the government is determined not only by the Constitution, but also — somewhat in parallel — by statutes, i.e. legislation adopted by the Sejm and the Senate.

The government is appointed by the President of the Republic, but on the basis of a required approval by at least a simple majority of the Sejm. In that context, and in accordance with the principle of separation of powers (the legislative and the executive), there is no justification for a practice of hearing candidates for members of the Council of Ministers before parliamentary committees (even if such practice exists in the presidential system applied in the USA). For the same reasons, the "problematic" resolutions adopted by the Sejm at the conclusion of plenary debates on a given problem, may only have an inspirational and propositional value (understood in political categories). Indeed, they have only an evaluative and propositional character in the political sense, and contain no legally binding elements. However, a refusal to pass a motion of confidence in the government has legal consequences, such as compelling the government to resign.

5. FINAL CONCLUSIONS

In general, the system of government established by the Constitution of the Republic of Poland dated 2nd April 1997 remains a rationalized parliamentary system based on the strengthened position of the Prime Minister and the government, as well as an active Presidency, separately legitimized by universal and direct elections[28]. Its aim is to ensure full legislative powers to the Sejm and the Senate. It is also characterized by the dominant position of the Sejm, as compared to the Senate, both in respect of legislative and controlling functions. The executive power has a dualistic nature, the position of the President has a political legitimation (resulting from universal and direct elections) different from that of the government (based on approval by a majority chosen in the course of

---

[28] W. Sokolewicz.: *Pomiędzy systemem parlamentarno-gabinetowym a systemem prezydencko-parlamentarnym: prezydentura ograniczona lecz aktywna w Polsce i w Rumunii* [*Between Parliamentary and Presidential-Parliamentary Systems: Limited but Active Presidency in Poland and Romania*], „Przegląd Sejmowy", No. 3(15)/96, p. 41–42, 44–54.

elections to the Sejm). The function of current direction, management and shaping of State policy is conferred on the government directed by the Prime Minister — whose position and powers in the system of government are strengthened. The President, despite his routine function of the head of state, possesses a wide range of constitutional prerogatives; beyond them, the official acts of the President require — for their validity — the signature of the Prime Minister and are subjected to political control exercised by the Sejm.

Wiesław Skrzydło
Ryszard Mojak

Professors, Marie Curie Skłodowska University, Lublin

PARLIAMENTARY AND CONSTITUTIONAL ACCOUNTABILITY

I. INTRODUCTORY REMARKS

The principle of parliamentary accountability of a government and its members is a universally accepted feature of the parliamentary government. It is associated with constitutional accountability which is applied less often. These two forms of accountability are known to the Polish legal system and have a long-standing and rich tradition of practical application. Moreover, they are recognised as a consequence of provisions of Polish constitutions which assigned to the Sejm the function of control of a government and its members. Recently, they have also been derived from the principle of a democratic state ruled by law in connection with the principle of sovereignty of the nation[1].

Transitions undergone over time by systems of government, including the parliamentary system, have also led to changes in the practice of the principle of parliamentary accountability. Since political parties have begun to play a leading role in parliament and the political unity of the Cabinet and the parliamentary majority has become consolidated, this accountability is accomplished through use of other mechanisms, which also means a diminishing role for the Opposition[2] participating in the exercise of the control function by a house of representatives. In this respect, the cohesion among parliamentary majority composed of a small number of coalition partners is of great significance because, under the

---

[1] Cf. L. Garlicki: *Parlament a rząd: powoływanie–kontrola–odpowiedzialność* [*Parliament and Government: appointment–oversight–accountability*], (in:) *Założenia ustrojowe, struktura i funkcjonowanie parlamentu* [*Basic assumption of the organization, structure and functioning of Parliament*], edited by A. Gwiżdż, Warszawa 1997, p. 239. See also: W. Sokolewicz: *Rozdzielone, lecz czy równe? Legislatywa i egzekutywa w Małej Konstytucji 1992 roku* [*Separated, but are they equal? The legislative and the executive in the Small Constitution of 1992*], „Przegląd Sejmowy" 1993, No. 1, pp. 23 and 27.

[2] This is rightly stressed by L. Garlicki, *op.cit.*, p. 240.

rule of such majority, accountability is effected by means other than parliamentary accountability. And, conversely, looser inner ties within a coalition lead to unstable configurations which, in turn, result in a traditional contradiction between parliament and government. The authors of Poland's constitution assumed that in a period of transformation, characterised by lack of an established system of political parties (being then under construction), there may be a political fragmentation of the Sejm. Therefore, they decided to set up classical institutions connected with parliamentary accountability, although subjecting them to relevant rationalizations.

II. PARLIAMENTARY ACCOUNTABILITY

1. Traditions of parliamentary accountability in Poland and its place in the system of government

This institution has a long tradition in Poland. The principle of political accountability was introduced by the Constitution of 3rd May 1791, the first written constitution in Europe, which allowed (in Article VII) for the dismissal of ministers by a two-thirds majority of votes of members of two houses of parliament. Its more developed form was applied by the constitution of renascent Poland, adopted in 1921, which stated (in Article 56) that the government as a whole and each minister individually resigns at the request of the Sejm. In both instances, as in the constitution of 1952, political responsibility had a parliamentary character. The government and ministers were accountable to both houses (1791) or to the Sejm only (1921). Under the rule of the Constitution of 1935, political responsibility had not only a parliamentary form, as the government and ministers were primarily accountable to the President of the Republic, by whom they could be recalled at any time (Article 28). Accountability to parliament was, however, continued — even if subjected to numerous limitations, specified in Article 29.

The Constitution of 1997 unequivocally adopts this principle and also specifies its premises. Firstly, parliamentary accountability to the Sejm is assumed collectively by the Council of Ministers and — individually — by members of the government. The second house of parliament, the Senate, was not granted the right to control the executive and, therefore, it cannot exercise parliamentary accountability.

Secondly, political responsibility is connected with the Sejm alone, the President of the Republic does not participate in it. However, he has a legal obligation to accept resignation of a government that, or of one of its members who, has lost support of the Sejm.

Thirdly, within the scope of parliamentary accountability, the Constitution provides for the participation of the Prime Minister who, as a result of a Sejm resolution unfavourable to the government, is obliged to offer the resignation of the Cabinet, which cannot be submitted by any member thereof. The Prime Minister alone is constitutionally entitled to submit a request to the President to effect changes in the composition of the Council of Ministers (a recall or appointment of its members).

The President is only constitutionally authorized to appoint a Council of Ministers, but in no case has he the right to recall it. He has only the right to accept the resignation of the government in circumstances specified by Article 162 of the Constitution. However, he may refuse to accept such resignation in one case only, i.e. when it results from the voluntary resignation of the Prime Minister.

Hence, parliamentary accountability is a constitutional institution regulated explicitly by the basic law which specifies the conditions of and procedure for its use, as well as the results of its practical application.

The institution of parliamentary accountability, as a guarantee of cohesion between government policy and that of a Sejm majority[3], assumes the existence of legal and political mechanisms which make it possible to find out whether the government enjoys, or does not enjoy, parliament's confidence, and whether there is still a parliamentary majority supporting the Cabinet.

The subjective scope of accountability is expressly determined by the Constitution and linked with the Council of Ministers as a whole (Article 158) — giving it a collective character — and to ministers (Article 159)

---

[3] See: W. Sokolewicz: Uwaga 10 do art. 66 Małej Konstytucji [Comment 10 to Article 66 of the Small Constitution] (in:) *Komentarz do Konstytucji Rzeczypospolitej Polskiej* [*Commentary to the Constitution of the Republic of Poland*], edited by L. Garlicki, Warszawa 1995.

— treating it as individual accountability. Such accountability covers the so-called departmental ministers, i.e. those directing a particular branch of administration and whose tasks are specified by statute, as well as ministers without portfolio, who do not head any government department and whose tasks are specified by the Prime Minister. The Constitution does not envisage the possibility of submitting a motion of no confidence in the Prime Minister. Such position is completely justified by the special place of the Prime Minister in the government, who manages its work as well as co-ordinates and controls the work of members of Cabinet. A resignation of the Prime Minister is tantamount to resignation of the whole Council of Ministers.

Article 159, governing of a vote of no confidence in individual ministers, does not relate to secretaries and undersecretaries of state[4]. Such accountability does not encompass heads of central administrative agencies and other persons not included in the composition of the Council of Ministers. Hence, the scope of parliamentary accountability is much narrower than that of constitutional accountability.

The Constitution does not specify the scope of parliamentary accountability. However, according to legal doctrine, from the essence of such accountability it follows that the requisite of such accountability includes a negative appraisal of policy pursued by the government or a minister, or the finding that the government in its current composition, or a minister heading a governmental department, is not in a position to effectively implement the political course approved by the parliamentary majority[5].

The holding of a government to parliamentary accountability is a consequence of both a refusal to grant a vote of confidence, passing a vote of no confidence or a refusal to adopt the discharge in respect of the implementation of the budget.

---

[4] Cf. W. Sokolewicz: *Odpowiedzialność parlamentarna rządu RP (wotum zaufania, wotum nieufności, absolutorium)* [*Parliamentary accountability of the Polish Government (vote of confidence, vote of no confidence, vote of approval of accounts)*], Warszawa 1993, p. 74.

[5] Cf. T. Mołdawa: *Legislatywa i egzekutywa pod rządami noweli kwietniowej i Małej Konstytucji* [*The Legislative and the Executive under the Rule of the April Amendment and the Small Constitution*], (in:) *Przeobrażenia ustrojowe w Polsce* [*Transformations of Poland's System of Government*], edited by E. Zieliński, Warszawa 1993, p. 226.

2. The institution of a vote of confidence

The Constitution authorizes only the Prime Minister to seek a vote of confidence in the government. This is a consequence of the Prime Minister's role in the system of government, specified in the basic law, by which he may seek a vote of confidence not only in the course of formation of a government (pursuant to procedures specified in Articles 154 and 155), but also during the life of a Cabinet (in accordance with Article 160) when its chief wants to obtain confirmation of the Sejm's support for government policy. Such confirmation may be needed for internal purposes, to override the parliamentary opposition, for relaxation of tensions within a coalition, etc., but also, externally, in the foreign policy area.

The expression of confidence by the Sejm must take place within a precisely specified time limit only in the event of creation of a new government. Within 14 days following the day of appointment of a government by the President of the Republic, the Prime Minister is obliged to present to the Sejm a political programme of activity of the government for which he wants to win the house's support, expressed during a vote on whether to pass a vote of confidence. It is, naturally, quite reasonable that no such time limits are required for motions made in accordance with Article 160, when the Prime Minister seeks support. Under the procedure provided for in Article 154(1) and (2), confidence is expressed by an absolute majority of votes in the presence of at least half of the constitutional number of Deputies. However, Article 155 which specifies the third procedure for appointing a government in circumstances of a lack of a clearly crystallized parliamentary majority, requires only a simple majority of votes. A similar requirement is contained in Article 160 concerning the passing of a vote of confidence to an already functioning Council of Ministers, i.e. confirming the Sejm's support therefor.

A vote of confidence is granted when government policy has been approved by a parliamentary majority. By contrast, disapproval of the presented policy outlines provides a basis for a refusal to pass a vote of confidence which results, automatically, in a government's obligation to submit, by the Prime Minister, the resignation of the Cabinet to the President of the Republic who is obliged to accept it.

The Constitution does not provide for an individual vote of confidence for a minister. Hence, a refusal to pass a vote of confidence relates exclusively to cases of collective accountability of the Council of Ministers and only in such form is it manifested in the basic law.

3. The institution of a vote of no confidence

A motion of no confidence is passed when parliament disapproves of government policy, including the manner in which it is implementing its programme previously accepted by a parliamentary majority. The relevant procedure is initiated, as a rule, by the Opposition[6]. In the light of Article 158 of the Constitution, a motion to this end may be moved by a group of at least 46 Deputies (i.e. 10% of the constitutional number of Deputies). The threshold applied in this respect is much higher than the requirement for establishing a Deputies' club (15 Deputies), which fact does not facilitate the exercise by the Opposition of its powers to control government activities. Such right is conferred only on Deputies, while Senators are explicitly denied such right.

The provisions specifying the character of a vote of no confidence have undergone substantial changes. The Small Constitution of 1992 contained a simple vote of no confidence, existing along with a constructive vote of no confidence (designed after the German model). However, the new Constitution has departed from the classical form of that institution. This was aimed at ensuring the stability of a government, in order to avoid the creation a negative parliamentary majority, opposing the policy pursued by the Council of Ministers, which very seldom leads to its transformation into a positive majority ready to create and support a new Cabinet.

The present shape of this institution is close to its German archetype. Pursuant to Article 158, a motion to pass a vote of no confidence should specify the name of a candidate for Prime Minister. In fact, this is aimed at obtaining a new majority in the Sejm, a majority of a positive character

---

[6] Transformation of Polish system of government knows an instance of a motion for a vote of no confidence submitted by a member of the ruling coalition (in February 1995). This step was intended to exempt the President of the Republic from the procedure of forming a new government. Moreover, in 1997, the Polish Peasant's Party (PSL) submitted a vote for no confidence in the government which it formed (in coalition with the Left Democratic Alliance — SLD).

which — having recalled the previous Cabinet — could form a solid basis for the creation and functioning of a new government.

The intention to ensure stability of the executive power is evident in two provisions of the Constitution. The first of them relates to a majority required for passing a vote of no confidence. According to Article 158, a motion in this respect should be passed by a majority of votes of the constitutional number of Deputies, i.e. not less than 231 Deputies in a Sejm composed of 460 members. The second provision is contained in paragraph 2 of this Article, which states that any rejection of such motion results in the prohibition against its resumption during the 3-month period following the submission of the first motion.

A motion to pass a vote of no confidence may be put to a vote no sooner than 7 days after its submission. This enables the ruling coalition to have the time to close ranks and look for support. The lack of constitutional definition of a time limit for putting a motion to vote may cause disputes and encourage manipulation. Article 158 is substantially supplemented by Article 61f of the Standing Orders of the Sejm. It establishes a requirement that the motion be considered and put to vote at the first sitting of the Sejm occurring 7 days after its submission. However, in the literature it is assumed that there are no legal obstacles for beginning the consideration of the motion before that time limit, since Article 158(2) specifies only the time limit for a vote.

The adoption of the motion means dismissal of the government, but with simultaneous avoidance of a political crisis connected with the seeking of a new majority, since such has already emerged when appointing a new Prime Minister. A relevant resolution of the Sejm definitely binds the President of the Republic who is obliged to accept the resignation of the previous Cabinet and appoint a new government. The role of the head of state is, therefore, somewhat limited, because the appointment to the office of a Prime Minister is exclusively decided by the Sejm, and the composition of the government by the Prime Minister.

By contrast, the rejection of a motion for a vote of no confidence not only results in leaving the government with its previous composition, but also secures it against subsequent attempts to destabilize it. This is guaranteed by the prohibition against submitting a subsequent motion of a like kind no sooner than after the end of 3 months from the day the previous motion was submitted. The intention of this provision is to protect the government from too frequent attempts to extinguish it by proposing trivial motions. Such threats may particularly appear in a situation of political turmoil in the Sejm, when small groups, abusing parliamentary procedures, are in a position to disorganize the normal functioning of the Sejm and government[7]. A departure from this requirement is allowed only if a subsequent motion has been submitted by at least 115 Deputies (one-fourth of their constitutional number) which would manifested a severe political crisis and strong resistance to the government's actions. Hence, the provisions of the Constitution exactly specify the limits of application of this institution, doing so in a manner preventing the Opposition from abusing it.

The procedure for expressing a vote of no confidence in a minister (Article 159(2)) is based on similar principles, except for the lack of the obligation to submit the candidature of a new minister and with an increased number (69) of signatures required for consideration of a motion. In this instance, we have a classical form of a vote of no confidence along with preservation of the Prime Minister's exclusive right to nominate candidates for members of the government. The recalled minister is replaced by a new one whose candidature is submitted by the Prime Minister to the President of the Republic for effecting change in the given post.

Summarizing our analysis of the institution of a vote of no confidence, we should notice that the Constitution (except for Article 158(2)) does not introduce any further limitations on time limits for the submission of a vote of no confidence in the government. Hence, there are no constitutional obstacles to their consideration by the Sejm in periods of application of extraordinary measures (i.e. in times of a state of siege, a state of emergency and a state of natural disaster). This is, indeed, possible due to giving the said institution a constructive character, which prevents Cabinet crises from emerging.

4. A vote of approval of the government accounts

It should be stressed that even if the legal systems of many European countries have regulations relating to the consideration by their par-

---

[7] Cf. L. Garlicki: *Parlament a rząd...*, p. 254.

liaments of government reports on the execution of the State Budgets, only in the Polish constitutions does this institution have so developed a form; this is evidence of an original contribution stemming from Polish legal thought[8].

In the Polish tradition, such reports are referred to the Sejm. Many European constitutions do not explicitly provide that rejection of a government report by parliament, or acceptance thereof with reservations, leads to particular legal consequences. Thus, it should be presumed that "the authors of the Constitution have assumed that such a situation is an important condition for assuming political responsibility by the government and political responsibility and/or constitutional accountability by its members, according to general rules concerning the enforcement of such accountability specified in a given constitution"[9].

The report relates to the implementation of the Budget Act and is presented together with information on the condition of the State debt. It covers the whole period of implementation of that act, i.e. the entire fiscal year, regardless of whether it is presented by the same government which prepared the Budget Bill, or the Cabinet has been changed in this period. Any failure to fulfil the requirement of presenting the above mentioned reports within the constitutional period of 5 months does not result in extinction of the obligation and, additionally, leads to government accountability for the violation of the Constitution[10].

The Sejm takes a position on this question on the basis of an opinion of the Sejm Public Finances Committee and an opinion submitted by the Supreme Chamber of Control. A resolution adopted in this respect by the Sejm relates to the Council of Ministers as a whole, without differentiating the responsibility of individual members of government (which has been applied in accordance with provisions existing before 1992). This is so, because it is the whole Cabinet that bears collective responsibility for the execution of the Budget Act. The resolution of the Sejm is adopted by a simple majority votes in the presence of at least half of the constitutional number of Deputies.

---

[8] See: W. Sokolewicz: Komentarz do art. 22 Małej Konstytucji [Comments on Article 22 of the Small Constitution] (in:) *Komentarz...*, p. 2.

[9] *Ibid*, p. 6.

[10] *Ibid*, p. 5–6.

A vote of discharge consolidates the government, since thereby the Sejm manifests its confirmation of confidence in it and support for its policy and management of finances. In the previous legal system, a refusal to pass a vote of discharge had the same consequences as a refusal to pass a vote of confidence, i.e. obliged the government to submit its resignation. The present Constitution is silent on this question and does not impose an explicit obligation on the Prime Minister to submit the resignation of the Cabinet. This, naturally, does not apply to a government which has executed the Budget, but no other exists at the time of passing the resolution by the Sejm. However, the problem arises in the case of the Council of Ministers which has functioned in the reporting period and which continues to exist at the moment of adoption of this resolution.

The new provisions give the Opposition the ability to adopt a resolution not to pass a vote of approval of the government, since its adoption requires a simple majority vote, compared with a qualified majority vote (of the constitutional number of Deputies) required to pass a vote of no confidence. The authors of the Constitution have no intention of introducing a solution facilitating the recall of a government. On the other hand, the Constitution does not specify the manner of conduct of a government in whom a vote of approval has not been passed. Obviously, there is a gap here, one which may be interpreted in different ways. An opinion has been expressed that the authors of the Constitution intended to protect the government against the possibility of its easy recall, therefore restrictions connected with the procedure for passing a vote of no confidence against it were introduced. From this a conclusion is derived that, on grounds of existing provisions, the government is under no obligation to submit its resignation after the Sejm has refused to give its approval thereto[11].

Another approach is also encountered, that based on making reference to previous legal regulations and that of practical application of so-called existing notions "whose understanding will exert influence on the interpretation of the new Constitution both by constitutional law doctrine and

---

[11] See: M. Markiewicz, (in:) *Konstytucja Rzeczypospolitej Polskiej oraz komentarz do Konstytucji z 1997 roku* [*The Constitution of the Republic of Poland and a Commentary to the Constitution of 1997*], edited by J. Boć, Wrocław 1998, p. 333.

by practice"[12]. A vote of discharge is undoubtedly an existing notion. A refusal to pass it obliges the government to submit its resignation. The authors of the Constitution do not provide any basis for any other understanding of this institution, although — which is the weak point of the adopted solutions — they do not specify all its consequences. Nevertheless, no change in the attitude of the authors of the Constitution to the question of a vote of approval should be presumed.

Legal doctrine, though yet underdeveloped on this point, also supports this interpretation of Article 226. An expert of the Constitutional Committee, Paweł Sarnecki, argues expressly that "However, the new Constitution does not impose an obligation of automatic resignation of a government in the event of failure to obtain a discharge: this is a response to certain facts from political reality where it happens that decisions on a vote of discharge are taken when the government which has executed a given Budget is not functioning. But let us suppose that the functioning government has not received a discharge. Then, it would seem impossible for such government to continue its activity. In practice, this would compel it to submission of resignation (cf. Article 162 (2)(3))[13].

A similar conclusion should be made from the analysis of the system of government applied by the Constitution, a system which is usually considered as a parliamentary system[14] or, according to others, a parliamentary system with some elements typical of a Chancellor's system[15].

[12] A. Szmyt, (in:) *Wybrane zagadnienia nowej Konstytucji* [*Selected issues of the new Constitution*], „Gdańskie Studia Prawnicze", vol. III, 1998, Gdańsk 1998, p. 5.

[13] P. Sarnecki: *Przemiany kompetencyjne Sejmu i Senatu dokonane w Konstytucji z kwietnia 1997 roku* [*Changes in competencies of the Sejm and the Senate effected in the Constitution of 2nd April 1997*], (in:) *Wybrane zagadnienia nowej Konstytucji...*, p. 118.

[14] M. Kruk: *System rządów w Konstytucji Rzeczpospolitej Polskiej z 2 kwietnia 1997 r.* [*System of Government in the Constitution of the Republic of Poland, dated 2nd April 1997*], (in:) XL Ogólnopolska Konferencja Katedr i Zakładów Prawa Konstytucyjnego [The 40th Polish Nationwide Conference of Constitutional Law Faculties], Kazimierz Dolny n. Wisłą, 4–6 June 1998, p. 33.

[15] Cf. R. Mojak: *Status ustrojowy Rady Ministrów w nowej Konstytucji RP (zagadnienia wybrane)* [*Status of the Council of Ministers in the system of government under the new Constitution of the Republic of Poland (selected issues)*], (in:) XL Ogólnopolska Konferencja Katedr i Zakładów Prawa Konstytucyjnego [The 40th Polish Nationwide Conference of Constitutional Law Faculties], Kazimierz Dolny n. Wisłą, 4–6 June 1998. p. 33.

Indeed, the basis for solving the issues of our concern should be derived from an analysis of the essence of the parliamentary system and from the content of Article 162 (2)(3) of the Constitution. As a reason for dismissal of the Prime Minister, this Article envisages resignation which may be provoked by many factors. A refusal by the Sejm to pass a vote of discharge for the government may obviously be included among these factors.

Not only the existence of a government based on a Sejm majority, but also the principle of that government's accountability to parliament, are the substantive characteristic features of our parliamentary system. Majority support for the government is manifested not only by means of passing a vote of confidence in it, but also (and undoubtedly) by discharge in respect of the implementation of the budget. A lack of such discharge is expressed by the refusal of the Sejm to give support to the government, which is tantamount to holding it politically responsible, necessitating — legally or at least politically — the submission by the Prime Minister of resignation of the whole Cabinet.

III. "CONSTITUTIONAL ACCOUNTABILITY" (IMPEACHMENT)

1. The concept of constitutional accountability, its place in the system of government, and its traditions in Polish constitutional law

Constitutional accountability has the character of legal accountability. It is the responsibility of persons holding the highest State offices for violation of the law, which is exercised, on parliamentary initiative, before a judicial body, a special court called the Tribunal of State[16].

The specific role of the institution of constitutional accountability in the system of government is evident even in a preliminary definition of the concept. In the subjective aspect, it encompasses holding the highest State officials accountable only and exclusively for actions which violate the law. Such accountability has a strictly individualized character and relates to particular persons performing specified official functions.

[16] See: L. Garlicki: *Polskie prawo konstytucyjne. Zarys wykładu, cz. II [Polish Constitutional Law. Framework of lecture, part II]*, Warszawa 1998, p. 195.

The objective scope of constitutional accountability reveals the diversity of solutions establishing the system of government. An essential part of acts covered by such accountability includes, naturally, actions and omissions violating the constitution and statutes. The name of constitutional accountability in its classical form originates from violation of constitutional norms. In models applied by various systems of government, constitutional accountability does not confine itself exclusively to actions inconsistent with the constitution or statutes. Its objective scope is extended to include actions not only being formal violations of the law, but also those encompassing situations of extremely flagrant but qualified transgressions of the law[17]. Such accountability sometimes covers gross breaches of the duties of service or office[18].

Nowadays, constitutional accountability, its character and purpose are derived from the doctrine of a democratic state ruled by law. It is one of the fundamental guarantees of the observance of the law and the exercise of oversight over rulers and holding them accountable for violations of the law. It is also a guarantee of a democratic state ruled by law, protecting its society against any abuse of power by the rulers[19].

Constitutional accountability is functionally connected with the oversight functions exercised by parliament, particularly over the executive power. Accountability of a government in modern systems of government is characterised by a dualism in its form. Presently, parliamentary accountability plays a leading role, while constitutional accountability has been limited to the role of an extraordinary procedure, potentially rather than actually practised[20]. Nowadays, constitutional accountability is related, in particular, to the President of the Republic being that organ of the

---

[17] Cf. *Prawo konstytucyjne [Constitutional Law]*, edited by P. Tuleja, Warszawa 1995, p. 296.

[18] Cf. M. Pietrzak: *Odpowiedzialność konstytucyjna w Polsce [Constitutional Accountability in Poland]*, Warszawa 1992, p. 39.

[19] Cf. *Ibidem*, p. 8 and 34.

[20] It should be stressed that the execution of constitutional accountability depends also on a particular composition of political forces, on public acceptance for activities of particular persons and their political status within the State. The issue of holding a person constitutionally accountable rests, in general, on particular political mechanisms rather than the very fact of violation of the law. Cf. *Trybunał Stanu w PRL [The Tribunal of State in the People's Republic of Poland]*, edited by Z. Świda-Łagiewska, Warszawa 1993, pp. 43–57.

179

State, which — due to the essence of his office — is not subject to parliamentary accountability.

The solutions of the Polish system of government also envisage the application of constitutional accountability to members of government and other persons holding top State offices. The connection between constitutional accountability and the control powers of parliament is reflected in entrusting it with the right to initiate such control or to impose sanctions resulting therefrom.

The institution of constitutional accountability, in its classical form, derives from the English institution of *impeachment*, adequately transformed and adjusted to the political concepts and circumstances of systems of government of individual states in the 18th and 19th centuries.

In the course of evolution of systems of government, the shape of constitutional accountability has been crystallized in a charge of violation of the law, as a form of accountability of ministers and other persons holding top State offices, including a President of the Republic. The development of constitutional accountability in the European constitutions of the 19th century led to a model of constitutional accountability exercised before a special judicial body, namely the Tribunal of State (*Staatsgerichtshof, Haute Cour Nationale*)[21].

Constitutional accountability, or an institution of supervision of the observance of the law by the rulers, was present beginning in the Constitution of the 3rd May of 1791. Pursuant to this Constitution, constitutional accountability was applicable if there had been a violation of the government statute (Constitution) or other law, and for that breach they might have been held accountable by the Sejm and heard by the Sejm Court composed of Deputies and Senators.

The procedure for constitutional accountability was also known to both constitutions of the II Republic, i.e. the March Constitution of 1921 and the April Constitution of 1935.

The March Constitution applied a classical solution, subjecting the President of the Republic and members of government to constitutional accountability for violation of the Constitution or a statute. The power to

---

[21] Cf. M. Pietrzak, *op.cit.*, p. 31–35.

present an accusation belonged to the Sejm, which was then heard by the Tribunal of State[22].

The April Constitution excluded the constitutional accountability of the President of the Republic, however it envisaged the possibility of charging the Prime Minister and ministers before the Tribunal of State for deliberate violations of the Constitution or other statute, committed in connection with the performance of their duties. It extended constitutional accountability to Deputies and Senators, and those who committed a breach of anti-corruption provisions might have been deprived of their mandate[23].

After World War II, the institution of constitutional accountability did not exist in Poland. The Constitution of the People's Republic of Poland did not established the Tribunal of State, nor did it introduce institutional guarantees of the observance of provisions of the Constitution.

The return to the institution of constitutional accountability was possible as a consequence of political events of 1980, in the face of a deep political and social crisis of the system of government of the State. A proposal to set up a Tribunal of State was connected with the notion of widening the control powers of the Sejm and the concept of holding persons responsible for State economic policy.

On 26th March 1982, by way of an amendment of the Constitution of the People's Republic of Poland, the Tribunal of State and the Constitutional Tribunal were established and, on that same day, an Act on the Tribunal of State was passed[24].

---

[22] The March Constitution refers regulation of constitutional accountability to the Act on Tribunal of State, adopted by the Sejm on 27th April 1923, Dziennik Ustaw RP [Journal of Laws of the Republic of Poland] No. 59, item 145. There were two attempts holding two ministers constitutionally accountable (Minister W. Kurowski in 1924 and Minister G. Czechowicz in 1929) but without concluding the proceedings to the stage of making a judgment by the Tribunal of State.

[23] Under the rule of the April Constitution, the institution of constitutional accountability was a dead letter. The Constitution of 1935 and the Act on the Tribunal of State of 14th July 1936 [Dz.U. RP No. 56, item 403], based thereon, had no application in the practice of government system.

[24] The principles of organization and functioning of the Tribunal of State, as specified in the Act of 26th March 1982, were mostly based on model solutions and character of this institution specified in the Act on the Tribunal of State of 1923.

The revival of the Tribunal of State and the institution of constitutional accountability in relation to persons performing top State offices had clearly political origins and intentions connected with the settlement of the socio-political conflicts of 1980–81 and provision of political legitimization, dictated by the existing state of affairs, of a new party-government group within the structures of the State power.

The practice of implementation of constitutional accountability in 1984 against Prime Minister Piotr Jaroszewicz and Deputy Prime Minister Tadeusz Wrzaszczyk, revealed its fictitious character within the mechanisms of government in a socialist state.

2. Legal grounds and scope of regulation of "constitutional accountability"

In Polish constitutional law, based on provisions of the Constitution of the Republic of Poland dated 2nd April 1997, constitutional accountability is one of basic institutional guarantees of a democratic state ruled by law.

The question of constitutional accountability and the institution of the Tribunal of State are dealt with in Chapter VIII of the new Constitution, titled *Courts and Tribunals* (Articles 198–201). Moreover, constitutional grounds for holding somebody constitutionally accountable are specified in Article 145 in relation to the President of the Republic; in Article 156 — in respect of members of the Council of Ministers and in Article 107(2) — in respect of Deputies and Senators. Detailed solutions concerning the rules and procedures for holding these persons constitutionally accountable are contained in the Act of 26th March 1982 on the Tribunal of State[25].

The Constitution of 2nd April 1997 does not introduce any essential change in the regulation of constitutional accountability in Poland; however, one may indicate certain modifications in comparison with the

---

[25] The Act on the Tribunal of State has undergone several amendments, particularly wide scope of amendments was introduced by the Act of 12th December 1992 on Amendment to the Act of 26th March 1982 on the Tribunal of State. This amendment took into account fundamental changes in Poland's system of government after 1989 in respect of the functioning of the Tribunal of State and related, partially, to defective operation of constitutional accountability after the change of government system, The consolidated text of the Act was published in Dziennik Ustaw of 1993, No. 38, item 172.

previously operating rules. There is need for amendment to the previous legal provisions as well as for the adjustment of the statutory regulations to the new constitutional provisions. In the present legal situation, inconsistent regulations of constitutional accountability may generate difficulties in interpretation.

An essential role in the legal regulation of constitutional accountability is played by the precise specification of the jurisdiction of the Tribunal of State.

The subjective scope of constitutional accountability to the Tribunal of State is limited to a group of persons holding top offices in the State, specified by constitutional provisions. This specification has an exhaustive character and cannot be subjected to extensive interpretation in the provisions of the Act on the Tribunal of State. In this respect, the Constitution of 1997 puts the previous solutions of the constitutional provisions into order and, at the same time, places the institution of constitutional accountability within the framework of standards of a state ruled by law[26].

In the present situation of constitutional law, the subjective scope of constitutional accountability encompasses three groups of holders of State offices (Article 198 of the Constitution).

The first group includes the President of the Republic. The scope of President's accountability to the Tribunal of State has not only the broadest, but also an exclusive character. In the light of provisions of the Constitution, doubts are raised about the scope of accountability of the Speaker of the Sejm, substituting the President of the Republic in the exercise of his office or temporarily performing the duties of the President of the Republic, which is prescribed in the existing provisions of the Act on the Tribunal of State (Article 2(3)). Today, the accountability of the Speaker of the Sejm does not very obviously find explicit support in the provisions of the new Constitution (Article 198, Article 131(2)).

---

[26] A positive and exhaustive definition of the substantive scope of constitutional accountability in the basic law was a *de lege lata* postulate based on Poland's previous constitutional provisions. Cf. *Prawo konstytucyjne [Constitutional Law]*, edited by R. Tuleja, *op.cit.*, p. 300, and also Pietrzak M.: *Odpowiedzialność konstytucyjna w Polsce w okresie przemian ustrojowych [Constitutional Acountability in the period of transition in Poland]*, „Państwo i Prawo" 1995, No. 3, p. 27.

The second group encompasses other persons holding top State offices, including: (a) the Prime Minister; (b) members of the Council of Ministers; (c) persons to whom the Prime Minister has granted powers of interim management over a ministry; (d) the President of the Supreme Chamber of Control; (e) the President of the National Bank of Poland; (f) members of the National Council of Radio Broadcasting and Television; (g) the Commander-in-Chief of the Armed Forces.

This group generally places under constitutional accountability all persons holding top offices within the executive power, except for the President of the Supreme Chamber of Control who does not stand within this category of broadly understood bodies of the executive power. In respect of the President of the Supreme Chamber of Control and the President of the National Bank of Poland, their constitutional accountability to the Tribunal of State is, in fact, the only form of oversight of their performance of office and, in practice, the only procedure for their removal from office before expiry of their term of office.

Judges, that is, persons exercising the judicial power, as well as the Commissioner for Citizens' Rights, are not brought within the concept of constitutional accountability.

The third group of persons subjected to constitutional accountability includes Deputies and Senators, to the extent specified in Article 107 of the Constitution.

The Constitution of 1997 extends constitutional accountability to include Deputies and Senators to the same extent as specified in the Constitution of 1935 and in the Act on the Tribunal of State of 1936. This approach is not commonly accepted by constitutional law study. Against such solution arguments are presented that constitutional accountability gives parliament a "supervisory arm" against functionaries of the executive power, which is also, to a certain degree, justified by the origins of the institution itself[27]. It seems, however, that such extension of constitutional accountability in the new Constitution has no anti-parliamentary denotation. Such solution may rather be justified by requirements of a state ruled by law. Subjecting the activity of parliamentarians to judicial review,

---

[27] Cf. *Polskie prawo konstytucyjne* [*Polish Constitutional Law*], edited by W. Skrzydło, *op.cit.*, p. 416.

to a degree generally exceeding the notion of activity connected with the exercise of the mandate, may also confirm prior argumentation.

The scope of matters to which accountability before the Tribunal of State is applied is diversified, mostly dependent on the character of acts whose commission involves the initiation of procedures for holding somebody accountable. This differentiation takes place also in respect of subjects covered by such accountability.

The substantial scope of accountability to the Tribunal of State encompasses accountability for violations of the Constitution or of a statute, committed within their office or within its scope, by persons subjected to accountability to the Tribunal of State (specified by Article 198(1) of the Constitution as constitutional accountability).

Hence, constitutional accountability includes liability for the commission of a "constitutional delict", i.e. an act which is not a crime, but which satisfies all of the following requirements: (a) it concerns violation of the Constitution or of a statute (it covers only breaches of norms contained in constitutional or statutory provisions); (b) it has been committed within the scope of performance of the office of particular persons (a person holding a State office operates within the scope of his competency, but with violation of the law); (c) it has been committed in connection with the office held (a person subjected to the cognition of the Tribunal of State undertakes actions exceeding the scope of his lawful competencies, but which are permitted due to the office held).

Constitutional accountability may concern only an act committed during the time of holding a given office, while the term "act" encompasses the broad legal meaning of the word. It includes actions undertaken by persons specified by the Constitution, as well as instances of refraining from the performance of certain actions despite a legal obligation to do so (delict of omission).

It should also be noted that execution of accountability for committing a "constitutional delict" is not limited to the period of holding a particular office. The Act on the Tribunal of State explicitly states that prosecution before the Tribunal of State is admissible within 10 years from the date of an act; and the fact that the perpetrator no longer holds the office or performs such duties does not constitute an obstacle to the institution or conduct of proceedings (Article 23(1))[28].

Guilt is not a constitutional determinant of constitutional accountability. It is, however, mentioned in Article 3 of the Act on the Tribunal of State, which seems to be inconsistent with constitutional requirements for "constitutional delict". The authors of the Constitution favour, as we can infer, giving constitutional accountability an objective character, i.e. allowing accountability in circumstances of a lack of guilt.

Constitutional definition of a "constitutional delict" does not include its material aspect, or the consequences and level of social detriment resulting from a breach of the Constitution or of a statute.

The objective scope of constitutional accountability in the Polish solution has, to a large degree, a juridical character and applies a very formal treatment of such accountability in the provisions of the basic law.

Indictment and accountability before the Tribunal of State is also admissible for reasons other than a violation of the Constitution, in particular for the commission of an offence. In such situation the Tribunal of State acts, and adjudicates, as a criminal court, however, this scope of its powers nowadays concerns only the President of the Republic and members of the Council of Ministers.

The President of the Republic may be held accountable before the Tribunal of State for a violation of the Constitution or statute, or for commission of an offence (Article 145(1) of the Constitution). Pursuant to the Constitution, the Tribunal of State has an exclusive jurisdiction in cases of offences committed by the President. Accountability of the President before the Tribunal of State covers all offences committed by him during the exercise of his office. Their connection with the office held does not matter, as the Tribunal of State is the exclusive criminal court competent for making the President of the Republic accountable for committed offences.

In relation to members of the Council of Ministers, the jurisdiction of the Tribunal of State in respect of offences has a limited character.

---

[28] Such solution causes controversies in the literature. It is stressed, in particular, that the institution of constitutional accountability should serve to recall from office a person who has committed a constitutional delict, when any other ways of dismissal of such person is either impossible or ineffective. Cf. *ibidem*, p. 417.

Pursuant to Article 156(1) of the Constitution, members of the Council of Ministers are accountable to the Tribunal of State only for offences committed in connection with the duties of their office.

Moreover, under the Act on the Tribunal of State, a member of the Council of Ministers may be held criminally responsible before the Tribunal of State for offences, if the Sejm, in a resolution on holding him constitutionally accountable, has found it advisable to jointly consider such acts (Article 2(4)).

The accountability of Deputies and Senators before the Tribunal of State is of a special character since it concerns only a breach of the prohibition against the performance of any business activity involving benefit derived from the property of the State Treasury or local government, or against acquiring such property.

Precise specification of these prohibitions is specified by the Act of 9th May 1996 on the Exercise of the Mandate of a Deputy or Senator[29], reference to which is found in the Constitution (Article 107(1)).

Accountability of Deputies and Senators before the Tribunal of State, defined in Article 198 as constitutional accountability, does not in fact cover the whole scope of classical accountability for a "constitutional delict", but is confined only to matters specified in Article 107(1) of the Constitution.

3. Constitutional position and organization of the Tribunal of State

As was already mentioned, constitutional accountability is realized before the Tribunal of State. The Constitution of the Republic of Poland states that the Tribunal of State is an element of the judicial power. Pursuant to Article 173 of the Constitution, the courts and tribunals constitute a separate power and are independent of other branches of power. Moreover, they have a monopoly over the exercise of the judicial power in Poland, in accordance with the jurisdiction specified in the basic law[30].

---

[29] Dziennik Ustaw of 1996, No. 73, item 350, as amended.

[30] See: A. Wasilewski: *Władza sądownicza w Konstytucji Rzeczypospolitej Polskiej* [*The Judicial Power in the Constitution of the Republic of Poland*], „Państwo i Prawo", 1998, No. 7, p. 6.

The Tribunal of State does not administer justice, but as an organ of the judicial power is exclusively empowered to adjudicate in respect of accountability for violations of the Constitution or statute. The Tribunal of State has also the competence to adjudicate in respect of offences committed by a category of persons strictly defined by the Constitution.

The Tribunal of State is not a "court" and does not "administer justice" within the meaning of Article 175(1) of the Constitution. Nevertheless, due to the nature of the independence of its judges and the nature of its tasks, consisting in adjudicating on alleged violations of law, the Tribunal of State is consistent with characteristic features of an organ of the judicial power[31]. At the same time, the Tribunal, in its organizational and functional aspects, is substantially connected with the Sejm.

The Tribunal of State is composed of a chairperson (the First President of the Supreme Court is chairperson, ex officio), two deputy chairpersons and 16 members chosen by the Sejm for the current term of office of the Sejm from amongst those who are not Deputies or Senators. Additionally, the Constitution states that the deputy chairpersons and at least one half of the members of the Tribunal of State should possess the qualifications required to hold the office of judge (Article 199(1)).

The substantial element of constitutional status of the Tribunal of State is the fact that its members, within the exercise of their office as judges, are independent and subject only to the Constitution and statutes (Article 199(3) of the Constitution).

Moreover, the members of the Tribunal of State are placed under special protection by law, being provided with the immunity of judges (Article 200 of the Constitution).

Although the Tribunal of State possesses the essential attributes of an organ of the judicial power, it is closely connected, both organizationally and functionally, with the Sejm. These connection gives the Tribunal of State the character of a "Sejm court" and indicates the political origins of its composition. In the practice of the system of government of the 1990s, there was applied a principle of political parity of individual parliamentary clubs in nominating candidates for the Tribunal of State. This principle

---

[31] Cf. L. Garlicki, op.cit., p. 199.

was intended to "neutralize" its excessively political character and subjecting it to the political interests of a current parliamentary majority[32].

4. The mode of proceedings in respect of constitutional accountability

Proceedings in respect of constitutional accountability are characterized by a large degree of complexity and are comprised of several stages. Such proceedings are not identical in respect of all the subjects covered by the jurisdiction of the Tribunal of State. Here, there exist certain disparities resulting in separate procedures for bringing to accountability the President of the Republic and for that of other persons subject to constitutional accountability.

The conduct of proceedings is partially governed by constitutional provisions specifying the competencies of the State organs, in particular those instituting proceedings in respect of holding a person accountable, as well as the provisions of the Act on the Tribunal of State (ATS). Additionally, provisions of penal law are applied, as appropriate, in the proceedings.

Proceedings in respect of accountability before the Tribunal of State involve three basic stages: (1) preparatory (preliminary) proceedings, encompassing the submission of a preliminary motion and proceedings in the Sejm, or in the National Assembly in respect of the President of the Republic; (2) consideration of a case by the Tribunal of State; (3) executory proceedings.

Preliminary (preparatory) proceedings begin by submitting a preliminary motion to the Speaker of the Sejm, then involve an inquisitional procedure before the Constitutional Accountability Committee, and end with the Sejm (National Assembly) passing a resolution to indict the President, or with discontinuance of proceedings. Proceedings at this stage are carried out, in general, in the Sejm.

Preliminary motions may be submitted:

(a) in respect of indictment of the President of the Republic — by at least 140 members of the National Assembly (Article 145(2) of the Constitution);

---

[32] This political custom was withdrawn in 1997 during the selection of the composition of the Tribunal of State which was fully dominated by the ruling coalition in parliament, i.e. Solidarity Election Action and Union for Freedom.

(b) in respect of accountability of members of the Council of Ministers — by the President of the Republic or at least 115 Deputies (Article 156(2) of the Constitution);

(c) in respect of accountability of other persons (except for Deputies and Senators) — by the President of the Republic or at least 115 Deputies, or an investigative committee of the Sejm (Article 6(2) of ATS);

(d) in respect of accountability of Deputies and Senators — by, respectively, the Speaker of the Sejm and the Speaker of the Senate (Article 107(2) of the Constitution).

A preliminary motion should be formulated in writing and satisfy the formal requirements strictly specified in the Act on the Tribunal of State. Otherwise, if the mover has failed to correct formal defects, no further action may be taken in respect of such motion (Article 6 of ATS).

The validity of a charge — as can be deduced from practice — including the political validity of bringing a given person to indictment[33], is considered by the Constitutional Accountability Committee of the Sejm. Proceedings at this stage have, similarly to criminal procedure, some attributes of preparatory proceedings, sometimes called a "Sejm investigation"[34]. This relates to all the concerned persons, including the President of the Republic. On the basis of collected material, the Constitutional Accountability Committee prepares a motion to indict a person or to discontinue the proceedings.

Indictment takes place by means of a relevant resolution of: (a) the National Assembly — in respect of the President of the Republic — passed by a two-thirds majority of at least two-thirds of the constitutional number of members of the National Assembly (Article 145(2) of the Constitution); (b) the Sejm, passed by a majority of at least three-fifths of the

---

[33] As is evident in the practice of Poland's system of government in the years 1990–97, constitutional accountability has possessed, and still possesses, some political aspects and political consequences. The fact of violation of the law is not considered a sufficient reason for institution of proceeding or formulation of charges against a given person. The existing political circumstances and, in particular, current political interests of parliamentary majority are elements of substantial importance. Political considerations and treating constitutional accountability as an instrument useful in political disputes lead to depreciation of this institution as a form of the exercise of oversight over the executive bodies by the Sejm. Cf. J. Pietrzak: *Odpowiedzialność konstytucyjna w Polsce w okresie...*, p. 24–25.

[34] See: *Prawo konstytucyjne [Constitutional Law]*, W. Skrzydło, *op.cit.*, p. 419.

constitutional number of Deputies, in respect of bringing members of the Council of Ministers to account (Article 156(2) of the Constitution) or by absolute majority vote requiring the presence of at least half of the total number of Deputies, in respect of holding other persons constitutionally accountable (Article 13(1) of ATS).

Examination of a case before the Tribunal of State has a two--instance character. As a court of first instance, the Tribunal of State adjudicates in a bench composed of chairperson and 4 members; as a court of second instance — in a bench composed of chairperson and 6 members, not including those judges who participated in consideration of the case in the court of first instance (Article 19 of ATS). In proceedings before the Tribunal of State provisions of criminal procedure are applied as appropriate. The indicted person has the right to defence.

The Tribunal of State may impose the following penalties for commission of acts covered by the indictment: (1) in respect of acts being "constitutional delicts" — loss of electoral franchise and eligibility for election (for a period ranging from 2 to 10 years); the prohibition against holding managerial posts and performing duties connected with special accountability within State organs or social organizations (for a period from 2 years and without limitation of time) as well as forfeiture of all or specified medals and decorations and loss of eligibility to receive them (for a period from 2 to 10 years) and (2) in respect of acts satisfying requirement of a criminal offence — sentences specified in penal statutes (Article 26 of ATS).

The Act states that, due to the special circumstances of a case, the Tribunal may refrain from inflicting a punishment and confine itself to a finding of guilt. It seems, however, that statutory rules governing the imposition of penalties by the Tribunal of State are not consistent with constitutional requirements for a "constitutional delict" and, in particular the requirement of guilt which is not included by the Constitution among the elements of a delict.

Executory proceedings in respect of judgments issued by the Tribunal of State is entrusted to the Warsaw Voivodship Court. Such proceedings should be conducted in accordance with the principles envisaged for penal cases by penal procedure provisions.

There is a tendency, observed in recent years in the practice of the Polish government system, to transform constitutional accountability in its classical form (i.e. accountability for a "constitutional delict") to penal responsibility, this is particularly evident in proceedings before the Constitutional Accountability Committee of the Sejm[35].

Such understanding and interpretation of constitutional accountability depreciates the specific character of "constitutional delict" within the system of government.

---

[35] See: J. Pietrzak: *Odpowiedzialność konstytucyjna w Polsce w okresie...*, p. 22.

Andrzej Gwiżdż

Janusz Mordwiłko

Professors, University of Warsaw

THE STATUS OF THE SEJM IN THE LIGHT OF THE CONSTITUTION OF THE REPUBLIC OF POLAND OF 2ND APRIL 1997

The authors of Poland's Constitution of 2nd April 1997 have accorded a particular position and specific rank to the Sejm in the system of government, reflecting its role in over 500 years of Polish parliamentary history.

The most fundamental question faced by the authors of the Constitution was to define the place and role of the Parliament in the system of State authorities. They rejected the concept, applied by the Constitution of 1952, of the superior position of Parliament over all State organs determined by the principle of unity of State power. They did not accept, following the Constitution of 1935, the subordination of Parliament to another authority (President of the Republic). It was decided that the place and role of Parliament would be determined, above all, by the principles of separation and balance of powers. Hence, Article 10 of the Constitution states that "The system of government of the Republic of Poland shall be based on the separation of and balance between the legislative, executive and judicial powers.

Legislative power shall be vested in the Sejm and the Senate, executive power shall be vested in the President of the Republic of Poland and the Council of Ministers, and the judicial power shall be vested in courts and tribunals."

The general position of the executive power is also specified by the principle of "cooperation" between the public powers. It seems to be a directive blunting the idea of "mutual checks of the branches of power".

The principle of separation of powers introduced to our constitutional order by the Small Constitution of 1992 provides, therefore, a point of departure for considerations concerning Parliament. However it should be complemented by the requirement of basing "the system of government of the Republic" on the principle of "balance" between powers.

The principle of separation of powers excludes a concentration of all State decisions and tasks in Parliament and requires that some balance exists between its individual branches. Such balance does not have to be of an absolute character, hence, both in the Small Constitution and the present basic law, there appears a certain preponderance of Parliament as compared with the executive power. This is reflected in Parliament's competencies. It exercises the legislative function, which results from the essential role of Parliament as "a legislative body". Moreover, typical of parliamentary system of government, Parliament plays a very significant role in appointing a government and has the power of control over the government and enforces the accountability of government.

Parliament is also involved in a system of checks and balances constituting fundamental elements of the principle of separation of powers. It is connected with the executive power by participation in the appointment of governments. It may also hold the government or ministers accountable to parliament, and — in respect of the President of the Republic — it may also hold him constitutionally accountable, under specified circumstances. The executive power, in turn, has at its disposal different means of influencing the exercise by Parliament of its legislative function. Fundamental examples of the balance between the legislative and the executive powers are the classical institutions of: the legislative veto of the President; the political and constitutional accountability of the government to the Sejm; the President's right to dissolve Parliament; the constitutional accountability of the President before the National Assembly (joint houses of the Sejm and the Senate). However, as we already mentioned, these institutions do not ensure a complete balance because of operation of weakening mechanisms contained therein. The right to dissolve Parliament is limited only to two situations and is, above all, an independent competence of the President, exercised without countersignature, therefore, the government cannot freely maneuver in relation to it. Political accountability is reflected in the so-called constructive vote of no confidence which is perhaps the least "dangerous" procedure for the government, even if there exists an individual political accountability of several members of government. The principle of permanency of debates of Parliament has excluded the institution of convening, suspending and closing parliamentary sessions by the President of the Republic, usually conducted with a government's countersignature, which is an institution typical of a system of checks and balances.

The adoption of the parliamentary government on grounds of the principle of separation of or balance between powers leads to an increasing intersection and overlapping of powers, if only because, in this type of separation of powers, the political and personal distance between the parliamentary majority and the government has been obliterated.

A connection between Parliament and the judicial power consists in adoption of statutes which bind judges in their exercise of adjudicatory functions. Parliament also influences the appointment of judges of the Constitutional Tribunal and of the Tribunal of State. The judicial power, in turn, may — via the Constitutional Tribunal — find statutes passed by Parliament as inconsistent with the Constitution and deprive them of their binding power.

As regards the organization of Parliament, there was a dilemma related to its uni- or bicameral character. In the Polish tradition, Parliament is usually bicameral. The existence of the Sejm and the Senate was envisaged by the March and the April Constitution which also gave the Sejm a stronger position.

The National Assembly which adopted the Constitution, decided by a small majority of votes for a Parliament of bicameral character, thereby accepting its shape as developed after the transformations of 1989. The adoption of such concept of organization of Parliament was not preceded by any careful analysis of this question. There was no more in-depth analysis of a proposal for change of principles governing the election of the Senate (e.g. as a representation of local government), which would make it possible to give that house a clearly different character from such political representation as is found in the Sejm.

The Constitution does not apply the principle of equal rights of the different houses, as such equality never existed in the Polish constitutional tradition. This is evident in general constitutional characteristics that show that the legislative power is jointly vested in the Sejm and the Senate, but the exercise of oversight over government is the exclusive domain of the Sejm.

Since 1989, the concept of the role of the Senate has undergone no change. Limitations on bicameralism are reflected in the far-reaching decline of the position of the Senate as compared to the Sejm, both in respect of competencies and organization. This is evident in a fundamental function of both bodies, namely the legislation. Whilst all statutes, with no exceptions, are also considered by the Senate, legislative initiatives may be instituted only in the Sejm, and the right to introduce bill is vested in the Senate only as a whole body. Statutes may be enacted in spite of objection (whole rejection thereof) by the Senate, since such objection may be relatively easily overridden as well as in relation to any amendments proposed by the Senate to bills adopted by the Sejm. The Senate cannot reject the Budget Bill, but the Constitution maintains its right to offer amendments to the Budget. It is the Sejm that has an exclusive right to consider and decide about the re-passing of a statute vetoed by the President of the Republic. Regulations having the force of statute, issued by the President of the Republic during a period of state of siege are subject to approval only by the Sejm. The right to order the holding of a referendum is vested in the Sejm which cannot express objections against such order because it does not consider this case. This defect is only partly compensated by the right of the Senate to give consent for ordering a referendum by the President of the Republic, since it relates to different situation, and the consent is envisaged as a check on anti-parliamentary (and, hence, anti-Sejm) implication of such referendum ordered by the head of state.

Some expansion of competence, as compared with the Small Constitution, is observed in respect of the process of amending the Constitution. Such an amendment would become effective only after the adoption of an identical text by the Sejm and the Senate, while the lack of consent of the Senate could not be validated by the Sejm. Similar acceptance by the Sejm and the Senate is also required for the adoption of statutes granting consent for ratification of international agreements which delegate to international organizations or international institutions the competence of organs of State authority in relation to certain matters.

Apart from being involved in the legislation, the Senate participates in the appointment of certain State authorities: the President of the Supreme Chamber of Control, the Commissioner for Citizens' Rights, partially

— the National Council of Radio Broadcasting and Television, and partially — the Council for Monetary Policy.

However, the Senate does not participate in the exercise of control functions over the government, nor does it take part in the appointment of the government nor hold it parliamentarily accountable, as these powers belong exclusively to the Sejm.

At this point, we must mention that the existence of the Senate is connected with the existence of the Sejm, because the terms of office of both houses are specified by the term of office of the Sejm and any dissolution of the Sejm results in a dissolution of the Senate.

Hence, in the situation of choice between two possible constructions, i.e. a house of resistance and a house of reflection and thought, the latter solution was taken for the Senate. This resembles the provisions of the March Constitution (1921), because now — similar to the situation existing under the rule of that Constitution — the Senate has rather to prevent unnecessary haste in the course of legislative process, and also has to be an additional forum for more comprehensive and in-depth consideration of juridical solutions contained in a statute and, during its work on a statute, should take into account criteria of legislative coherence and harmonization of solutions concerning the system of government with the Constitution rather than purely political considerations.

Due to the unequal position of the Senate within Parliament as a whole, our further comments will concentrate on the Sejm.

Organization of Parliament, and its method of functioning, have been established in connection with the principle of Parliament's autonomy, and more precisely — of its houses. This principle applies not only in shaping internal organization or parliamentary procedures, but also provides to Parliament (its houses) the necessary guarantees for unrestricted performance of its constitutional duties, and for unobstructed exercise of their mandate by parliamentarians.

The general principle of Parliament's autonomy (and of its houses) has been developed in a form of personal autonomy (exclusive right to determine membership of its internal bodies), financial and budgetary autonomy (exclusive right to determine the budget and the manner of its implementation), territorial autonomy (separateness of the seat of Parliament and its exclusive right to manage its precincts), jurisdictional (exclusiveness of decisions in immunity and disciplinary matters).

Pursuant to the principle of autonomy, each house adopts its own rules of procedure. In the light of judgments of the Constitutional Tribunal, the rules of procedure of the Sejm are considered as a normative act, being an independent act issued directly on the basis of the Constitution. The Constitution maintains a broad concept of parliamentary rules of procedure (established in the Polish tradition) stating that they should govern "the internal organization", "conduct of work" and "the procedure for appointment and operation of organs of the house", as well as "the manner of performance of obligations, both constitutional and statutory, by State organs in relation to the Sejm".

Parliament's autonomy has led to very considerable limitations on the scope of review of conformity of the rules of procedure with the Constitution. In its practice, the Constitutional Tribunal has stressed the imperative of considerable moderation in oversight of norms established in relation to this autonomy and a particularly strong presumption of conformity of the rules of procedure with the Constitution.

We must add that certain questions related to Parliament are also regulated in a statutory fashion, e.g. by Acts on elections to the Sejm and to the Senate which do so fragmentarily (requirements for the expiry of a mandate). Moreover, there exists an Act on the exercise of the mandate of a Deputy or a Senator, whilst certain elements of the functioning of the houses and parliamentarians can be found in other statutes, e.g. in Anti-corruption Act, Budgetary Law or the Act on the Tribunal of State.

The Constitution resolves some issues essential for the functioning of the houses of Parliament. Above all, it maintains their traditional 4-year term of office.

The term of office of the Sejm begins on the day on which the Sejm assembles for its first sitting (the term of office of the Senate begins on the same day) and continues until the day preceding the first sitting of the Sejm of the succeeding term of office. Hence, an inter-term break has been eliminated. Such solution ensures continuity of existence of Parliament, as the term of a current Parliament cannot expire before the constituting of a new one, which is also true in respect of a dissolved Parliament. The applied system of specifying the term of office means that for a certain period (i.e. between the day of election and the day of the first sitting) Parliaments of the preceding and new terms exist together. However, this does not cause any constitutional problem, since during that period the new parliament is only a potential being without a capacity to act.

It is therefore generally impossible, on grounds of the Constitution, to prolong the term of office of the Sejm (and, hence, that of the Senate); the only exception might be in the event of an introduction of extraordinary measures and within the period of 90 days following their termination, then the term of office (provided that its expiry falls within this period) could be appropriately prolonged.

Nevertheless, the Constitution envisages the possibility of shortening the term of office of Parliament. This may happen as a result of: (1) the Sejm's own decision (self-dissolution); a resolution on self-dissolution is passed by the Sejm by a majority of at least two-thirds of the votes of the constitutional number of Deputies. Such resolution may be taken at any time and for any reason, provided that there is no prohibition against shortening of the term of office during the period of introduction of extraordinary measures and within the period of 90 days following its termination; (2) decision taken by the President of the Republic. Such dissolution of Parliament is an instrument connected with the principle of separation of and balance between powers, and was introduced to the Polish system of government as early as in the 1989 Amendment to the Constitution of 1952, then repeated in the Small Constitution and maintained by the present Constitution. Dissolution of Parliament has been, and still is, limited by the Constitution to specific situations in the State. Nowadays, the President of the Republic may shorten the term of office of Parliament only in two instances: (a) obligatorily — in the course of formation of the government, in the event that the Sejm has failed to pass a vote of confidence in the government appointed by the President or failed to appoint its own government; (b) facultatively — in the course of adoption of a Budgetary Bill — in the event of failure to pass it by the houses within a period of 4 months.

The Constitution does not provide for any other possibility of dissolution of the Sejm, which may manifest the stronger position of Parliament in relation to the President in the Polish model of separation of and balance between powers, especially in comparison to possibilities of dissolution of Parliament in certain European democracies.

The President of the Republic dissolves the houses of Parliament by means of an order which does not require a countersignature but only the seeking of the opinion of speakers of both parliamentary houses. Such opinions have no binding character, as final decision is taken exclusively by the President.

Dissolution of Parliament results in ordering and holding of early elections for a new Parliament, however, the powers of the dissolved Parliament still continue, since its term of office, even if shortened, should last until the day preceding the first sitting of the Sejm of a new term. After the dissolution of Parliament, the position and competencies of the President of the Republic do not change, as well as the situation of the government. In such circumstances, only the perspective of swift elections and the possibility of establishing, by its result, of a new political majority should induce the government to moderation in undertaking important and controversial matters. However, such limitations result from good political habits, rather than constitutional prohibitions.

As concern the method of functioning of Parliament in the course of its term, the Polish Parliament operates under the system of permanency. The Constitution continues this system, applied by the Small Constitution, and specifies only the time of sitting of the houses. Distinguishing between ordinary and extraordinary sittings and the conditions for their convening have been left to the decision of houses of Parliament — which fact manifests the complete autonomy of the houses. This is connected with the lack of a right to suspend or close parliamentary debates by any external factor, which is possible under the sessional system. Hence, the term of Parliament has a uniform character, it cannot be divided into sessional and inter-sessional periods.

The orders of the day have an utmost importance for determining the time of sittings — the sitting lasts until all business is dealt with. The Polish parliamentary tradition allowed for sittings lasting several days, and in 1991 (beginning with the first term of the Sejm of the Republic of Poland) there appeared the practice of intermittent sittings, exceeding the period of one week. The rhythm of sittings is determined by the scope of matters considered by the houses. They are specified on the basis of plans accepted by executive bodies of the houses, and are convened by the speakers of the houses.

The orders of the day are established by the Speaker of the Sejm after hearing an opinion of the Council of Seniors (an opinion-making body composed of chairpersons of political parliamentary clubs), while controversial matters are resolved by the house. The rules of procedure concerning the fixing of the orders of the day, to a large degree, protect the interests of the parliamentary minority.

The Constitution maintains the principle of the public nature of debates in the houses, being of fundamental importance for its work, however, making it possible to waive this rule, provided that an appropriate resolution has been adopted by the house. The Sejm may resolve to hold a debate in secret if so required in the "interests of the State". In practice, withdrawal of the public nature of debates of the house has been rare and related only to selected items of the orders of the day. The application of the principle of public nature of debates is more limited in respect of sittings of internal bodies of the house, including Sejm committees. Attendance of the representatives of the mass media at the sitting of a committee is allowed upon consent of its chairman; a committee may also decide to hold a sitting *in camera*, some committees (e.g. Special Services Committee or investigative committees) impose limitations on the public nature of their functioning.

The rules of procedure of Sejm debates do not differ from general patterns developed by the practice of Parliaments in established democracies, as well as old Polish parliamentary tradition. An analysis of changes in the rules of procedure of the Sejm, effected in the 1990s, reveals a tendency to create and strengthen institutions and solutions increasing the role and powers of the political opposition in shaping the work of the Sejm. However, in the light of experience of several Western countries, the rules of procedure of the Sejm do not provide clear guarantees of the pluralistic character of internal bodies of Parliament.

In the internal structure of the house, we can easily distinguish executive bodies — the Speaker of the Sejm (Speaker of the Senate), the Presidium of the Sejm (Presidium of the Senate), as well as a special political and consultative bodies — the Council of Seniors, and auxiliary bodies — Sejm (Senate) committees.

The Speaker, the Presidium and committees are bodies of the houses and, therefore, are composed exclusively of Deputies (or Senators) and their composition is directly determined by the Sejm (the Senate). In the internal structure of the Sejm and the Senate, understood as a system of internal bodies, we can distinguish organizational structures of Deputies (Senators) which are designed to elaborate and formulate joint political position in respect of matters subject to consideration of the house or its committees. Among such voluntary organizations of parliamentarians, particular position belongs to Deputies' (Senators') clubs, as well as other quasi-political organizations, such as groups and groupings.

The Constitution states that the Speaker of the Sejm is its executive body. Moreover, the rules of procedure also establish a collective body as an internal executive, i.e. the Presidium of the Sejm, composed of the Speaker and Vice-Speakers whose number is determined by the Sejm at the time of their election.

In the light of the Constitution, establishing the office of Speaker of the Sejm as its executive body, this body concentrates powers connected with presiding over the debates of the Sejm, safeguarding the rights of the Sejm as well as representing the Sejm in external matters.

Selection of the Speaker of the Sejm is made in accordance with political criteria, as the office of the Speaker falls to a group composing a majority coalition, which does not necessarily mean that it should be its strongest club. The concept of the Speaker of the Sejm as a politically determined office may weaken his role as a neutral arbitrator and organizer of the house's work. Offices of Vice-Speakers are usually entrusted to significant groups and a custom has been established in Parliament to entrust the position of one Vice-Speaker to a representative of the strongest Opposition group.

The Council of Seniors is a body which ensures co-operation between parliamentary clubs in respect of matters connected with the activities and course of Sejm work. It is, therefore, a political body in which the most important decisions on the house's activity are taken. The Council is composed of the Speaker and Vice-Speakers, as well as chairpersons of Deputies' clubs and representatives of alliances composed of at least 15 Deputies. Sejm committees are specialized internal bodies designed to consider, provide opinions and elaborate matters subject to debates in the Sejm. The Constitution distinguishes standing, special and investigative committees. Presently, the rules of procedure of the Sejm provide for appointment of 28 standing committees. The committee system is based on a departmental or problem criterion (around 20 committees operate according to this principle) or a functional criterion (the scope of activities of these committees is connected with functions or powers exercised by the Sejm). While, in the sphere of legislation, committees play an evidently auxiliary role to the house, their role in the exercise by the Sejm of its function of control increases and is characterized by a large extent of independence and autonomy.

It is very important for proper exercise of the parliamentary mandate that a Deputy possesses certain guarantees of independence, which on the one hand makes it difficult to exert different pressure on the Deputy from outside and, on the other hand, protect him against any potential threat connected with conflict of interests. Two fundamental guarantees are formulated in this respect by the Constitution, i.e. (1) parliamentary immunity, (2) the principle of incompatibility.

The provisions of the Small Constitution concerning parliamentary immunity have remained almost unchanged. The Constitution maintains substantive immunity (non-liability or privilege) of parliamentarians, covering "activity performed within the scope of a Deputy's mandate". The protection guaranteed by this privilege covers the activity performed within the scope of a mandate, provided however that such activity has not infringed the rights of third parties. Activities falling into the scope of exercise of a mandate are specified by the pre-constitutional Act on the Exercise of the Mandate of a Deputy or a Senator. It enumerates such activities as moving of motions, delivery of speeches and voting at the sittings of the houses and the National Assembly and their organs, at the sittings of parliamentary clubs, as well as other activities indispensable for the exercise of the mandate of a Deputy (or a Senator).

Non-liability (privilege) is of an absolute (immovable) character, since there is no procedure enabling its withdrawal. The Constitution states that for activities covered by such privilege, a Deputy may be held accountable only before the Sejm, and only in accordance with the disciplinary procedure.

Non-liability has a permanent character, as it also functions after the expiry of the mandate, however, of course, only in respect of actions which have taken place in the period of the exercise of the mandate.

Formal immunity has been continuously present in constitutions from the times of the March Constitution. Such immunity relates to those acts, committed by a Deputy irrespective of his exercise of the mandate, which could be subject to criminal responsibility. The Constitution extends this immunity to the sphere of criminal responsibility. However, the Act on the Exercise of the Mandate of a Deputy or Senator expands its scope to prosecution before a criminal-administrative court. This immunity does not cover civil or professional liability. It prohibits the institution and conduct of criminal proceedings against a Deputy. If criminal proceedings have already been instituted against a person before the day of his election as Deputy, they may be continued, unless the Sejm requests suspension of such proceedings.

This immunity has a conditional character, as it may be withdrawn. In the light of the Constitution, such withdrawal may be made by the Sejm itself, by means of a resolution taken by a qualified majority of two-thirds of votes. However, such majority requirement results from the rules of procedure of the Sejm, because the Constitution fails to include this requirement, such withdrawal may be also made by granting consent for it by the Deputy concerned. A waiver of immunity by the Deputy excludes any further procedural actions of the house in this respect.

Many controversies are caused in the Polish doctrine by the institution of waiver of immunity. This results from the consideration that such immunity represents not only a privilege of a Deputy, but also a guarantee of independence and freedom of performance of its functions by the whole house.

Formal immunity has no permanent character and it expires with the expiry of the mandate.

Inviolability is an integral part of formal immunity. Pursuant to the Constitution, a Deputy cannot be detained without the consent of the Sejm, except in cases when he has been apprehended in the commission of an offence and in which his detention is necessary for securing the proper course of proceedings. Any such detention shall be immediately communicated to the Speaker of the Sejm, who may order an immediate release of the detained person.

The principle of incompatibility may also be considered in two aspects: material and formal.

Such material incompatibility, aimed at preventing corruption of a deputy and protecting him against the threat of conflict of interests, is specified by the Constitution which states that Deputies are not permitted, to the extent specified by statute, to perform any business activity involving any benefit derived from the property of the State Treasury or local government or to acquire such property.

The formal aspect of incompatibility means prohibition against the exercise of the mandate jointly with other State functions or offices. Hence, the mandate of a Deputy cannot be exercised jointly with almost any constitutional State offices, except for those in the Council of Ministers and secretaries of state in the government administration. This exception refers to one of the fundamental principles of the parliamentary system of government which states that "a government emanates from Parliament". The prohibition extends to positions in government administration and in the Chancelleries: of the Sejm, of the Senate and of the President of the Republic, as well as the position of ambassador.

Incompatibility also encompasses persons performing functions of a judge, public prosecutor, officer of the civil service, soldier on active military service or functionary of the police or of the services of State protection. The catalogue of functions indicated by the Constitution may be extended by means of a statute.

The wide scope of rights and duties of Deputies and Senators is determined by the Act of 1996 of the Exercise of the Mandate of a Deputy or Senator. The Act specifies the rights and duties connected with the exercise of the mandate, connected with the activity of the house and its organs, as well as those relating to the individual legal situation of a Deputy or a Senator. As concerns the latter, we should mention (apart from the above discussed immunity and incompatibility) the Deputy's right to receive a parliamentary per diem allowance, the right to free travel by means of public passenger transport throughout the national territory and the right to benefits from the social welfare fund. We should also add that Deputies (Senators) who dedicate themselves exclusively to their parliamentary activity are entitled to the salary which is paid to a Deputy in a lump-sum form.

Among different duties of Deputies connected with the exercise of a parliamentary mandate, we want to stress one, established by the Small

Constitution, and currently having the rank of a statutory norm, namely their obligation to lodge a statement relating to their financial status. A Deputy is obliged to lodge a statement relating his financial assets (including those held within the matrimonial community of the spouses). Such a statement should be lodged immediately after assumption of the mandate and, annually, before 31st of March and 2 months prior to the date of the next elections. The statements are subject to review by a Sejm committee.

The most important tasks and competencies of the Sejm concern, of course, legislation.

The legislative function of Parliament (with the Sejm particularly playing a leading role in this respect) has been strengthened and specially widened by precise and exhaustive enumeration of universally binding acts and by the elimination (except for emergency measures) of acts having the force of statute but issued by another (extra-parliamentary) authority of the State.

The Sejm exerts special influence on issuing universally binding acts, since the legislative function performed by it includes participation in making constitutional amendments, adoption of bills (including the Budgetary Bill) as well as granting consent for the ratification of certain international agreements.

Universally binding provisions of law are, as a principle, created by means of a statute.

The authors of the Constitution do not give any definition of the legislative function, nor do they explain expressly the notion of a statute. Hence, they apply the existing meaning of this concept as understood by the views of established doctrine and practice of the courts. Moreover, the Constitution itself contains elements (in particular, over 120 references to statutes) which makes it possible to construct the characteristics of a statute.

In the light of an analysis of this constitutional material and pursuant to the traditional understanding of the notion of statute, it should be assumed that a statute is an act of Parliament, having a normative character and being of the highest rank in the domestic system of sources of law (although subordinate to the Constitution), with unlimited scope of regulation, and also provided that some matters may be regulated only by means of a statute or only upon an explicit statutory authorization. A statute is an act which takes effect in accordance with a specific procedure whose fundamental elements are determined in the Constitution.

It is exclusively Parliament that may adopt statutes which are legal acts playing a leading role in the system of universally binding sources of law. Statutes are enacted with the participation of both houses of Parliament, however a key role is assigned to the Sejm. With only one exception (consent for the ratification of an international agreement which delegates to an international organization the competence of organs of State authority — given by means of a statute adopted by way of a referendum), the Constitution does not envisage the possibility of enacting statutes by way of a referendum.

The basic law does not provide for issuing of acts (decrees or regulations) having the force of statute by other authorities, although one exception is made for the President of the Republic who may issue — during a period of state of siege — regulations having the force of statute. Such regulations are subject to approval by the Sejm at its next sitting.

A statute has an unlimited scope of application, which means that all matters may be regulated thereby, provided that the normative (general) character of its provisions is maintained and that it is consistent with the Constitution and international agreements ratified upon prior consent granted by statute.

A characteristic feature of statute, rooted in the tradition of Continental constitutionalism, is the principle of the exclusiveness of statutes. This principle requires that certain most important spheres of life of society and the State be governed exclusively by statute. And even if such exclusiveness of statute has not been explicitly specified in the Constitution (which does not mean that it cannot be inferred from its provisions), an analysis of the Constitution, the practice of the Constitutional Tribunal and doctrinal views enable us to distinguish two spheres of affairs reserved for exclusive regulation by means of statute and implementing acts issued strictly on a statutory basis.

The first sphere concerns the legal status of citizens (and similar subjects, e.g. associations, cooperatives etc.), and hence encompasses the sphere of rights and duties of citizens in private law and public law relations. The second sphere relates to the establishment of fundamental elements of the system of organization of the apparatus of State authority, in particular their creation, organization, competencies and mode of functioning.

The Constitution contains provisions concerning the legislative procedure, limiting in some instances the internal autonomy of the houses, but at the same time guaranteeing a democratic method for adopting statutes. The constitutional elements of the legislative procedure include: (a) specification of the holders of the right to introduce bills, including the right of legislative initiative given to 100 000 citizens; (b) making a distinction between two fundamental modes of legislative work, i.e. "ordinary" and urgent; (c) deciding on the number of "readings" of bills; (d) regulation of the right to introduce amendments; (e) specification of formal requirements for passing of statutes and constitutional amendments; (f) deciding on the possibility of withdrawal of a bill and the time limits therefor.

The right to introduce bills belongs to Deputies to the Sejm, and to the Senate, but also to holders of the executive power, namely the President of the Republic and the Council of Ministers. There applies a principle of equal treatment of all bills, which means that bills introduced by the President or the Council of Ministers do not enjoy any preferential treatment in the course of their consideration by Parliament. However, the Council of Ministers may classify a bill introduced by itself as urgent. This results in privileged treatment for such bill, manifested inter alia in the considerable shortening of time periods for consideration and signing of a bill. A decision on whether to subject a bill to an urgent procedure is taken by the government. The Sejm cannot oppose such decision, but it is obviously possible not to pass a bill classified as urgent.

Certain bills, due to their significance, cannot be considered under an urgent procedure. The qualification of a bill as urgent cannot be given to tax bills, bills concerning electoral rights, bills governing the organization and jurisdiction of public authorities and to draft law codes. Such enumeration has an exhaustive character, which means that any bill concerning other matters (except, however, for the Budgetary Bill and a bill on amendment of the Constitution — by virtue of specific constitutional provisions) may be classified by the Council of Ministers as urgent.

As already mentioned, the Constitution also provides for popular legislative initiative, under which a bill may be introduced by a group of 100,000 citizens having the right to vote in elections to the Sejm; there has been no statute regulating this type of legislative initiative.

Substantial limitations on the right of legislative initiative apply to two types of bills: (a) the Budgetary Bill and other bills directly determining the situation of State finances — the initiative in this respect belongs only to the Council of Ministers; (b) a bill on the amendment of the Constitution — the initiative belongs to Deputies (but a higher number of signatures of Deputies supporting it is required than in the case of an ordinary statute), the Senate and the President of the Republic; the Council of Ministers does not have such right.

The Sejm considers bills in three readings (pursuant to the Constitution) divided by work conducted in Sejm committees. The number of readings of a bill increased, as compared to the pre-constitutional period when two readings were applied. Such solution is designed to better arrange Sejm work on bills and to extend the amount of time spent on their consideration and, hence, to improve the course of the legislative process. The extent and depth of legislation in a period of transformation leads to a situation where, in spite of the increased number of readings and intensified use of expert services by the legislators, there is no possibility to avoid defects in the statutes adopted.

The consideration of a bill by the Senate is a necessary stage of the legislative process, however the acceptance by the Senate of the text adopted by the Sejm is required only in the event of amendment to the Constitution; in all other cases, the Sejm may reject proposal made by the Senate.

Cooperation by the Senate in the enactment of a bill consists of, within 30 days of submission of a bill, adopting it without amendment, adopting amendments or resolving on its complete rejection. A resolution of the Senate rejecting a bill, or an amendment proposed in the Senate's resolution, is considered accepted unless the Sejm rejects it by an absolute majority vote with a quorum of half of the constitutional number of Deputies.

After the completion of the procedure in the Senate (or, potentially, for the second time in the Sejm), the Speaker of the Sejm submits an adopted bill to the President of the Republic for signature. The President may apply any of the available procedures for questioning the bill. Firstly, the President may refer it to the Constitutional Tribunal for an adjudication upon its conformity to the Constitution. Secondly, he may use a legislative veto, i.e. refer the bill to the Sejm for its reconsideration. We will return to these two powers when discussing the oversight function of the Sejm. At this point we can only note that under the Small Constitution, the President might use these instruments jointly or separately. In the light of the Constitution (of 1997), such powers may be exercised only separately.

After the completion of the procedure connected with signing of a bill by the President, the President orders the bill to be published in the Journal of Laws [*Dziennik Ustaw*], a promulgation institution envisaged by the Constitution. Statutes, in general, come into force 14 days after their official promulgation, whereas *vacatio legis* is rather a statutory than a constitutional institution.

The Constitution expressly formulates the oversight function as, above all, oversight over the activity of the government. From the point of view of parliamentary oversight exercised within the framework of parliamentary system of government, the relations between Parliament and the President of the Republic as an element of the executive power are of substantial importance.

The function of arbitration is mostly evident in the relations with the legislative and the judicial powers. The President has several competencies connected with the organization and personal shaping of these two powers, making it also possible to check their functioning. Almost all of these competencies may be exercised independently by the President, without a requirement to seek countersignature. The adoption of the concept of the rationalized parliamentary system assumes some degree of active behaviour by the head of state, particularly in a situation where the Sejm has failed to obtain a stable majority.

The election of the President of the Republic is made directly by the Nation, but the houses of Parliament, acting as the National Assembly, may declare a President's permanent incapacity to exercise his duties due to the state of his health or may indict the President before the Tribunal of State, which may be the first step to his dismissal from office.

In accordance with the assumptions of the parliamentary system of government, the President of the Republic is not politically accountable to Parliament, but may only be held constitutionally accountable in the event of violation of law. The President's independence is limited, to some extent, by the requirement of countersignature by the government of his official acts. Nevertheless, the constitutionally specified list of official acts issued by the President, and which require no countersignature of the Prime Minister, is wide.

The President has at his disposal a range of measures applicable in relation to Parliament, including: the legislative initiative, the right to order the holding of a referendum (however, with the consent of the Senate), and certain checks, including legislative veto, the right to question statutes before the Constitutional Tribunal within the framework of *ex post* or *ex ante* (preventive) oversight, as well as the right to dissolve houses of Parliament. The right to dissolve Parliament, already discussed, may be exercised only in situations enumerated by the Constitution.

The President of the Republic, before signing a bill, may impose a legislative veto. The Constitution defines this action as "referring the bill to the Sejm for its reconsideration". Such veto cannot relate to Budgetary Bills, interim budget bills and bills on the amendment of the Constitution. The President may refer a bill to the Sejm for its reconsideration for any reason, either political or legal. Submission of a veto does not require countersignature by the Prime Minister. Nevertheless, the presidential veto has no absolute character, since it may be overridden by the Sejm. Hence, if the said bill is repassed by the Sejm (or overrides a veto) by a three-fifths majority vote with the quorum of a half of the constitutional number of Deputies, then, the President of the Republic is obliged to sign the bill.

Another check, an alternative to a legislative veto, is a presidential application to the Constitutional Tribunal for adjudication of conformity of a bill to the Constitution. Preventive oversight of a bill may be conducted only on request of the President. The President may refer to the Constitutional Tribunal any bill (including a Budgetary Bill), however it is not clear whether this relates also to a constitutional act. Any judgment of the Constitutional Tribunal on the conformity of a bill to the Constitution is of a binding force, the President of the Republic has an absolute obligation to sign a bill which has been judged by the Constitutional Tribunal as conforming to the Constitution. A bill which the Constitutional Tribunal has judged not to be in conformity to the Constitution dies (is not effective), and the legislative procedure must start with introduction of a bill. A judgment of the Constitutional Tribunal finding a bill to be in conformity to the Constitution, made at the stage of preventive (*ex ante*) oversight (i.e. before its signing by the President of the Republic) does not exclude the possibility of repeated questioning of that bill before the Constitutional Tribunal at the stage of *ex post* oversight. We have already mentioned that by application to the Constitutional Tribunal, the President of the Republic gives up his right to a legislative veto, since — contrary to the provisions of the Small Constitution — current constitutional regulations treat these actions as an alternative.

The Council of Ministers is, like the President of the Republic, an organ of the executive power. There exists a political link between it and Parliament, but in fact exclusively the Sejm, since under parliamentary system of government the government has to enjoy permanent confidence of a parliamentary majority. The Council of Ministers and its particular members are politically accountable to the Sejm for their political (parliamentary) activity, and — individually — are also constitutionally accountable before the Tribunal of State.

The Council of Ministers, as an organ of the executive power, is equipped by the Constitution for the most important solutions concerning the conduct of current policy of the State. The Constitution establishes, within the framework of the system of executive power, a presumption of competence on the part of the government, since it states that the Council of Ministers conducts the affairs of State not reserved to other State organs or local government.

The concept of rationalized parliamentarianism, applied by the Constitution, assumes the existence of permanent support to the Cabinet by the majority of the Sejm. The procedures for appointment, recall and accountability of the Council of Ministers has been subjected to this concept.

The Council of Ministers is appointed in accordance with a complex procedure which requires cooperation between the President of the Republic and the majority of the Sejm. The Council of Ministers is appointed by the President who always should take into account the position of the Sejm majority. The Constitution envisages three successive stages (while the Small Constitution provided for five such stages) in the formation of a government. As compared to the Small Constitution, the role of a person designated to the office of Prime Minister has increased. The process of formation of the Council of Ministers includes several stages, established in such a manner so that only a failure at one stage results in moving on to the next.

The government is politically responsible to the Sejm for its activity and may be compelled to resign if it finds itself in conflict with a parliamentary majority. Such disapproval may be expressed by a vote of no confidence. However, the Constitution also envisages a mechanism of a constructive vote of no confidence, designed to stabilize the functioning of a government. Pursuant to the Constitution, the only way to pass a vote of no confidence for the government is connected with a simultaneous appointment of a new Prime Minister. This evident influence of the provisions of the German Constitution (or even correspondence to its provisions) means that the Sejm may achieve the collapse of a government only on the condition that a positive majority, capable of formation a new Cabinet, is established within the Sejm. In the light of the Constitution, there is no possibility of using an ordinary vote of no confidence. At this point, we must admit that the Small Constitution allowed for both forms of a motion requiring a vote of no confidence: ordinary and constructive. For passing a vote of no confidence a simple majority of votes of the constitutional number of Deputies is required, which is a condition more restrictive than the requirement of an absolute majority vote calculated on the basis of the number of Deputies participating in a vote.

Apart from political accountability exercised collectively, the Constitution provides for political accountability of particular ministers (individual responsibility). A motion to pass a vote of no confidence in an individual minister (or other member of government) should be submitted by at least 69 Deputies. This means a more restrictive requirement than in the case of a motion requiring a vote of no confidence in the government as the support of only 46 Deputies is required for the latter. The President of the Republic is obliged to recall a minister in whom a vote of no confidence has been passed by the Sejm by a majority of votes of the constitutional number of Deputies. Submission of subsequent motions of a like kind is subject to various limitations.

Apart from political responsibility, the Prime Minister and members of the Council of Ministers also bear the so-called constitutional accountability for the violation of the Constitution or statutes or for committing of an offence in relation to the office held. Decisions on whether to hold them constitutionally accountable are taken by the Sejm upon a motion submitted by at least 115 Deputies or by the President of the Republic. A resolution in this respect is adopted by the Sejm by a three-fifths majority of the constitutional number of Deputies. The case is heard by the Constitutional Tribunal. It is true that in a parliamentary system of government, constitutional accountability plays an auxiliary role to political responsibility which is exercised directly by an instrument of a vote of no confidence.

Among different forms of oversight exercised by the Sejm over the government, the most important is its control in the course of passing a Budgetary Bill and consideration of a report on the execution of the Budget for the previous year. The complex matters of public finances have been regulated relatively precisely in the Constitution, which was not the case in the previous constitutions.

The Sejm adopts the State budget for a fiscal year and considers a report on the implementation of the Budget by the government and, on the basis of this report, passes an approval for government's accounts, the government is also obliged to present information on the condition of the State debt. There is a new competence for the Sejm, i.e. to consider reports on the achievement of the purposes of monetary policy, submitted to it by the Council for Monetary Policy (an institution unknown to the Small Constitution).

It should also be added that the exclusive subordination of the Supreme Chamber of Control (an independent constitutional body) to the Sejm has been maintained. Thereby, the Sejm has at its disposal a professional and specialized audit institution independent, to a considerable degree, from the government. The specific position of the Supreme Chamber of Control in the system of government consists, on the one hand, in the separation of the Chamber from the structures of government and the President (hence, in fact, from the whole executive power) and, on the other hand, subordinating it to the Sejm. Such subordination manifests itself in both the power of the Sejm to determine the personal composition of the

Chamber and subjecting the substantial activity of the Chamber to the needs of an effective execution of parliamentary (Sejm) supervision. The most important role is played by a professional audit (conducted by the Chamber) during the adoption of the State Budget and consideration of a government's report on its implementation. The Supreme Chamber of Control presents to the Sejm, inter alia, an analysis of the implementation of the State Budget and the purposes of monetary policy, as well as an opinion concerning the vote to accept the accounts for the preceding fiscal year presented by the Council of Ministers.

Among the instruments and measures applied by the Sejm to supervise the government and the whole government administration subordinate thereto, one should mention oversight activity of standing committees of the Sejm and the constitutionally provided possibility of appointing an investigative committee. Traditional forms of individual parliamentary oversight, including interpellations and Deputies' questions have been maintained or even developed. The Constitution distinguishes two types of Deputies' questions: apart from questions being a simplified form of an interpellation it also introduces "questions on current issues" [raised in the course of each sitting of the Sejm], which seems to be the first step on the way to appointment of a separate form of supervisory activity, the so-called "Question Time " (known to parliamentary procedures in many countries).

The supervisory function of the Sejm manifests itself also in its appointment competencies. Such competencies (sometimes exercised together with the Senate) consists in direct appointment and recall of other constitutional organs of the State and persons composing these organs. The role of the Sejm in this respect is fundamental, while that of the Senate is of a limited character.

The Sejm plays a leading role in the appointment and dismissal of the government but, as regards individual members of the Council of Ministers, their appointment in the course of individual changes in the composition of the Council of Ministers takes place without cooperation of the Sejm. However, we must bear in mind that it may, at any time, pass a vote of no confidence in a particular minister, which obliges that member of government to resign from office.

The Sejm chooses individually the entire composition of the Constitutional Tribunal. Judges of the Tribunal are chosen for a term of office of

9 years from amongst persons distinguished by their knowledge of the law. However, the Constitutional Tribunal Act requires from them the qualifications necessary to hold the office of a judge of the Supreme Court. The Senate (like other organs) does not take part in the process of making decisions about filling the posts in the Constitutional Tribunal. The principle of independence of judges makes the judges of the Tribunal practically irremovable during the period of their term of office.

The eighteen members of the Tribunal of State are chosen by the Sejm for the current term of office of the Sejm from amongst those who are not Deputies or Senators. The First President of the Supreme Court is, by virtue of the Constitution, the chairperson of the Tribunal of State.

The Sejm, with the consent of the Senate, appoints the President of the Supreme Chamber of Control for a period of 6 years. Also with the consent of the Senate, the Sejm appoints the Commissioner for Citizens' Rights for a term of 5 years.

Moreover, the Sejm appoints four (out of 9) members of the National Council of Radio Broadcasting and Television.

The Sejm (on request of the President of the Republic) appoints — for a period of 6 years — the President of the National Bank of Poland. It also appoints (in equal numbers, together with the Senate and the President) members of the Council for Monetary Policy.

The Sejm chooses (from amongst its Deputies) several members of the National Council of the Judiciary which is designed to participate in making most important decisions concerning the judiciary and to safeguard the independence of courts and judges. The three branches of power are represented in the National Council of the Judiciary with, however, predominant position for judges and their self-governing bodies.

The Constitution, adopted after a long period of work in Parliament, is a result of a broad social compromise. The Constitution establishes institutions and instruments of the system of government amalgamating 200 years of Poland's constitutional tradition and 500 years of the tradition of Polish Parliament, as well as the experiences of constitutionalism established in modern democracies.

The model of Parliament applied by the Constitution contains these already mentioned attributes typical of the whole Constitution. In this context, we may hope that this Parliament will meet the expectations of the present generation, i.e. to ensure representation of the Nation and effectiveness of its governments — in the framework of a democratic state ruled by law.

References:

D. Chrzanowski, W. Odrowąż-Sypniewski: *Analiza projektów ustaw wniesionych do Sejmu* [*An Analysis of Bills Submitted to the Sejm*], „Przegląd Sejmowy", 1998, No. 2/25.

Z. Czeszejko-Sochacki: *Prawo parlamentarne w Polsce* [*Parliamentary Law in Poland*], Warszawa 1977.

K. Działocha: *Dostosowanie ustawodawstwa do nowej Konstytucji w świetle jej artykułu 236* [*Adjustment of the Legislation to the New Constitution in the Light of its Article 236*], „Państwo i Prawo" 1997, No. 11–12.

L. Garlicki: *Polskie prawo konstytucyjne. Zarys wykładu* [*Polish Constitutional Law. Framework of lecture*], (Second edition), Warszawa 1998.

Komentarz do Konstytucji Rzeczypospolitej Polskiej [*Commentary to the Constitution of the Republic of Poland*], edited by L. Garlicki, Warszawa 1995–1997. (It relates the provisions of the Small Constitution).

P. Sarnecki: *Funkcje i struktura parlamentu według nowej Konstytucji* [*Functions and Structure of Parliament under the New Constitution*], „Państwo i Prawo", 1997, No. 11–12.

W. Skrzydło: *Konstytucja Rzeczypospolitej Polskiej. Komentarz* [*The Constitution of the Republic of Poland. A Commentary*], Kraków 1998.

Założenia ustrojowe, struktura i funkcjonowanie parlamentu [*Basic assumption of the organization, structure and functioning of Parliament*], edited by A. Gwiżdż, Warszawa 1997.

Janusz Trzciński

Professor, University of Wrocław

COURTS AND TRIBUNALS.
A COMMENTARY TO CHAPTER VIII
OF THE CONSTITUTION

1. Chapter VIII of the Constitution, titled "Courts and Tribunals", is divided into three subchapters (Courts, Constitutional Tribunal, Tribunal of State). It is a new chapter, both in respect of concepts and content, which has no equivalent in constitutional provisions existing before the adoption of the Constitution of 2nd April 1997[1]. The constitutional provisions continued in force pursuant to the Small Constitution of 17th October 1992 contained a separate chapter (Chapter 7), titled "The Courts and the System of Public Prosecution", which specified the position of the Supreme Court, the common courts and special courts in the system of government. Tribunals, including the Constitutional Tribunal and the Tribunal of State, were dealt with in another chapter (Chapter 4) jointly with the Supreme Chamber of Control, the Commissioner for Citizens' Rights and the National Council of Radio Broadcasting and Television. That chapter was titled "The Constitutional Tribunal, the Tribunal of State, the Supreme Chamber of Control, the Commissioner for Citizens' Rights, the National Council of Radio Broadcasting and Television". Such joint regulation of the position of the Tribunals in the system of government, in one chapter with the above mentioned institutions resulted from the assumption that State authorities are built on the basis of the principle of unity of State power, but also on a lack of understanding of the basic nature of the Constitutional Tribunal and the Tribunal of State, as well as their distinctions. Changes in the concept of the Constitution as a normative

---

[1] This concerns the provisions of the Constitution of 1952 continued in force pursuant to Article 77 of the Constitutional Act of 17th October 1992 on the mutual relations between the legislative and executive institutions of the Republic of Poland and on local self-government (Dziennik Ustaw of 1992, No. 84, item 426, as further amended).

act, evident after the set up of the Constitutional Tribunal and the Tribunal of State, were also important[2].

2. The fact that the regulation of Courts and Tribunals are contained in a joint chapter seems to evidence that an opinion predominated in the Constitutional Committee, according to which Courts and Tribunals share some features, in a degree justifying their inclusion in a joint branch of power[3]. Pursuant to the provisions of Article 173 which states that "[T]he courts and tribunals shall constitute a separate power and shall be independent of other branches of power", in comparison with Article 10 of the Constitution, the said organs are treated as institutions of the judicial power. Such approach resulted, inter alia, from some similarities among the principles of organization and functioning of Courts and Tribunals, and also from the belief that the provisions of Article 10(1) of the Constitution which states that "[T]he system of government of the Republic of Poland shall be based on the separation of and balance between the legislative, executive and judicial powers" form the basis for construction of a system of State authorities where each constitutional authority is subordinated to one of the three powers specified in Article 10 of the Constitution. Such common regulation of Courts and Tribunals might have also resulted from the lack of proper distinction between the Constitutional Tribunal and the Tribunal of State — which is undoubtedly a court. In my opinion, it is doubtful whether the Constitutional Tribunal, taking into account the basic nature of its activity (i.e. a review of constitutionality of laws), belongs to

---

[2] In this respect see also: J. Trzciński: *Rola konstytucji w procesie demokratycznych przemian ustrojowych* [*The role of the constitution in the process of democratic transformations in the system of government*] (in:) *Sądownictwo konstytucyjne* [*Constitutional Jurisdiction*], fascicle 1, „Studia i Materiały" vol. II, Warszawa 1996, p. 113 et seq.

[3] L. Garlicki: *Polskie prawo konstytucyjne. Zarys wykładu* [*Polish Constitutional Law. Framework of lecture*], second edition, Warszawa 1998, p. 295. He argues that "Even if there are substantial differences between courts and tribunals, it is possible to indicate their common attributes which constitute *differentia specifica* of the judicial power. These include: (1) the principle of independence of judges, which applies to courts and tribunals; (2) the activity of the judicial power is based exclusively on law; (3) settlement of legal matters and solution of disputes arising in the course of application of law or in its making, are entrusted to the judicial power; (4) the functioning of the judicial power is based on formalized procedures which strongly accentuate the principle of contradictoriness."

the judicial power and thus whether it should be regulated jointly with the Courts[4].

3. The position of Courts and Tribunals in the system of government is, above all, determined by Article 173 of the Constitution which states that "[T]he courts and tribunals shall constitute a separate power and shall be independent of other branches of power". The accentuation of the separateness of the judicial power (there is no such provision in respect of the legislative and executive powers) should be understood in the context of Article 10 formulating the separation of powers principle.

The basic nature of the concept of separation of powers adopted by the Constitution does not consist in rigid separation of powers, i.e. their division , but "is based on the separation of and balance between the legislative, executive and judicial powers".

In the light of the current Constitution, such formula is true in respect of the relation between the legislative and the executive powers. Separation of power, i.e. separation of organizational structures and separateness of functions are accompanied by adequate links, whose basic nature consists in co-operation of powers and their mutual checks. This is manifested in the process of making law as well as in the process of functioning of State organs, in particular in relations between the Sejm, the Senate, the President of the Republic and the Council of Ministers. The examples include the institution of the legislative veto and countersigning of the acts of the President.

In this respect, the relation of the legislative and executive powers to the judicial power seems to be different[5]. Here, separation of power is

---

[4] See J. Trzciński: *Czy Trybunał Konstytucyjny jest władzą sądowniczą? [Is the Constitutional Tribunal an organ of the judicial power?]*, „Prawo i Życie", 10th January 1998, as well as critical remarks on my position by W. Sokolewicz: *Czy rak może być rybą a Trybunał sądem? [Can a lobster be a fish and the Tribunal be a court?]* (in:) *Państwo prawa. Administracja. Sądownictwo. [A State ruled by law. Administration. Courts].* The work dedicated to Professor Janusz Łętowski. Warszawa 1999, p. 243 et seq.

[5] In this respect, see very interesting remarks by E. Łętowska and J. Łętowski: *Co wynika z sądów dla konstytucyjnej zasady podziału władz [What are the consequences of courts for the constitutional principle of separation of powers]*, (in:) *Konstytucja i gwarancje jej przestrzegania [The Constitution and Guarantees of its Observance]*, Warszawa 1996, and also L. Garlicki: *Polskie prawo konstytucyjne [Polish Constitutional Law]*, first edition, Warszawa 1997, p. 101–102.

understood, above all, as division or rigid separation of power. Article 173, stating that courts and tribunals are a separate power excludes such a standpoint. Emphasis on the separateness of the judicial power in this context is based on doctrinal concepts of the division of power. The second element (specified in Article 10 of the Constitution) typical of the separation of power principle, i.e. a balance in relations between the judicial power and the legislative and executive powers is limited to the obligation of the judicial power to "function on the basis of, and within the limits of, the law" (Article 7) and to be subjected "to the Constitution and statutes" (Article 178(1) of the Constitution).

The separation discussed in Article 173 should be understood in its organizational context, which means that the judicial power is a separated, autonomous organizational structure existing within the system of State authorities, and also in its functional context, which means that the course of functioning of the judicial power is not affected by the legislative and executive powers, which fact guarantees the independence of the judicial power.

Courts and Tribunals are not only separate, but also independent from other branches of power. The independence of the courts is also provided for by Article 45(1) of the Constitution and in Article 186(2) of the Constitution as a distinct attribute, but in the context of Article 173 it should be interpreted jointly with the attribute of separateness. Moreover, an emphasis should be put on the fact that Article 173 does not treat courts and tribunals as "independent" in general, but rather as independent from other branches of government, i.e. the legislative and executive powers. In this context, the notion of independence of courts and tribunals supplements the notion of their separateness, as one of the attributes of the principle of separation of powers considered in the context of the relation: the judicial power — the legislative and executive powers.

Such understanding of the concept of independence (also in the light of Article 173 of the Constitution) has been stressed in the literature[6].

---

[6] See Z. Czeszejko-Sochacki: *Prawo do sądu w świetle Konstytucji Rzeczypospolitej Polskiej* [*The right of access to courts in the light of the Constitution of the Republic of Poland*], „Państwo i Prawo", fascicle 11–12, pp. 98–100, as well as A. Murzynowski, A. Zieliński: *Ustrój wymiaru sprawiedliwości w przyszłej konstytucji* [*The Structure of Administration of Justice in the Future Constitution*], „Państwo i Prawo", 1992, fascicle 9, p. 3.

The above — outlined attitude to the understanding of the concept of independence of courts, as applied by Article 173 of the Constitution, does not exclude other ways of interpreting this concept as found in Article 45(1), Article 178(3) and Article 186(2) of the Constitution. For example, in an adjudication of the Constitutional Tribunal (K.3/98) the notion of independence of the courts is used as a synonym of independence of the judiciary[7].

4. Article 175 of the Constitution entrusts the administration of justice to the Supreme Court, the common courts, administrative courts and military courts. The new Constitution abolished the previously-existing possibility of establishing special courts. This means that in a situation where the legislator would like to subject a particular scope of matters to the jurisdiction of the courts, he should do so by attributing it to one of the courts specified in the Constitution[8]. The Constitution permits the establishing of extraordinary courts or summary (i.e. simplified) procedures only during a time of war.

The Constitution does not specify the structures of common courts. Pursuant to the Act — the Structure of Common Courts Act — they include appellate courts, provincial courts and district courts[9]. The Constitution does not distinguish the structures of administrative courts which, up to date and according to the Act on the Chief Administrative Court, is a single-stage proceeding[10]. This is inconsistent with the provisions of Article 176(2) which states that court proceedings shall have at least two stages. However, by virtue of Article 236(2) of the Constitution, this inconsistency may last for no longer than 5 years from the coming into force of the Constitution.

---

[7] See: Orzecznictwo Trybunału Konstytucyjnego. Zbiór Urzędowy [Judgments of the Constitutional Tribunal. An Official Collection], No. 4, 1998, p. 334.

[8] As for example when establishing the Lustration Court, the legislator entrusted its functions to the Appellate Court in Warsaw.

[9] See: Article 1 §2 of the Act of 29th June 1985 the Act — Law on the Structure of Common Courts (consolidated text: Dziennik Ustaw of 1994, No. 7, item 25 as amended). Provincial courts replaced voivodship courts pursuant to the Act of 18th December 1998 on the Amendment to the Act — Law on the Structure of Common Courts (Dziennik Ustaw, No. 74, item 368 as amended).

[10] See: the Act of Chief Administrative Court (Dziennik Ustaw No. 74, item 368 as amended).

The structure of military courts is not regulated in the Constitution, but is dealt with by the Act on the Structure of Military Courts. The Act establishes provincial courts and garrison courts (Article 3 § 1)[11].

According to a principle applied by the Constitution, the common courts implement the administration of justice concerning all matters save for those statutorily reserved to other courts, i.e. the Supreme Court, administrative courts and military courts.

From the comparison of Article 173 of the Constitution (''The courts and tribunals shall constitute a separate power and shall be independent of other branches of power'') and Article 175(1) (''The administration of justice in the Republic of Poland shall be implemented by the Supreme Court, the common courts, administrative courts and military courts'') and Article 176(1) (''Court proceedings shall have at least two stages'') it should be inferred that the notion of court used in chapter VIII relates only to courts implementing administration of justice and, hence, to courts in the meaning of exercising judicial power. Therefore, disciplinary courts of various type are not courts in this meaning of the word[12]. Moreover, the conclusion that only courts may implement administration of justice results also from an analysis of the cited decisions. The principle, known to Polish constitutional law before the adoption of the Constitution, providing for participation of the citizenry in the administration of justice has been maintained (Article 182 of the Constitution).

5. Judges are appointed for an indefinite period by the President of the Republic on the recommendation of the National Council of the Judiciary (Article 179 of the Constitution). Specific procedures for nomination of candidates and conditions required from candidates for judges of the courts referred to in Article 175 are regulated by the respective Acts defining the structure of common courts, military courts, the Chief Administrative Court and the Supreme Court.

The status of a judge is governed, above all, by Article 178(1) which formulates the principle of independence of judges — ''Judges, within the

---

[11] See: the Act of 21ˢᵗ August 1997 — Law on the Structure of Military Courts (Dziennik Ustaw No. 117, item 753).

[12] In this respect, see P. Przybysz: *Prawo do sądu w sprawach dyscyplinarnych [The Right of Access to Court in Disciplinary Matters]*, „Państwo i Prawo", fascicle 8, 1998, in particular p. 75–76.

exercise of their office, shall be independent and subject only to the Constitution and statutes." Independence of judges means their freedom from dependence on the parties to the proceedings and on public authorities. Its purpose is to make it possible for a judge to take an impartial decision, consistent with his/her conscience. Limitations on such independence are imposed by statutes in force and by the Constitution.

In its various provisions, the Constitution provides guarantees of the principle of independence that is thereby established[13]. These guarantees include:

a) appointment of a judge for an indefinite period (Article 179 of the Constitution) which in practice means permanent office (i.e. until age of retirement at 65 years);

b) irremovability of a judge (Article 180 of the Constitution), recall of a judge from office may only occur by virtue of a court judgment and only in those instances prescribed in statute;

c) on the same terms (Article 180 of the Constitution) a judge may be suspended from office or removed to another bench or position against his/her will[14];

d) judicial immunity (Article 181 of the Constitution) — "A judge shall not, without prior consent granted by a court specified by statute, be held criminally responsible nor deprived of liberty. A judge shall be neither detained nor arrested, except for cases when he has been apprehended in the commission of an offence and in which his detention is necessary for securing the proper course of proceedings";

e) political neutrality of a judge (Article 178(3) of the Constitution) — "A judge shall not belong to a political party, a trade union or perform public activities incompatible with the principles of independence of the courts and judges";

f) accountability before disciplinary courts for a breach of the duties of a judge;

g) adequate remuneration consistent with the dignity of their office and the scope of their duties (Article 178(2)).

---

[13] See more about this issue, L. Garlicki: *Polskie prawo konstytucyjne* [*Polish Constitutional Law*], 1998, p. 306–307.

[14] It is worth noting that no other profession has such guarantees.

6. The Constitution, like other constitutions of the European countries, provides for the existence of a National Council of the Judiciary, as an organ which "shall safeguard the independence of courts and judges"[15]. Any classification of this organ from the point of view of the separation of power principle is impossible. It should be assumed that it is a collegial organ of a structure dominated by judges, but composed also of representatives of the legislative and executive powers. It safeguards the independence and separateness of the judicial power[16].

The National Council of the Judiciary is composed of:

1) the First President of the Supreme Court, the Minister of Justice, the President of the Chief Administrative Court and an individual appointed by the President of the Republic;

2) 15 judges chosen from amongst the judges of the Supreme Court, common courts, administrative courts and military courts;

3) 4 members chosen by the Sejm from amongst its Deputies and 2 members chosen by the Senate from amongst its Senators.

The term of office of the National Council of the Judiciary is 4 years.

Detailed competencies of the National Council of the Judiciary are specified in the Act on the National Council of the Judiciary[17]. These include in particular:

1) consideration of candidacies for the offices of Judge of the Supreme Court, of the Chief Administrative Court, of common courts and military courts, and submitting to the President of the Republic recommendations for their appointment;

2) consideration of and taking decisions on motions concerning the removal of a Judge to another bench for reasons connected with the Judge;

3) determination of the number of members of the Disciplinary Court and the High Disciplinary Court and indication of the number of members of disciplinary courts elected, respectively, by general assemblies of judges of the Supreme Court, the Chief Administrative Court, a con-

---

[15] The National Council of the Judiciary was introduced to the Polish constitutional law as a result of the amendment made in December 1989.

[16] See: L. Garlicki: *Polskie prawo konstytucyjne* [*Polish Constitutional Law*], p. 303.

[17] The Act of 20th December 1989 on the National Council of the Judiciary (Dziennik Ustaw No. 73, item 435 as amended), Article 2.

ference of general assembles of judges of appellate courts, a conference of representatives of general assemblies in voivodship courts, and by the Assembly of Judges of Military Courts;

4) granting consent for continued holding of an office by a Judge who has attained the age of 65 years;

5) expression of its opinion about rules of judicial ethics;

6) hearing of information provided by the First President of the Supreme Court, the Minister of Justice, the President of the Chief Administrative Court and chairman of the Higher Disciplinary Court about the activities of courts and expression of their view on the condition of the judges;

7) expression of viewpoint on the proposals of changes in the structure of courts, and in other matters relating to the conditions of their functioning;

8) acquainting itself with normative acts concerning the judicature;

9) provision of opinion on programmes of training for apprentices, the scope and methods of conducting the judicial examinations and establishing their results, as well as principles of assessment of work of assistant judges;

10) expressing opinions in matters concerning judges and courts, which have been submitted for deliberation of the Council by the President of the People's Republic of Poland, other State organs and also by general assemblies of judges."

7. The present Constitution corresponds in its basic solutions with the previously existing model of review of the constitutionality of law.

Pursuant to the provisions of the Constitution, the Constitutional Tribunal performs four major functions:

a) adjudicating on the conformity of the law to the Constitution (Article 188(1)–(3) of the Constitution);

b) adjudicating on the conformity to the Constitution of the purposes or activities of political parties (Article 188(4) of the Constitution);

c) settling disputes over authority between central constitutional organs of the State (Article 189 of the Constitution);

d) adjudicating on complaints concerning infringements of constitutional rights, as specified in Article 188(5) and Article 79 of the Constitution.

Under provisions of the Constitutional Tribunal Act (Article 4)[18], the Tribunal also submits to competent law-making organs observations concerning ascertained formal inconsistencies and gaps in the law, removal of which is necessary to insure the integrity of the legal system. This is the so-called indicative function.

The basic function of the Constitutional Tribunal is to adjudicate regarding the conformity of the law to the Constitution (Article 188(1)–(3)) in the course of *ex post* review. This notion, pursuant to the Constitution, includes following three situations:

1) adjudicating regarding the conformity of statutes and international agreements to the Constitution[19];
2) adjudicating regarding the conformity of a statute to ratified international agreements whose ratification required prior consent granted by statute;
3) adjudicating regarding the conformity of legal provisions issued by central State authorities to the Constitution, ratified international agreements and statutes.

The following may make application regarding the above mentioned matters:

a) in any instance — the President of the Republic, the Speaker of the Sejm, the Speaker of the Senate, the Prime Minister, 50 Deputies, 30 Senators, the First President of the Supreme Court, the President of the Chief Administrative Court, the Public Prosecutor-General, the President of the Supreme Chamber of Control and the Commissioner for Citizens' Rights,
b) the National Council of the Judiciary, to the extent that a challenged act relates to the independence of courts and judges (Article 191(1)(2));
c) local councils (i.e. councils of appropriate units of local self-administration — a commune, a district or a voivodship), national organs of trade unions and national authorities of employers and professional organizations, as well as churches and other religious organizations, if the challenged normative act relates to matters relevant to the scope of their activity.

---

[18] The Constitutional Tribunal Act was newly adopted after the passing of the Constitution. See: the Constitutional Tribunal Act of 1st August 1997 (Dziennik Ustaw No. 102, item 643).

[19] The question which international agreements require prior consent granted by statute is governed by Article 89(1) of the Constitution.

In this connection, the Constitutional Tribunal Act provides for preliminary qualification of matters submitted to the Constitutional Tribunal by the subjects specified in sub-para. a.

Proceeding for ascertaining the conformity of the law to the Constitution may also be initiated in the form of a question of law. This institution has existed in Poland since the establishment of the Constitutional Tribunal. Article 193 states that "[A]ny court may refer a question of law to the Constitutional Tribunal as to the conformity of a normative act to the Constitution, ratified international agreements or statute, if the answer to such question of law will determine an issue currently before such court".

The list of subjects authorized to initiate the proceeding, compared to that existing before the coming into force of the Constitution, was extended and the possibility to formulate questions as to the conformity of a normative act to ratified international agreements was introduced.

8. The Constitution introduces a constitutional complaint not only as a means to initiate the proceeding to examine the constitutionality of a normative act, but also as a measure for protection of freedoms and rights granted to citizens. Pursuant to Article 79 of the Constitution, "[I]n accordance with principles specified by statute, everyone whose constitutional freedoms or rights have been infringed, shall have the right to appeal to the Constitutional Tribunal for its judgment on the conformity to the Constitution of a statute or another normative act upon which basis a court or organ of public administration has made a final decision on his freedoms or rights or on his obligations specified in the Constitution".

Relevant provisions of the Constitutional Tribunal Act, particularly those governing the adjudication regarding constitutional complaints (Articles 46–52) correspond with the above cited provision of the Constitution.

According to the Polish model of constitutional complaint, it concerns the unconstitutionality of a legislative act, on the basis of which a judgment or a final decision has been made. A decision ascertaining the unconstitutionality of a normative act, made in the course of consideration of question of law, is a basis for re-opening proceedings, or for quashing the decision or other settlement in a manner and on principles specified in provisions applicable to the given proceedings.

9. Apart from *ex post* review, the Constitution (Article 122(3)) provides for preventive review of the constitutionality of the law. It is only the President of the Republic who can submit a relevant application. His application to the Constitutional Tribunal is, in a sense, an alternative to the exercise of his right to refuse to sign a bill[20]. In contrast to previously existing provisions, in the event that only particular provisions of a bill have been found to be unconstitutional, the new Constitution allows the President of the Republic, after seeking the opinion of the Speaker of the Sejm, to sign the bill with the omission of those provisions considered as being in non-conformity to the Constitution. In such event, the judgment of the Constitutional Tribunal must contain a statement that those unconstitutional provisions are not inseparably connected with the whole bill, i.e. that their omission will not affect the application of the bill (Article 122(4)). This is a pragmatic solution which does not frustrate the purposes of Parliament, nor does it paralyse public life of the State in the situation where such regulation is necessary. Before the coming into force of the Constitution, a judgment of the Constitutional Tribunal on the constitutionality of a bill, made under the procedure of preventive review, prevented the President from signing the bill.

10. Judgments of the Constitutional Tribunal are of universally binding application and are final (Article 190(1)). This principle departs from the previous one according to which judgments of the Constitutional Tribunal on the unconstitutionality of statutes might be rejected by a two-thirds majority vote in the presence of at least half of the constitutional number of Deputies. There is, however, an exception to this general rule specified in Article 239(1) which states that, within 2 years of the day on which the Constitution comes into force (i.e. from 17th October 1997 to 17th October 1999), judgments of the Constitutional Tribunal on the non-conformity to the Constitution of statutes adopted before its coming into force are not final and that the Sejm may reject them under the existing principles by a two-thirds majority vote in the presence of at least half of the constitutional number of Deputies. This provision does not concern only judgments issued in response to questions of law submitted to the Constitutional Tribunal. *Ratio legis* of the above mentioned exception is

---

[20] Under the Small Constitution of 1992, the President of the Republic could enjoy both prerogatives, a right of veto and then, a complaint to the Constitutional Tribunal.

inexplicable. Its inexplicability (except for political reasons) is particularly manifested in the situation where the Sejm would decide to reject a judgment of the Constitutional Tribunal, made as a result of a constitutional complaint, and thereby exclude the citizen's possibility to claim his rights, as well as in the situation where the Sejm would decide on the conclusion of a judgment which refers to an international agreement binding upon the State[21].

There is a principle according to which a judgment of the Constitutional Tribunal takes effect from the day of its publication (in the official publication in which the original normative act was promulgated, e.g. *Dziennik Ustaw* [Journal of Laws]). Pursuant to the existing principles, such day is the day of publication of *Dziennik Ustaw*. However, the Constitution prescribes exceptions to this principle (Article 190(3)). The Constitutional Tribunal may specify another date for the end of the binding force of a normative act. It may not exceed 18 months in relation to a statute or 12 months in relation to any other normative act. In each instance of change in the time limit of the expiry of a normative act, where such judgment has financial consequences not provided for in the Budget Act, the Constitutional Tribunal specifies a date for the expiry of the binding force of the normative act, after seeking the opinion of the Council of Ministers.

11. The Constitutional Tribunal is composed of 15 judges chosen individually by the Sejm for a term of office of 9 years from amongst persons distinguished by their knowledge of the law (Article 194)[22]. Moreover, the Constitutional Tribunal Act specifies that only a person who possesses the necessary qualifications to hold the office of the judge of the Supreme Court or the Chief Administrative Court may be a judge of the Constitutional Tribunal. Candidates for the office of a judge are nominated by at least 50 Deputies or by the Presidium [the Bureau] of the Sejm. A resolution on the election requires an absolute majority of the votes cast in the presence of at least half of the total number of Deputies. As concerns the term of office and composition of the Constitutional Tribunal, an

---

[21] See, (in:) *Wyroki sędziów czy posłów* [*Judgments made by Judges or by Deputies*], „Prawo i Życie", 6th December 1997.

[22] Prior to the passing of the new constitution, it was composed of 12 judges. The extension of competencies of the Tribunal required the extension of its composition.

important principle is applied. According to this principle, judges are elected individually, which means that *en bloc* voting for a group of candidates for the office of a judge is not permitted. Apart from obvious advantages, such solution has a defect, since a majority of parliamentarians may exercise (even if only for a short time) discretion in shaping the composition of the Constitutional Tribunal.

The President and Vice-President of the Constitutional Tribunal are appointed by the President of the Republic from amongst candidates proposed by the General Assembly of the Judges of the Constitutional Tribunal. Previously, they were appointed by the Sejm.

The legal status of a Judge of the Constitutional Tribunal is established by the Constitution on the same principles as that concerning judges of the Supreme Court, of the Chief Administrative Court and of common courts[23]. There is, however, a difference: judges of the Constitutional Tribunal, in the exercise of their office, are subject only to the Constitution (judges of other courts — to the Constitution and to statutes).

12. The organization of the Constitutional Tribunal, as well as the mode of proceedings before it, are specified by an appropriate statute adopted after the coming into force of the new Constitution (see: footnote 18) and Resolution of the General Assembly of the Judges of the Constitutional Tribunal dated 22nd October 1997 on the Rules of Procedure of the Constitutional Tribunal (Official Gazette of the Republic of Poland *Monitor Polski*, No. 81, item 788, as amended in 1998, No. 11, item 191).

13. Besides courts and the Constitutional Tribunal Chapter VIII of the Constitution regulates the position of the Tribunal of State in the system of government. The Tribunal of State was known to Polish pre-war history[24] and was again introduced to the Polish system of law in 1982[25].

The Tribunal of State is an organ to which persons holding offices specified in the Constitution[26] are constitutionally accountable for viola-

---

[23] See: section 5 of this study.

[24] See: M. Pietrzak: *Odpowiedzialność konstytucyjna w Polsce [Constitutional Accountability in Poland]*, Warszawa 1992.

[25] See: Constitutional Act of 1982, Dziennik Ustaw No. 11, item 83 and the Act of 6th March 1982 on the Tribunal of State, a consolidated text Dziennik Ustaw of 1993, No. 38, item 172, as amended.

[26] Pursuant to Article 198(1), these include: the President of the Republic, the Prime Minister and members of the Council of Ministers, the President of the National Bank of

tions of the Constitution or of a statute committed by them within their office or within its scope (Article 198), i.e. for committing a "constitutional delict". Where a constitutional delict satisfies the features of a criminal act, and the resolution on holding a person accountable has deemed it advisable to do so, such persons may also be held criminally responsible. However, in the absence of a relevant resolution, it is possible to conduct criminal proceedings against these persons (except for the President of the Republic) before a common court.

The right to indict the President of the Republic is exclusively vested in the National Assembly, and a motion to this end may be submitted by at least a quarter of the total number of members of the Sejm and Senate[27]. The right to indict other persons constitutionally accountable to the Tribunal of State is exclusively vested in the Sejm, upon the motion of the President of the Republic, an investigative committee or Deputies, being at least 115 in number.

The Tribunal of State shall be composed of a chairperson, two deputy chairpersons and 16 members chosen by the Sejm for the current term of office of the Sejm from amongst those who are not Deputies or Senators. The deputy chairpersons of the Tribunal and at least one half of the members of the Tribunal shall possess the qualifications required to hold the office of judge. The First President of the Supreme Court shall be chairperson of the Tribunal of State. The members of the Tribunal of State, within the exercise of their office as judges of the Tribunal, shall be independent and subject only to the Constitution and statutes.

The fact that the Tribunal of State may impose penalties prescribed by penal statutes, i.e. to make judgments as a criminal court, justifies the view that the Polish Tribunal of State may be treated as one of the organs of administration of justice and in this meaning it is, obviously, a court.

Poland, the President of the Supreme Chamber of Control, members of the National Council of Radio Broadcasting and Television, persons to whom the Prime Minister has granted powers of management over a ministry, and the Commander-in-Chief of the Armed Forces. Deputies and Senators are also constitutionally accountable to the Tribunal of State (Article 198(2) to extent specified in Article 107 which states that "Deputies shall not be permitted, to the extent specified by statute, to perform any business activity involving any benefit derived from the property of the State Treasury or local self-government or to acquire such property (Article 107(1)).

[27] See: Article 2(4) of the Act on the Tribunal of State.

Andrzej Bałaban

Professor, University of Szczecin

UNITY AND DECENTRALIZATION OF THE STATE

The principle of the unity of the State belongs to the very essence of the phenomenon of the State, and its different manifestations result from historical circumstances and from the legal model of specific State organization. From the formal point of view, the unity of a State is given by the form of the unity of the State machine and the legal system that protects the national system of values and State symbols. The unity of a functioning State may be ensured by different methods, which is evident from the typology of States and forms of government. Nowadays, however, the unity of a State is relatively seldom ensured by the use of the method of centralization of power. Authoritarian systems of different origin have not provided any effective way of strengthening a State, either in its internal aspect — this led to a processes of alienation of the State power and its rejection by the Nation, nor in its external context existing currently on the basis of international democratic standards. The contemporary, universally accepted model of the State rests its power and unity on the participation of citizens in government and international cooperation. The principle of subsidiarity, strongly accentuated in documents establishing the European Union, assumes that, wherever needed and possible, the processes by which a State is governed should be decentralized and socialized.

Every modern State has its own experiences concerning centralization or decentralization of its power and authority. In Poland's case, very complex historical experiences and state-building processes have developed today's model of State unity based on a decentralized model contained in the new Constitution of 2nd April 1997.

Poland's history is a very interesting process. As concerns State power, this process was characterized — during the feudal period — by gradual limitations imposed on the king's authority and the creation of a system of class privileges and grant of powers to representatives of the estates and to the Sejm. This model had proved its uselessness by the 18th century, in the circumstances of centralization of State power in countries neighbouring Poland, i.e. Russia, Austria and Prussia, leading to the annexation of a part of Poland's territory by these countries in 1772 in the so-called first partition. The attempts to improve Poland's system of government took the form of a struggle for a new constitution. That constitution, adopted finally on 3rd May 1791, was the first written constitution in Europe[1]. It was based on the ideals of the French Revolution and attempted to build a new civil society and new system of government. However, it was adopted too late and its provisions were, in all probability, too radical. The hopes that it inspired threatened Poland's neighbours, leading soon to the second and third (final) partitions, respectively in 1793 and 1795. Until 1918 Poland was deprived of its sovereignty and the Polish Nation appeared in the history of the invaders as a very insubordinate element. It was only in circumstances of military defeat and weakening of these states that Poland was able to regain its independence in 1918. Soon thereafter, on 21st March 1921, the so-called March Constitution was adopted. It was based on a collection of the then most democratic principles of a system of government. Poland became a parliamentary republic. However, serious economic and political problems of that time were resolved (as elsewhere in Europe) by methods of concentration of power. As a consequence of gradual adjustments of the system of government, the so-called April Constitution (dated 23rd April 1935) was adopted. The April Constitution was based on the principle of unity of State power concentrated in the President of the Republic but who bore neither political nor legal responsibility. After Poland's collapse as the result of German, and Soviet, invasion of September and October 1939, the April Constitution became a legal basis for the functioning of a government in exile in London — existing until 1991, when the State insignia was handed over to Lech Wałęsa, after his election as President in a general election.

After the expulsion of the German troops by the Red Army, for many years the shape of the Polish State remained but an imitation of the Soviet model. Constitutional documents alone do not provide a clear picture of that

---

[1] Cf. R. Ludwikowski, W.F. Fox: *The Beginning of the Constitutional Era*, Washington 1993.

system, since it was based on extralegal mechanisms used by the communist party to rule the country and on police means of oppression. Initially, transitional constitutional documents referred to "democratic principles of the constitution of 1921" and refused the "fascist constitution of 1935". On 22nd July 1952, a new constitution was adopted. It consistently avoided any provisions accentuating the principles of concentration of power. However, in the doctrine of law, the leading principle of the Constitution was defined (gradually but perceptibly) as a "unity of State power" understood as a centrally planned system, regulated, to a high degree, by extralegal means. Under this system, the State organs including Parliament and local councils pursued the current aims of programmes determined by the party executive thereby pushing legal considerations into the background. Subsequent modifications and adjustments of communist doctrine built a new concept of "developed socialist society" with the appearance of a democracy[2].

The inefficiency of Poland's economic system and the failure of its communist ideology, evident particularly on 13th December 1981 at the time of the introduction of the state of siege, combined with the growing strength of a political opposition supported by a working class disposing of the strike "weapon", led to the "Round Table" contract of 5th April 1989 and, then, to the constitutional reforms of 29th December 1989 and 19th October 1992. They transformed the system of government, above all, by changing the catalogue of fundamental principles of the Constitution, now seriously treated and implemented: thus -

(1) the principle of the "unity" of the ideological State was replaced by the principle of a democratic state ruled by law;

(2) the principle of the class nature of society was replaced by the principle of the Nation's sovereignty;

(3) the monopoly of the communist party was replaced by the principle of ideological pluralism and freedom to form political parties;

(4) local government was considered as a basic instrument of decentralization of the State;

(5) monopoly of State ownership in basic sectors of the economy was replaced by a dominant position accorded to private property and economic liberalism;

---

[2] Cf. A. Bałaban: *Theorie moderner sozialistscher Verfassungen*, „Jahrbuch des Offentlichen Rechts der Gegenwart" 37/1988, Tübingen.

(6) the system of State organs subordinate to Parliament was subjected to the principle of separation of [the three] powers.

These and several other changes have produced a new picture of the State and the law[3]. On the basis of these principles, work on a new constitution was undertaken, however, they are discussed in a separate part of this book.

In the Constitution of 2nd April 1997, the principle of unity of the State did not find explicit legal regulation. Its most direct manifestation can be found in Article 3 of the Constitution which states that "the Republic of Poland shall be a unitary State". In its Preamble and Article 1, the Constitution puts specific solidarity accents on the national unity of society, stating that "the Republic of Poland shall be the common good of all its citizens". On grounds of experience with centralization of power in the communist system and in comparison with the episode of government introduced by the April Constitution of 1935, accentuating the unity of State power in its formal and legal aspect was not considered an acceptable solution. Further development of the principle of State unity, as such, does not seem to be necessary in a situation where the protection of such unity is a natural consequence of State organization and a natural consequence of a centrally enacted system of law — almost exclusively by parliamentary methods. Protection of State unity appears as a permanent element of the tasks of all constitutional bodies. This is most evident in respect of the office of a President as "the supreme representative of the Republic of Poland and the guarantor of the continuity of State authority..." (Article 126 of the Constitution). In relation to law-making activity, determining the relations between Poland and international society and international law, as well as management of the national economy (particularly by means of a Budgetary Act) the unity of the State is protected, respectively, by both houses of the Polish Parliament. This aim is also realized by the Council of Ministers which determines international and socio-economic policy, and by the organs of administration of justice and enforcement of law, which pursue a uniform policy of application of the law in accordance with a system of basic constitutional values.

---

[3] Cf. A. Bałaban: *Developing a new Constitute for Poland.* „Cleveland State Law Review", 3/1993.

Legal elements guaranteeing the unity of State are dispersed in the framework of legal regulation in a concealed way, so to speak, however evident those norms are that are devoted to different forms of State decentralization and "socialization" of the State power. They are visible also because of their relative legal novelty. By this, I mean the newness of their actual legal expression, since concepts of decentralization in legal doctrine — if only at the level of academic study — were continuously present during the period of communist rule.

Fundamental spheres of State activity, in which the problem of decentralization has appeared, include both the political and economic system, at the level of forms of local representation and new forms of public administration, along with regulation of the economy and development of supplementary forms of local legislation. Decentralization is not always achieved by way of establishing new institutions. We can observe other forms of "socialization" of power by its transfer to professional self-governing bodies or even by withdrawal of the State from certain types of activity, and such lacunae are filled by social activity that is not licensed, but rather registered in a form of partnership, association, society etc. Another problem, discussed in a separate chapter of this book, is connected with the interference of international law and international organizations in the fields of activity traditionally reserved to the exclusive jurisdiction of the State in the shape of its central organs.

As regards the traditional issue of the political system, the most important change relates to political pluralism. The ease of creation of political parties, their multitude and diversity has resulted in many law-making initiatives and has become a source for the work of State organs. However an abundance of political parties can produce the problem of excessive political disintegration of society and, above all, disintegration of representative bodies. This has led to adjustments in electoral law, including the use of electoral thresholds and national lists. Proposals are often made to replace proportional representation by a majority system. Moreover, experience of the mutual relations between ruling and opposition parties has led to adjustments in the parliamentary rules of procedure and parliamentary practice aimed at an improved functioning in political mechanisms. More problems have been caused by increasing politicization of the activities of State administration, par-

239

ticularly in the circumstances of frequent changes of government. Therefore, we must consider as particularly valuable those provisions of the new constitution that guarantee the non-political character of the judicial power or those which introduce a corps of civil servants to the organs of government administration (Article 153). There is also a growing awareness that there is no need for political bias in the activities of the President. Another irritating feature is the type of politician who seeks advantage from political divisions and raking up old faults, but who lacks creativity and social usefulness at any level of authority. However, this model of behaviour is subject to evolving political habits and political culture.

It was a real shock for the system of government, directly influencing the issue of unity and decentralization of the State function, to experience a complete shift in the principles underlying the operation of the economic system. Under communism there was a concentration of all means of production in the hands of the State, along with centralization of economic decisions, and the dominance of ideology replaced the calculation of economic effectiveness, as well as guaranteeing the monopoly of State ownership. The reforms of 1989 and 1992 subverted this system and introduced freedom of economic activity and gave a predominant position to private ownership in the context of a market economy. Privatization of the economy and making it accessible to international markets became a principal slogan in this respect. The Constitution of 1997 makes certain adjustments to this system by introducing the principle of a social market economy (Article 20). The new Chapter X of the Constitution, titled "Public Finances", apart from formulating elementary principles of financial management, also introduces the institutions of the National Bank of Poland and the State Treasury which represents State assets.

In addition to the above, briefly-presented historical, political and economic implications, the problem of the unity and decentralization of the State is determined, above all, by the scope of competencies of State power and forms of their exercise. The departure from a centralized and bureaucratic model of the State is accomplished through the process of socialization of central authority and the process of decentralization of its powers. This is conducted on grounds of a new philosophy of thinking about the State, rightly expressed in the preamble to the constitution by the application of the principle of subsidiarity as a concept of a State currently obliged to "strengthen the powers of citizens and their communities".

The contemporary shape of State unity consists in a different model of the exercise of powers, even those which completely belong to State organs, because such organs are chosen in accordance with democratic procedures and are subjected to a diverse social supervision (by the press, mass media, citizens' initiatives, referenda, etc.). The principle of separation of power (into three branches) has made it possible to prevent subordination of the State machine by any group of State organs. In this state of affairs, the unity of State is, above all, manifested in unity of the law, and particularly by a constitution prevailing throughout its framework. The dominant position of the constitution is protected by the principle of its direct application, by the citizen's right of constitutional complaint and by the independent position of the Constitutional Tribunal which takes final decisions on the conformity to the Constitution of statutes and international agreements. The Constitutional Tribunal also ensures the observance of the principle of primacy of statute as another guarantee of unity of the law.

The problem of decentralization of State powers is being resolved gradually in the course of transformation of the system, mostly through the implementation of reforms of local government. Among the unattained ideals of communist doctrine there was also a promise that, in the future, local government would become a basic form of governing State affairs, gradually replacing the State machine. However, this stage never arrived, even if — from time to time — the political propaganda declared the beginning of a new era of "social development", e.g. stepping into the stage of a "developed socialist society" whether in Brezhnev's Soviet Union or in satellite countries. The departure from that system does not mean that the proposal to increase the role of local government in the organization of the State's life and the replacement of the State machine by activities of local bodies (where appropriate) has lost any of its topicality. The need and possibility for the participation of local government in the conduct of State affairs has become more important and real than ever before. In this situation, the problem of determining which spheres of State activity are suitable for the transfer to local government and how they can be transferred has emerged in all its complexity.

Undoubtedly, a referendum is the most developed form of people's participation in government. By means of a referendum, the Nation takes legal or political decision about the future directions of State development. At least four types may be distinguished (law-making, opinion-making, veto and popular initiative) and they guarantee that society is a bearer and executor of rights.

People's participation in the sphere of politics assumes the right of founding political parties irrespective of their programmes (provided that, as a rule, particular constitutionally sanctioned purposes of the State and fundamental values of the society are not violated.)

The economy is another important sphere of people's participation (or self-administration). The existing model of exerting influence by workers on the employer will be subject to limitations that will vary proportionally with the growing scope of private ownership in the economy. Limitations upon workers' rights in this respect will, however, find very considerable compensation in the form of employee stock ownership plans and in the positive consequences of increased productivity resulting from the reforms. Nevertheless, any potential limitations of employees' participation in this respect may lead to a growing need for the protective activities of trade unions as an alternative form of protection of employees' interests. Additionally, self-administration is developed, above all, in religious and professional life, national minorities, cooperatives, cultural life and many other spheres of public life.

In any of the above-mentioned fields, self-administration may take two forms. First is the local government created in accordance with the principle of concession of the powers of the State, however, self-governing bodies may also participate as opinion-making organs or may decide on substantive matters. Irrespective of the scope of participation in the decision-making process and the character of consultations (facultative or obligatory) accompanying such process, the most important fact is that the State has the right to decide — in the most democratic shape — to apply supervisory procedures. This type of self-administration power assumes the competence of State organs in respect of a given category of matters and their partial and temporary delegation to local government.

The second model form of self-administration is based on the principle of the autonomous separation of its functions from the domain belonging to State organs. In this case, the competencies of local government organs may be derived from historical processes (e.g. the autonomy of Swiss communes) or from the recognition that such concessions from the State machine to local government are evidently of benefit to both sides. In the autonomous model, any positive results of the functioning of self-administration may lead to a widening in the scope of its competencies, as well as entrusting to it (temporarily and on particular conditions) functions normally falling within the cognizance of the State machine.

Local government has a particular position among the above-mentioned types of self-administration. It is a special form of organization of social life in its local elementary form, where the right to make decisions on both matters concerning the community at large and matters concerning individual citizens is exercised according to principles similar to those applied by State organs of local levels (ruling powers, contact with inhabitants of the commune and accountability to them) and, additionally, in forms accessible and appropriate to self-administration.

Local government provides the best way to coordinate other special, above-mentioned forms of self-administration. The existence of local government assumes that its decisions are recognized as binding by organs of State administration and also that local authorities have the right to control the activities of organs of State administration at the same level of competency (as a rule, in the form of special administration). Over-developed system of self-administration in basic units of territorial division of the country results in the need to establish higher-level structures of local government, able to coordinate its activity in different spheres and relations.

After the above general comments on local government, let us devote some place for questions of legal comparisons. The period of reconstruction of Poland's political and State system affords an extraordinary opportunity for taking benefit from experiences of others in a situation where the legislator has a wide range of choice among the best principles of the system or to adjust the details of the applied solutions. The direction of Poland's reforms means that, on the one hand, organizational concepts are assessed without ideological bias, and, on the other hand, that local government — unlike any other institution of the system of government — is connected with the historically established nature of State organisms, and therefore — is less subject to comparison and not suitable to a simple adaptation.

The idea of self-administration may be found in all modern constitutions of democratic States. It is treated as a logical consequence of the basic principles of the system of government and a supplement to democratic rules for the functioning of the State machine. Participation of citizens in governance is a consequence of the applied rules of organization of public life, as well as the accomplishment of the principle of efficiency in the work of the State machine, achieved inter alia by the introduction of State administration only where it is really necessary.

The possibility of unrestricted shaping of the forms of local government, frequently observed in practice, may result from according precedence to the concept of self-administration over the concept of the State (which is the case in Switzerland established as a union of previously existing sovereign cantons and communes) or transformation of the predominant idea of federalism to the sphere of local government (in the USA). For those reasons, the model of local government in the USA has not received uniform legal solutions. The inefficiency of self-administration resulting therefrom leads to a situation where competencies are transferred to county agencies of local government or specialized agencies of government administration are organized (special districts) to supplant the tasks of local government. This example shows how excessive democracy can finally lead to its limitation.

The changes to German legislation concerning its system of territorial government have aimed at improving the efficiency of local government and the principles of its cooperation with local administration. They have led to the increase of territory of the commune and equipped it with additional technical means enabling its adjustment to new and nationally unified tasks. To compensate for the loss of sense of community by the local population, attempts have been made to create — apart from basic division — local councils of local scope and to increase the efficiency of State administration.

The diversity of organizational concepts of the commune is, in the nature of things, greater in states with a federal structure, and the system of relations, due to the complex nature of territorial divisions, is more complicated than that in unitary states. Of course, France, whose territory was divided into 36,548 communes is a model example of this second group. To perform their tasks, these communes have at their disposal more than one half of the funds of the State Budget allotted to financing of activities of local communities in the country. The considerable scope of powers delegated to communes produces the necessity of a precise coordination of their tasks with other elements of the State system. This is guaranteed both by the status of the mayor who is an executory organ of the commune and at the same time the government's representative on its territory, as well as by a developed system of supervision exercised over the commune by departmental and regional institutions (particularly regional audit chambers, an administrative court and the Ministry of Internal Affairs).

In addition to the French system, the legal provisions concerning local government of Italy or Scandinavian states may also be regarded as model solutions. Nevertheless, the successes of European integration provide more attractive patterns in this respect. In 1985, the Standing Conference of Local and Regional Authorities of Europe (CLRAE) prepared the draft of a Charter of Local Self-Government which will influence the evolution and unification of legislation in the field of local government and local authorities in the coming years. This draft deserves very careful consideration.

Basic principles of the Charter include the proposal that self-administration issues be recognized in the constitution (Article 2). Public affairs of the local population should be managed by local authorities composed of members freely elected by secret ballot on the basis of direct, equal and universal suffrage (Article 3). Local authorities should, within the limits of the law, have full discretion to exercise their initiative with regard to any matter which is not excluded from their competence nor assigned to any other authority. Powers given to them should be full and exclusive, and matters concerning directly local communities should be decided in consultation with relevant local authorities (Article 4). The Charter applies as a long-term postulate the principle that local taxes and charges might be used as financial resources of local authorities (Article 9). This principle may be inconsistent with the scope of tasks ascribed to local authorities particularly in an initial stage of its existence (the case of Poland and East European countries). Moreover, it is also inconsistent with the practice of financing local authorities in Western Europe and with the postulate of necessary unification of their tasks, which assumes equality of incomes which cannot be obtained under self-financing procedures. The Charter emphasizes local authorities' need and right to co-operate in order to jointly carry out tasks, and to permanently associate for the protection of their common interests (Article 10). The right of recourse to a judicial remedy should be a fundamental method of securing principles of local government (Article 11).

When seeking for a model of legal solutions for, and organizational details of, self-administration, one cannot ignore the traditions of the Polish system of government, particularly from the period of inter-war Poland. Prior to the adoption of the Constitution of 17th March 1921, self-administration was organized fragmentarily on the basis of the legal systems of the three powers participating in the partitions of Poland, supported by transitional legislation adopted during the first years of the post-war period. The provisions of the March Constitution on self-administration accelerated the process of its unification and contained principles whose significance has not disappeared at the present time.

Based on the clause of a comprehensive, so far as possible, accomplishment of the principle of sovereignty of the nation in all classical forms, the Constitution assumed:

— the right to confer on social self-administration a part of the scope of legislation in order to implement the constitutional principle of wide autonomy (Article 3);

— a three-tier structure of local government, corresponding to units of State territorial division (Article 65);

— local councils chosen in elections and the collective nature of their executive bodies composed jointly with the representatives of State administration and under their direction (Article 67);

— establishing of a range of other forms of self-administration, including agricultural chambers, trade and industrial chambers, paid employment and other chambers, linked to the Main Economic Chamber of the Republic (Article 68), self-administration of national minorities (Article 109) and religious self-administration (Article 113);

— State oversight of self-administration exercised only via self-administration of a higher level and by administrative courts (Article 70).

This concept of self-administration, briefly outlined above, had no chance of application, at first due to more urgent legislative needs in other spheres of life and, later, in consequence of a change in political concepts of the position of local government within the framework of the State structures. The Act of 23rd March 1933 on Partial Change of the System of Local Government was adopted at a time when the application of the principle of the State administration's omnipotence was developing. Finally, the April Constitution (of 23rd March 1935) adopted a principle permitting central government to supervise local government (Article 75(4)).

In the practices of the system of government of a totalitarian state, the practice of governance detrimental to the performance of a real and independent role by local government was more important than the provisions of the Constitution. In inter-war Poland, there was — in fact — no self-administration at voivodship [provincial] level (except for the Poznań and Pomeranian voivodships). Local government in the autonomous Silesian voivodship was organized in a different way.

One may consider the establishment of supporting institutions operating within its structure as a considerable success of the self-administration of that time. Self-administration found financial support in the Polski Bank Komunalny S.A. [Polish Municipal Bank plc.] running a loan and relief fund and providing support to regional unions of municipal savings banks. The Komunalny Bank Kredytowy [Municipal Credit Bank] in Poznań operated according to similar principles. The Państwowy Bank Rolny [State Agricultural Bank] specialized in providing support for mostly agricultural communes. In 1934, the Union for Local Government Scrutiny was established by virtue of the Order of the President of the Republic of Poland, as a State institution of supervision and assistance for self--administration. In these years, the activities of local government were supported by the Union of Polish Towns, the Union of Communes and the Union of Districts of the Republic of Poland.

The process of building local government in Polish lands was interrupted by World War II. In the post-war period, in spite of continuance in force of the March Constitution until 1952, in fact, its ideals (including those relating to local self-administration) were systematically abandoned.

According to the newly adopted doctrine, local councils were treated as a form of universal influence of citizens on the State affairs, however, its actual aim was to ensure State influence on citizens and to guarantee control over their initiatives by the system of councils. All the stages of development of the councils (including the years: 1944–50, 1950–58, 1958–72, 1972–83 and 1983–1988), delimited by subsequent statutes amending its concept, correspond to different forms of inability of politically incapacitated councils — ranging from their participation in pseudo-elections to party instructions concerning everyday activity.

One can hardly consider this system as a step on the path of development of the concept of self-administration and the Constitution of inter-war period. It cannot be regarded as an introduction to present Polish solutions, however, we must recognize its special logic and constitutional cohesion. Moreover, it is worth considering how it would function in circumstances of political pluralism and application of democratic procedures for choosing local councillors.

Obviously, its important merit was the fact of existence of the system of councils at communal and voivodship (provincial) level, uniform in nature, with a highest representative organ and supervised by a specialized organ called the Council of State.

On 8th March 1990, the previously existed system of local councils was abolished and replaced — by virtue of the Act on the Amendment of the Constitution of the Republic of Poland and the Local Self-Government Act — with a completely new system of communal self-administration and, then, also by a new system of local organs of central government administration. The new concept of local government resulted from the adoption and development of the principle of sovereignty of the nation, which formed the basis for the adjustment of the Constitution of 1952. This principle, compared with the previous one, was much more explicit — namely, democratic. Above all, it gave no possibility to manipulate the notion of a sovereign reflecting subsequent political concepts which eliminated from its contents "proponents of capitalism", individual farmers, political opposition, Zionists, etc.

The new form of realization of the nation's sovereignty in the local area has a novel nature, in both constitutional and statutory contexts. The applied concept of self-administration means a local government autonomous from the State and treated as original and dominant in relation to local bodies of State administration. This was resolved by a constitutional clause stating that local government is the basic form of organization of public life in the commune, and the commune satisfies the collective needs of the local community (Article 43), and by adoption of the statutory principle according to which inhabitants of the commune constitute, by virtue of law, a self-governing community (Article 1). The commune should encompass an area as uniform as possible from the point of view of settlement and spatial organization as well as social and economic links ensuring the capacity for performance of public tasks (Article 4(2)). Of no less importance was the provision of the Act according to which the scope of operation of the commune encompassed all public issue of local significance which had not been reserved to other subjects (Article 6, para. 1). These important provisions were confirmed in the form of specific constitutional and statutory solutions concerning legal personality, judicial protection of the commune's rights and its financial powers, etc.

Interpretation of the nature and sense of legal regulation concerning local government depends on awareness of the fundamental role of the above-mentioned principles of local government reform and its consti-tutional status, and of the fact that the Act of 8th March 1990 on Local Government constitutes a *lex generalis* in relation to subsequent statutes which have sometimes undermined the original intentions of the legislator.

The lack of full consistency in the work of the legislator and difficulties with the implementation of self-administration reform resulted from various causes. One of them was the fact that communes were created on the basis of a mostly mechanical division of the country's territory, paying no attention to historically established economic and social integrities. Although Article 4 of the Act on Local Government allows the creation, assembly and abolition of communes and the right to change their boundaries (which should be considered an inherent power of communes, which was subsequently confirmed by a regulation of the Council of Ministers), however, communes will not be inclined to engage in such difficult undertakings, since they have more pressing problems.

Another problem lacking successful regulation by the legislator is the wide disparity between the tasks of rural and urban communes, which has not been reflected in an appropriate statutory differentiation of their status, competencies and organization. The Act of 18th May 1990 on the System of Local Government of the Capital City of Warsaw may be considered as the legislator's admission of this defect. Nevertheless, other relatively large conurbations have to operate within the limits prescribed for a conventional commune.

The reform of self-administration, based on provisions of temporary constitutional acts and the Act of 8th March on Local Government, as well as numerous specific statutes, has been implemented by the end 1998 only in the form of commune self-administration. There existed voivodship self-governing assembly at the level of voivodship [province], but its powers were very restricted. The years 1990–98 have seen a very rapid popularization of the concept of local government as a form of political, social and economic life. The existence of communal self-administration illustrates the appearance of a new category of a public administrative authority and the foundation of a new, and swiftly developing, branch of law. The limited capacities of one-stage local government have led to a situation where the authors of the new constitution decided to extend local government to a multi-form system based on a three-tier territorial division of the State. It is the preamble to the new Constitution of 2nd April 1997 which contains the principle of subsidiarity, which also forms a basis for the development of the principle of self-administration. Apart from the formulation of a general concept of the State as the common good of all its citizens (Article 1), a democratic state ruled by law (Article 2), based on the separation of and balance between the powers (Article 10), the Constitution adopts, as its fundamental principle, that "The territorial system of the Republic of Poland shall ensure the decentralization of public power" (Article 15).

A separate chapter (VII) of the Constitution deals with the issue of local government. The primary jurisdiction of local government is indicated by the presumption of competence, since it performs public tasks not reserved by the Constitution or statutes to other public authorities (Article 163). The commune remains to be the basic unit of local government (Article 164). Other units of regional or local government are specified by statute (Article 164). Units of local government possess legal personality and have rights of ownership, and may also use public funds. Their local councils are chosen in elections. Supervision of the legality of activity of local government is exercised by constitutionally specified organs, including the Prime Minister, voivodes and regional audit chambers (Article 171). Units of local government have the right to associate in stronger unions and structures, also with participation of local and regional communities of other states (Article 172). Jurisdictional disputes between units of local government and units of central government administration are settled by the administrative courts (Article 166).

As a result of the legislative work, conducted in 1998 on the basis of the existing constitutional solutions, a new model of local government was prepared. It contained a previously existing form of communal self--administration (i.e. around 2,500 communes) and a new form of district self-administration (over 300 districts plus around 70 city-districts) as well as a regional one (16 voivodships). The statutes enacting this reform of local government came into force on 1st January 1999.

Work on the reform has encountered some obstacles. It provoked some political disputes and protests were staged against it by local communities. This was mostly connected with the departure from the previous model of 49 voivodships (introduced in 1975 as an element of a two-tier division of the country's territory) and replacing them with new units, i.e. voivod-ship-regions. The newly proposed concept of voivodship has proved not to be clear and convincing. It has broken with the tradition of the system of government which makes it possible to link the concept of voivodship with an old Polish "province". This new concept of voivodship is mostly based on economic presumptions and calculations, and resembles the concept of regions applied in West European countries, which is rather subordinate to the doctrine of decentralization of the state. Local communities have proved to be accustomed to the concept of a small voivodship (introduced in 1975) not only as a symbol of social advance (particularly of smaller administrative entities), but also as a sign of stability of administrative structures in the country[4]. In the course of the creation and drawing of boundaries (which falls within the competence of the government, and not the Sejm), there were not so many protests, as this activity has not involved any liquidation of existing structures, but only granting a new status (though not to all aspirants).

Local government, in its new form, makes it possible to delegate substantial competencies of central administration and territorial govern-

---

[4] I wrote on this subject in the Polish official newspaper "Rzeczpospolita", 28th April 1998, *W niewoli pojęć [In the captivity of notions]*.

ment administration to self-governing bodies of the commune, the district and the voivodship. The commune remains as the general and primary form of local government. Districts and regions are not appellate structures in relation to administrative decisions of the commune. Appeals from decisions of any of three levels of self-administration are lodged with special appellate boards as organs of second instance (and also, where appropriate, with administrative courts).

Voivodship self-administration will deal with categories of matters entrusted to it by statute. These are: (1) to determine strategies for development in the field of culture, local economy, environment, etc.; (2) to pursue voivodship policy in the field of economy and finance, and to support science and education; (3) to prepare comprehensive programmes of development of a voivodship. District self-administration is to undertake actions in the area exceeding that of a commune, but also smaller than that of a region. A considerable part of its competence will be transferred from territorial units of central government administration and departmental areas. In particular, districts will provide technical means for combating disasters and maintain local infrastructure, maintain public utilities of supra-communal character, health protection, social assistance, secondary education, etc. City districts located in the largest cities will fulfil, simultaneously, competencies of the commune and those of the district.

The new shape of local government creates very wide opportunities for evolution of the traditional concept of the State and State machine. Even at the level of the commune, it has developed a very imposing activity in the field of local initiatives, and in the form of associations of communes sharing unsolved problems. Therefore, by way of national agreement, a new body, unknown to statute law, namely the National Assembly of Local Authorities has been appointed. The communes located along the Polish frontier have developed intensive cooperation with foreign local authorities, establishing 22 "Euroregions"[5]. One may reasonably expect that districts, and especially self-governing voivodships, will treat international cooperation as one of their priorities — and to an ever-increasing extent.

The existence of three-level territorial self-administration will mean not only relieving the State of some administrative duties, but also more

---

[5] Cf. W. Malendowski, M. Ratajczak: *Euroregiony [Euroregions]*, Atla 2, Wrocław 1998.

accurate drawing up the outlines of its major policies. Nevertheless, the central character of strategic policies, including — inter alia — foreign, defence and financial policy, will be maintained.

One of the most important methods of protecting the unity of the State is to maintain unity of the law, accomplished by way of precedence of the Constitution and statutes and preserving the State's exclusive power to conclude treaties. Local government will also require some changes in this area. This is so, as the organs of local government have the right to enact universally binding local enactments, issued "on the basis and within limits specified by statute" (Article 94 of the Constitution). It is worth noting that, in this context, the notion of "basis" and "limits" may be understood as relatively discretionary, and the intensity of exercise of law-making powers and their variety may be very considerable. This, in turn, leads to the need for new forms of legislative oversight, not only on the part of a voivode as a government representative in the region, but also central organs responsible for law-making and review of the legality of such legislation.

The process of actual and legal democratization of Poland's system of government consists in the application of a wide range of legal solutions guaranteeing an optimal shape of the State. Methods of socialization and decentralization of power have appeared among the methods of democratization of life in Poland. The lack of such decentralization led to the collapse of the communist formation and loss of chances for the development of Poland. Different forms of decentralization of State power means an adjustment of Poland's system of government to international standards[6]. The local government reform, in its extended form, will provide new opportunities. The unity of the State in today's Poland, under the rule of the new Constitution, is guaranteed by connecting central and local forms of the exercise of State power and by stimulating public participation.

---

[6] Cf. A. Bałaban: *International Constitutional Standards and the Polish Constitution*, „Archiwum Iuridicum Cracoviense", Vol. XXIX–XXX, 1996–1997, p. 115–122.

Krzysztof Wójtowicz

Professor, University of Wrocław

THE RECEPTIVITY OF THE CONSTITUTION OF THE REPUBLIC OF POLAND TO INTERNATIONAL AND SUPRANATIONAL LAW

1. The political transformations of the end of 20th century effaced the line of division between two hostile political blocks separating the modern world and laid the foundation for a real process of universalization of international law based on commonly understood principles of democracy, respect for the rule of law — both within the states and in relations between them — and, finally, respect for human rights irrespective of where and under whose rule a person lives.

The transformation of the governmental system of Poland also produced a change in attitude towards international law, which can be observed in the provisions of the new Constitution of the Republic of Poland.

The constitutional definition of international law status hitherto existing in the Polish legal system proved less than adequate. Provisions of the former Constitution of the Polish People's Republic ignored this issue, allowing for theoretical legal discussions about it and leaving it to the decision of the courts in particular cases. As a result, pragmatists and theoreticians could not develop a common position on the matter, a situation that produced uncertainty in the administration of law. Judges, seeking a sound basis for their judgments, had to rely on the relevant provisions of the Polish legal system then in force. If its provisions did not repeat or refer directly to international legal norms, these latter were considered as non-binding within the national legal system. Regarding the former doctrine of law, the treatment of the existing loopholes as a threat to observance of international obligations resulted in a conception that international law is binding "by its own virtue" (*ex proprio vigore*). However, this doctrine was not applied in the adjudication practices of courts and seemed practically of little worth[1].

---

[1] See: decision of the Supreme Court of 25th August 1987, IPRZ 8/87 item. 199, judgment of the Chief Administrative Court of 26th August 1988, OSP 1990, No. 10, p. 750.

The provisions of the so-called Small Constitution of 1992, regulated the principles and procedures for ratification (conclusion) and notification of denunciation of international agreements in a very fragmented manner.

The new attitude of the democratic Polish State to the issue of international law was confirmed, first, at an international forum. On 27th August 1990, Poland acceded to the Vienna Convention of 1969 on the Law of Treaties which stated amongst other matters that "Every treaty in force is binding upon the parties to it and must be performed by them in good faith" (Article 26) and that "A party may not invoke the provisions of its internal law as justification for its failure to perform a treaty (...)" (Article 27).

Both the above cited provisions of the Convention, as well as our own Polish experience, suggested the need to resolve doubts regarding the principles of application of international norms within the national legal system. Obligations resulting from international treaties are between states, but they influence to a significant degree the legal situation of individuals through conventions regarding human rights, conventions of the ILO, agreements regarding intellectual property or protection of the natural environment; all are typical examples.

2. In relation to these issues, it was assumed in the preparatory stage that the Constitution, being — according to the rule of a state of law — the basis for the binding force of all legal norms within the state, should adopt rules that allow for a precise definition of the place of the international legal norms within the national legal system. In consequence, the Polish legal system became open — at least in part — for the first time in the postwar period, to the provisions of international law.

Article 9(1) gives evidence of such openness. It states that: "The Republic of Poland shall respect international law binding upon it". This provision remained within the fundamental constitutional provisions of the Republic of Poland defined in Chapter I, opening the Constitution. At the same time, the international community was informed, in a very general way, that Poland remains a state ruled by law also in respect of conduct of international relations. It should be also noted that the principle adopted enjoys a broader scope of binding force than the earlier mentioned principle of the Vienna Convention *"pacta sunt servanda"*. It refers to all spheres of international law, among them, to customary international law.

The assessment of the above principle is not unambiguous in the context of Polish legal doctrine[2]. There are views that Article 9(1) constitutes a declaration that is binding within the ambit of international relations only, without any direct legal effect in the national legal system. These latter effects would result only from detailed constitutional provisions or provisions of certain statutes which might specify the applicability of the declared principle. Consequently, the omission to include international custom in the sources of universally binding law might indicate the impossibility of applying such custom within the national legal system. On the other hand, however, the normative character of the constitutional provisions within the constitutional law, to which Article 9 belongs, is unquestionable. The above-discussed principle may constitute grounds for defining an obligation to consider the provisions of the international law both by parliament in the process of law-making and its implementation, and by the organs of administration and courts. Customary international law, as law incorporated into the Polish legal system by means of the constitutional provision, might constitute the base for adjudication in proceedings before the courts since, according to the provisions of Article 178(1), "Judges (...) shall be independent and subject only to the Constitution and statutes" and the provisions of Article 8, "The provisions of the Constitution shall apply directly, unless the Constitution provides otherwise". Nevertheless, the lack of opportunity for the Constitutional Tribunal to adjudicate upon the conformity of statutes to ratified international agreements and customs included in the provisions of Article 188 of the Constitution results in a situation where the Tribunal cannot ground its judgments on principles included only in customary international law.

A desire to establish a so-called closed system of law sources was the reason for excluding customary international law from the list of law sources mentioned in Article 87. It has been thought that this system cannot include customary norms which are not subject to duty of promulgation and about which we cannot unambiguously state whether and to what extent they are binding.

---

[2] See further: C. Banasiński, *Pozycja prawa międzynarodowego w krajowym porządku prawnym (w świetle Konstytucji z 1997 r.)* [*Position of international law in the domestic legal system (in the light of the Constitution of 1997)*], „Przegląd Prawa Europejskiego", No. 2(3) 1997, p. 8.

As a result, the constitutional provisions regulate, in a not very consistent way, only the status of the international agreements within the Polish legal system, attaching different importance to them depending on the mode by which they have been concluded.

3. The provisions of Article 87 generally define the status of the international agreement within the Polish legal system. The Constitution, statutes, ratified international agreements and regulations are listed in this Article as sources of universally binding law.

It results *a contrario* from the provisions of this article that international agreements, not subject to ratification, do not constitute sources of universally binding law; however, agreements mentioned in other provisions of the Constitution, that is, agreements approved by the Council of Ministers according to Article 146(4)(10) as well as agreements concluded by the simplified procedure, also constitute such sources. This situation imposes on the appropriate state organs conducting negotiations a duty to consider whether the agreements approved by the Council of Ministers do include universally binding norms. However, the status of agreements concluded by the simplified procedure, e.g. concluded only by means of signature remains unclear as these agreements include often legal norms that have a universally binding character. It is, in my view, senseless to wait for adoption of a national regulation which may make the internal application of such norms possible. This would also depreciate the significance of the simplified procedure which is designed to advance the conclusion and full effectiveness of the agreement[3].

We may differentiate, on the basis of the constitutional provisions, several methods leading to ratification of an international agreement.

The most simple procedure for the ratification of an agreement is ratification concluded by the President pursuant to the provisions of Article 133(1)(1) with notification to the Sejm and the Senate that this has been done. The Prime Minister notifies the Sejm about the intention to

---

[3] This may refer to e.g. an agreement allowing the Armed Forces of a foreign state to perform military manoeuvres on Polish territory and regulate the principles subjecting members of the Armed Forces of such state to the jurisdiction of the national courts. See: A. Wyrozumska: *Projekt Konstytucji Rzeczpospolitej Polskiej w świetle badań nauki prawa konstytucyjnego* [*The draft Constitution of the Republic of Poland in the light of constitutional law study*], Gdańsk 1998, p. 138.

submit to the President documents subject to ratification under this mode. Parliamentary practice dictates whether this notification shall have only an informative character or become the basis of a debate and, if needed, a change of the mode of ratification.

The mode of ratification of agreements referring to: 1) peace, alliances, political or military treaties; (2) freedoms, rights or obligations of citizens, as specified in the Constitution; (3) the Republic of Poland's membership in an international organization; (4) considerable financial responsibilities imposed on the State; (5) matters regulated by statutes or those in respect of which the Constitution requires the form of a statute; is more complicated. Certain problems may be caused by the lack of precision of this provision, a topic of some discussion in the appropriate literature[4]. It seems that due to the unlimited objective scope of a statute and the internal results of the statutory agreement for ratification, it is Parliament, not the executive organs, which should decide whether the ratification of the agreement requires statutory consent or not.

Such agreements are ratified prior to a consent granted in a statute i.e. by a simple majority vote, in the presence of at least half of the constitutional number of Deputies (Article 120).

The procedure for ratification of an agreement delegating the competence (of public authorities) to an international organization or international institution is especially complicated. The statute giving consent for the ratification of such agreement should be passed by a two-thirds majority votes in the presence of at least half of the constitutional number of members of both chambers. Granting consent for ratification of such agreement may also be done by a nationwide referendum (Article 90).

The statute granting consent for the ratification of an international agreement remains within the cognizance of the Constitutional Tribunal and, in a case finding that this statute is inconsistent with the Constitution, the process of ratification is inadmissible.

A model for the detailed transformation in respect of all agreements ratified has been adopted and, according to provisions of Article 91(1), following promulgation thereof in the Journal of Laws of the Republic of

---

[4] See: W. Sokolewicz: *Ustawa ratyfikacyjna* [*The ratification statute*], (in:) *Prawo międzynarodowe i wspólnotowe w wewnętrznym porządku prawnym* [*International and Community law in the domestic legal order*], edited by M. Kruk, Warszawa 1997, p. 102–106.

Poland (*Dziennik Ustaw RP*), they constitute part of the national legal order and are applied directly, unless application depends on the passing of a statute. We may wonder whether the second part of the above mentioned article referring to the direct application of the agreements is necessary. If the agreement is of a self-executing character it is naturally directly applied. Additional underlying of this phenomenon in the Constitution may only mean that national organs applying the law, especially in the field of human rights protection, are supposed to consider presumption of self-execution of the agreements.

It has been provided, pursuant to Article 88(3), that international agreements ratified with prior consent granted by statute shall be promulgated in accordance with the procedures required for statutes. However, the principles of promulgation of other international agreements shall be specified by statute. The adopted solution implies the duty to promulgate all international agreements but on a different basis. This is consistent with the concept of the state ruled by law and attempts to change the present not very satisfactory practice in this field[5].

Transformation is the process introducing international agreements into the national legal order; however, the main issue remains how to establish the precedence of these agreements in the case of their conflict with provisions of the national legal order.

The provisions of the Constitution explicitly determine only the status of agreements ratified prior to a consent granted by statute. The norm of competence referred to in Article 91(2) provides that such an agreement "shall have precedence over statutes if such an agreement cannot be reconciled with the provisions of such statutes". Consequently, the Constitutional Tribunal may adjudicate upon the conformity of statutes to ratified agreements whose ratification required prior consent granted by statute (Article 188(2)).

As regards the status of international agreements ratified according to the provisions of former constitutions, according to Article 241(1), all international agreements, previously ratified by the Republic of Poland pursuant to the constitutional provisions in force at the time of their

---

[5] See: R. Szafarz: *Międzynarodowy porządek prawny i jego odbicie w polskim prawie konstytucyjnym* [*International legal order and its reflection in Polish constitutional law*] (in:) *Prawo międzynarodowe...*, op.cit., p. 40.

ratification and promulgated in the Journal of Laws of the Republic of Poland (*Dziennik Ustaw RP*), are considered as agreements ratified with prior consent granted by statute and subject to the provisions of Article 91 of the Constitution — if it is assumed that their contents refer to the categories of issues mentioned in Article 89(1). It should be noted that the above-mentioned solution provides for the supra-statutory effect of, inter alia, agreements concerning human rights ratified in the period when the provisions of the Constitution of the People's Republic of Poland and the so-called Small Constitution were in force[6].

Nevertheless, there is a lack of explicit provision defining the status of agreements which do not require statutory consent for their ratification. They certainly have precedence over acts that are not normative since they are listed in Article 87 before the regulations, and since the Constitutional Tribunal has been granted the right to adjudicate upon the conformity of legal provisions issued by central State organs to ratified international agreements (Article 188(3)). In this context, the relation of such agreements to statutes seems to be not so obvious. There is tendency to attach to them less importance than to statutes. However, there are also arguments found in certain countries, derived from their practices, that the lowest position within the hierarchy of legal acts given to ratified agreements is that of a statute[7]. This suggests that certain disputes over status and precedence are solved according to the principle *lex posterior derogat legi priori*[8].

All international agreements binding on Poland should be in conformity to the Constitution. The Constitutional Tribunal, pursuant to the provisions of Article 188(1), adjudicates upon the conformity of international agreements to the Constitution. Another advantage of this principle is that the President may ask the Tribunal to adjudicate upon the conformity of an international agreement to the Constitution prior to its ratification (Article 133(2)). In the light of constitutional provisions, subsequent review of the conformity of agreements to the Constitution is not to be excluded although recognition of an agreement as inconsistent

[6] See: M. Masternak-Kubiak: *Umowa międzynarodowa w prawie konstytucyjnym* [*International agreement in constitutional law*], Warszawa 1997, p. 124.

[7] See: M. Masternak-Kubiak, *op.cit.*, p. 123.

[8] Compare: A. Wyrozumska: *Projekt Konstytucji Rzeczpospolitej Polskiej w świetle badań nauki prawa konstytucyjnego*, Gdańsk 1998, p. 140.

with the Constitution cannot affect international law. The provisions of Article 241(2) help to order this situation as they impose on the Council of Ministers an obligation to submit a list of international agreements with provisions that are inconsistent with the Constitution within 2 years of the date the Constitution comes into force. This refers to all categories of agreements independent of the mode of their conclusion by Poland. As a result, there might occur a necessity for denunciation or re-negotiation of certain agreements.

On the other hand, there are guarantees ensuring the conformity of national enactments to the norms of international law. According to the provisions of Article 188(2) and (3), the Constitutional Tribunal adjudicates upon the conformity of statutes to international agreements whose ratification required prior consent granted by statute as well as on the conformity of legal provisions issued by central State organs to ratified international agreements. Additionally, every court has been granted the right to refer a question of law to the Constitutional Tribunal as to the conformity of a normative provision to ratified international agreements (Article 193).

The separate category of "acceptance" of an agreement has not been specified in the provisions of the Constitution although this is done in Article 14 of the Vienna Convention on the Law of Treaties. As certain international agreements provide that the mode of acceptance is the only way to bind oneself to these agreements, it is not possible to exclude such practice when the provisions of the present Constitution are in force. Such phenomenon has been observed earlier[9].

As regards renunciation of international agreements, the previously cited constitutional provisions provide that denunciation of such agreement, whose ratification requires prior consent granted by statute, also requires consent granted by statute.

4. From the beginning, the work on the draft Constitution was accompanied by the idea that it should include provisions enabling Poland to have future access to the European Union. This idea was the result of an intention, underlined by the subsequent governments of the Third Republic

---

[9] Compare: R. Szafarz: *Międzynarodowy porządek prawny i jego odbicie w polskim prawie konstytucyjnym* (in:) *Prawo międzynarodowe i wspólnotowe w wewnętrznym porządku prawnym*, edited by M. Kruk, Warszawa 1997, s. 35.

of Poland, to include our country in the process of European integration. This produced, on 16th December 1991, the Europe Agreement establishing an association between Poland and the European Communities and their member states, as well as the submission, on 8th April 1994, of a motion for admission to the European Union.

From this point of view, the main problem that had to be solved referred to the constitutional formula allowing an organization of a "supranational" character to discharge some powers of the state. Nevertheless, the European Union is not a typical international organization, access to which might be achieved pursuant to the provisions of Article 89(1)(3) of the Constitution of the Republic of Poland i.e. by prior consent granted by statute for ratification of an international agreement relating to membership in an international organization. It is known that the legal order of the Communities, on which the whole legislation of the Union is based, is not an order typical of classical international law. It has not been clearly stated in the EC Treaty however, that the Court of Justice of the European Communities has established in its jurisdiction that member states delegating their respective competencies to the Communities, equipping them with separate institutions, legal personality and capacities as well as establishing a system of legal norms binding on the citizens of these states, thus limited their sovereign rights.

Taking this situation into account, a special provision has been included in our Constitution, namely, Article 90(1), pursuant to which: "the Republic of Poland may, by virtue of international agreements, delegate to an international organization or international institution the competence of organs of State authority in relation to certain matters".

The contents of this Article require explanation. First of all, it should be noticed that in contrast to the provisions of the constitutions of the member states [10] and to the early jurisdiction of the Court of Justice of the European Communities, the Article discusses neither limitation of sovereignty nor delegation of sovereign rights to the organization [11]. Following

---

[10] Compare: Preamble to the Constitution of the French Republic of 1946 in force at the time of signing of the Rome Treaty, Article 11 of the Italian Constitution, Article of the Basic Law of the German Republic.

[11] Compare: case 6/64 *Costa versus ENEL.*

the example of other member states, a more politically neutral formula of delegation of "competence" has been adopted[12].

Inevitably, this limited the area for ideological and political disputes in the referendum campaign preceding adoption of the Constitution. Nevertheless, it should be noticed that the idea of sovereignty constitutes the possibility of taking independent decisions in such spheres of public activity as: the law-making process, administration of justice or money issue. Accession to the Union means that, in areas determined by the establishing (constitutional) treaties, Poland will lose its capacity to act independently and that appropriate decisions concerning the law-making process, as well as administration of executive and judicial powers, shall be performed by Community organs. Irrespective of the discussion whether we delegate competence or the right to its execution, limitation of state sovereignty[13] remains the main issue. The fact that, after taking the sovereign decision concerning accession, Poland shall participate together with other member states in common execution of certain sovereign activities, protecting at the same time its own interests, does not contradict this statement.

It might be assumed, from the discussion about delegation of competence in "certain matters", that the delegation of competence regarding all matters is out of the question. We may then wonder, whether the areas that are not subject to such delegation should be determined, since we do not know exactly which kind of competence has been considered.

The modern doctrine of constitutionalism suggests two solutions in such a case. The first provides for a clear reservation, that in regard to certain areas, the process of delegation is not possible. It has been reserved, e.g. in § 5 of Chapter 10 of the Act on the Form of Government of Sweden that: "it shall not be possible to delegate the right to adopt, amend or repeal

---

[12] Compare: Article 92 of the Constitution of the Netherlands; Article 20(1) of the Constitution of Denmark; Article 28(2) of the Greek Constitution.

[13] Compare: J. Galaster: *Konstytucyjnoprawne aspekty przystąpienia RP do Unii Europejskiej* [Legal and constitutional aspects of Poland's access to the European Union] (in:) *Wejście w życie nowej Konstytucji Rzeczypospolitej Polskiej* [Coming into force of a new Constitution of the Republic of Poland], Toruń 1998, p. 71; J. Barcz, *Konstytucyjnoprawne problemy stosowania prawa Unii Europejskiej w świetle dotychczasowych doświadczeń państw członkowskich* [Legal and constitutional problems with the application of the UE law in the light of experiences of its member states], (in:) *Prawo międzynarodowe i wspólnotowe w wewnętrznym porządku prawnym*, Warszawa 1997, p. 207.

fundamental laws, the Act on the Riksdag, electoral laws or statutes establishing restriction on rights and freedoms, as specified in chapter 2".

The Italian Constitutional Tribunal issued a ruling similar to the Swedish parliament, although it lacked explicit constitutional justification. The Tribunal stated that, although execution of competence regarding the law-making process as well as the executive and judicial powers by the state may be limited by establishment of the Communities, this kind of delegation cannot result in violation of "basic principles of the constitutional order" and "inalienable rights of an individual"[14]. The French Constitutional Council assumed as inadmissible the adoption of international commitments by France (among them those relating to the delegation of competence) which would be "inconsistent with the duty of a state to ensure respect for the institutions of the Republic and the continuity of the state as well as the duty to guarantee citizens' rights and freedoms"[15] or would "violate fundamental conditions relating to the exercise of national sovereignty"[16].

Provisions of Article 23 of the Basic Law of the Republic of Germany illustrate the second solution. These provisions allow for membership of the Republic of Germany in the development of the European Union, provided that the Union respects the principles of democracy, state ruled by law, social and federal principles together with principle of subsidiarity as well as guaranteeing the protection of fundamental laws to an extent comparable to the provisions of the Basic Law.

It may be expected that adoption of the open principle of delegation of competence in the future Polish Constitution will result in the necessity for the Constitutional Tribunal to adjudicate on the scope of such delegation. Perhaps the provisions of Article 5 of the Constitution will be the basis for such activity, in that "the Republic of Poland shall safeguard the independence and integrity of its territory and ensure the freedoms and rights of persons and citizens, the security of the citizens, safeguard the national heritage (...)". However in special matters, the necessity to amend certain constitutional provisions before Poland's accession to the Union is presently obvious. The possible accession to the future monetary union might be treated, for example, as the delegation of competence "in certain

---

[14] See: decision of 27th December 1973 concerning Frontini case.
[15] See: decisions of 22nd May 1985 and 25th July 1991.
[16] See: decision of 9th April 1992.

matters". However, this will require amendment of Article 227(1) of the Constitution according to which the National Bank of Poland has the exclusive right to issue money as well as to formulate and implement monetary policy. It will also be necessary to adjudicate on the conformity of Article 52(5) of the Constitution — which states that anyone whose Polish origin has been confirmed in accordance with statute may settle permanently in Poland", to the law of the union.

The procedure for taking decisions regarding delegation of competence has been defined in Article 90(2), (3) and (4) of the Constitution. Thus, in accordance with those provisions, "(2) a statute, granting consent for ratification of an international agreement referred to in para. 1, shall be passed by the Sejm by a two-thirds majority vote in the presence of at least half of the constitutional number of Deputies, and by the Senate by a two-thirds majority vote in the presence of at least half of the constitutional number of Senators. (3) Granting of consent for ratification of such agreement may also be passed by an nationwide referendum in accordance with the provisions of Article 125. (4) Any resolution in respect of the choice of procedure for granting consent to ratification shall be taken by the Sejm by an absolute majority vote taken in the presence of at least half of the constitutional number of Deputies."

The majority required in the Sejm in this case is identical to the majority required to amend the Constitution[17], however, as concerns the Senate in regard to amending the Constitution an absolute majority of votes is required. This majority is easier to obtain than the two-thirds majority of votes required to grant consent for ratification.

A similar solution can be found in the constitutions[18] of other countries though justified by far-reaching consequences regarding ratification of the agreement on the accession to the international organization.

---

[17] Article 235(4) of the Constitution.

[18] In Greece, ratification of such agreements or arrangements requires adoption of a statute by two-fifths majority of votes of the general number of Deputies (Article 28(2) of the Greek Constitution). In Spain, granting consent for ratification is by means of an organic law adopted by an absolute majority of votes (Articles 93 and 81). In Sweden "a decision on delegation shall be adopted under the procedure required for the amendment of fundamental laws. In case of any difficulties in using the required procedure, Riksdag shall take the decision by five-sevenths of the Deputies voting, and which shall constitute no less than three-fourths of all Deputies" (§ 5 of Chapter 10).

As regards the possibility of holding a referendum, the part of the provision defining the procedure for granting consent for ratification of a statute delegating competence was, in both draft Constitutions of 5th June and 27th August 1996, as follows: "The Sejm may, before passing a statute (*granting consent for ratification*) submit to a nationwide referendum the issue of granting consent for delegation of competence of the State organs to an international organization or to an international organ".

As can be noted, such referendum might possibly be held before the passing, under special procedure, of a statute authorizing the delegation of competence.

This solution was ineffective. The possibility of the existence of alternative procedures was more reasonable. The statute authorizing the delegation is passed either by the parliament, and then the referendum is not held, or the Sejm holds the referendum in which the nation decides about grant of consent for ratification and then special majorities in both chambers are not necessary.

This logically constructed procedure might become complicated when the result of the referendum is not binding or the number of participants is lower than half of the number of those having the right to vote (Article 125(3) of the Constitution). Considering the hitherto low turnout in universal elections after 1989, such a possibility might occur. So, should the order to hold a referendum mean the final closing of the parliamentary procedure? In the case where the result of a referendum is binding — and is either positive or negative — this is the right situation since the constitutionally-binding decision of the sovereign nation cannot be questioned by any State organ. If the sovereign nation does not express its will in a way that is binding — i.e. it does not "make use" of its right, the Sejm may then order return to the parliamentary procedure: applying any another solution would mean that an act which is legally not binding (due to lack of participation) would have results identical to a legally binding act (a "no" vote with the required number of participants). This may result in refusal to grant final consent for ratification of the accession agreement.

As regards the ratification procedure, it is to be observed that the President, pursuant to Article 133(2) of the Constitution of the Republic of Poland, may, before ratifying an international agreement, refer it to the

Constitutional Tribunal with a request to adjudicate upon its conformity to the Constitution.

There arises the question whether the Constitutional Tribunal, enjoying pursuant to the provisions of Article 188 the right to adjudicate upon the constitutionality of statutes, may adjudicate upon the conformity to the Constitution of an act granting consent for ratification pursuant to the provisions of Article 90 of the accession agreement.

We should distinguish two different situations. We deal with the first, when the above mentioned consent is granted by a statute. In this case we cannot exclude the jurisdiction of the (Constitutional) Tribunal. This act, although passed under special procedure by majority of votes more restricted than in the case of amendment of the Constitution, will remain a statute in the light of the provisions of Article 188. The President before signing the bill, in exercising preventive control, may refer it to the Constitutional Tribunal with a motion to adjudicate upon its conformity to the Constitution. In Article 191 of the Constitution, among other matters, 50 Deputies or 30 Senators may make application to the Constitutional Tribunal for adjudication on the constitutionality of an already-passed statute granting consent (for ratification). When a statute has been judged inconsistent with the Constitution, the statute should be amended before the ratification procedure, pursuant to provisions of Article 235, which provides exclusively for this purpose. The act of delegation of competence pursuant to the provisions of Article 90 cannot be understood as an "implicit" amendment of the Constitution.

If a consent for ratification of the accession agreement is granted in a referendum, pursuant to the provisions of Article 188, adjudication on the constitutionality of such consent will not be within the competence of the Constitutional Tribunal.

5. The problem of application of community law in the national legal order of the Republic of Poland remains another constitutional problem connected with our membership in the European Union.

As is known, community law consists of so-called primary law (i.e. the establishing treaties together with treaties which amend or supplement them as well as conventions and additional protocols constituting integral parts of the treaties) and secondary law (legal acts passed by the Community organs under provisions included in treaties i.e. regulations, directives and decisions). Additionally, the sources of community law are constituted by general principles and basic laws as well as international agreements concluded by the Communities).

Community law has precedence over national law according to the jurisdiction of the Court of Justice of the European Communities. As a result, individuals within the member states may refer to provisions of the law of the Communities before national courts e.g. in cases where national legal norms stand in contradiction to this law. Provisions of community law may have direct effect on the national legal order i.e., when conditions resulting from certain norms of community law are fulfilled this then results in the emergence of rights and duties which refer directly to individuals without consideration of national norms. These rules result from the idea of an autonomous legal order which constitutes the basis of community law and which has to be respected independently of whether it has been incorporated or not into the national law.

There are provisions in the Constitution of the Republic of Poland which might be referred to principles of application of either primary or secondary law.

As regards the primary law of the Union which is to be adopted by Poland in the future by virtue of the accession agreement, the lack of specific regulations suggests that the law should be subject to the provisions of the Constitution referring to ratified international agreements. Pursuant to Article 87(1), ratified international agreements belong to the sources of universally binding law of the Republic of Poland, and pursuant to Article 97(1), after having been promulgated in the Journal of Laws of the Republic of Poland (*Dziennik Ustaw RP*), they constitute part of the national legal order and are directly applied — provided their application does not depend on the passing of a statute.

Besides, pursuant to the norm of competence of Article 91(2) referring to the primary law, "an international agreement ratified upon prior consent granted by statute shall have precedence over statutes, if such an agreement cannot be reconciled with the provisions of such statutes".

Such legal structure raises interpretative doubts as regards the status of community law within the Polish legal order.

First of all, the Constitution does not make a difference between the status of ratified international agreements although, it implements three different procedures for granting consent for their conclusion: the first procedure, in which consent for ratification of an agreement is granted in normal legislative procedure (Article 89); the second, in which consent is granted by a statute passed by special majorities of votes (Article 90); and the third, in which consent for ratification is not granted by virtue of a statute but is passed by a national referendum (Article 90(3)). Although, at first glance, these three procedures differ among themselves as regards political and legislative importance, it should be considered that in the absence of other provisions relating to them, an international agreement has, in all these three cases, precedence over a statute though not, however, over the Constitution, and the Constitutional Tribunal may in every case adjudicate upon the constitutionality of the primary law.

Principles of application of secondary law have been regulated in Article 91(3): "If an agreement, ratified by the Republic of Poland, establishing an international organization so provides, the laws established by it shall be applied directly and have precedence in the event of a conflict of laws". It should be assumed, in case of *a contrario* interpretation, that this provision sanctions precedence of the Constitution over the secondary law.

It has also to be observed that the approval of the precedence of both categories of community law over all norms of the national law (including constitutional provisions) would be in accordance with the views expressed in many judgments of the Court of Justice of the European Communities. On the other hand, we cannot wholly ignore objections to the claim of precedence of community law over constitutional provisions which has been expressed by the constitutional courts of certain member states (e.g. Germany and Italy).

In this situation, the passing of the following norm of competence would be advisable: "the right of the international organization as referred to in Article 90(1) of the Constitution shall be applied in the legal order of the Republic of Poland pursuant to the principles of the treaty constituting this organization". Thus, there would be no conflict between provisions of the Constitution and judgments of the Court of Justice of the European Communities.

As regards other constitutional provisions which might be probably cited with respect to the application of community law in the Polish legal order, the usefulness of legal questions and complaints concerning constitutional infringements addressed to the Constitutional Tribunal should be considered.

The provisions of Article 193 of the Constitution provide for the possibility for a court to address questions of law to the Constitutional Tribunal regarding "the conformity of a normative act to the Constitution, ratified international agreements or statute, if the answer to such question of law will determine an issue currently before such court".

Thus, according to Articles 164 and 177 of the EC Treaty, only the Court of Justice of the European Communities is competent to give final explanation of an interpretation of the community law and national courts (of the member states) address applications for preliminary judgment specially to the Court.

As regards the right to appeal to the Constitutional Tribunal, Article 79 of the Constitution states that it belongs to everyone whose constitutional freedoms or rights have been infringed regarding "conformity to the Constitution of a statute or another normative act upon which basis a court or organ of public administration has made a final decision on his freedoms or rights or on his obligations specified in the Constitution".

Considering rather carefully the scope of the appeal, it can be assumed that this provision relates to normative acts issued by organs of the Republic of Poland. Considering this issue in a broader context may produce the question whether the appeal will be admissible when the national court bases its decision on, for example, community regulations constituting a normative act. Such regulations has precedence only over a statute. The problem would be more serious when the national court issued its decision after having obtained the preliminary judgment of the Court of Justice of the European Communities. It seems, that after giving consent for the admissibility of an appeal, the Constitutional Tribunal would be limited by the interpretation of the Court of Justice pursuant to Article 5 of the Treaty establishing the European Communities, imposing on all organs of the member states a duty to fulfill commitments resulting from activities taken by the community institutions. These activities must be legal in the context of community law; however, the Court of Justice of the EC remains the main judicial institution. Nevertheless, the Polish Constitutional Tribunal may follow the path indicated by the German

Tribunal in the Brunner case — to show whether the Communities, in passing of certain provision, acted in conformity to the competence given to them in the provisions of the Treaties. Infringement of competence would mean that the above mentioned provision has no support in the provisions of the accession act and thus, is not in conformity to the Constitution under the provisions of which the consent for delegation of competence in regard to certain matters, specified in the act of accession, had been granted.

In conclusion, we may state that constitutional provisions ensure at least a partial effectiveness of "classical" international law in the Polish legal system and, despite a certain ambiguity, they create a suitable basis for Poland's accession to the European Union. More complicated situations might occur in relation to the application of community law in Poland, especially in cases putting the constitutionality of this law at issue. The future practice of the Constitutional Tribunal of the Republic of Poland will have to resolve such matters.

TABLE OF CONTENTS

Table of Contents

KANCELARIA SEJMU

Opracowanie, druk i oprawa Wydawnictwo Sejmowe
Arkuszy wydawniczych 18,7. Arkuszy drukarskich 17,25
Wydanie pierwsze
Warszawa 1999